The Never-Resting Mind

The Never-Resting Mind

Wallace Stevens' Romantic Irony

Anthony Whiting

Ann Arbor
THE UNIVERSITY OF MICHIGAN PRESS

Published in the United States of America by
The University of Michigan Press
Manufactured in the United States of America
⊗ Printed on acid-free paper

1999   1998   1997   1996   4   3   2   1

A CIP catalog record for this book is available from the British Library.

Library of Congress Cataloging-in-Publication Data

Whiting, Anthony, 1951–
    The never-resting mind : Wallace Stevens' romantic irony / Anthony Whiting.
        p.   cm.
    Includes bibliographical references and index.
    ISBN 0-472-10659-7 (hardcover : alk. paper)
    1. Stevens, Wallace, 1879–1955—Criticism and interpretation.
    2. Romanticism—United States—History—20th century.   3. Irony in literature.   I. Title.
    PS3557.T4753Z945   1996
    811'.52—dc20   96-2557
                                                                    CIP

For Caroline

Acknowledgments

Not the least of the pleasures of seeing a book into print is having the opportunity to thank those who have been helpful. I am especially grateful to A. Walton Litz, George Stade, and Carl Woodring for their support of this project. Each has given generously of his time and learning, and each has significantly influenced my thinking about Stevens. I was fortunate to have George Lensing and Robin Schulze as my outside readers. Their insightful comments helped me to clarify key points in my argument. I am indebted to Nancy Kranich for many courtesies. Without her help, research for this book would have been a great deal more difficult. I wish to thank two individuals at ITT Hartford who were also helpful in my research. Barry Kramer sent a marvelous cache of items on Stevens, while Eric Rennie provided information about Stevens' daily life at the Hartford. My thanks also to Bonnie-Jean Radtke for sending material on Stevens and for providing more details on Stevens' life at the insurance company. Debts to a parent are not easily articulated, especially within the confines of a preface. I can here only gratefully acknowledge my mother's support in this endeavor, as in everything. The Elliott V. K. Dobbie Fund of Columbia University kindly provided a grant to assist in the publication of this study. An earlier version of chapter 2 was published in *The Wallace Stevens Journal* 16, no. 2 (fall 1992). The book is dedicated to Caroline, who encouraged me along the way and whose appreciation of Stevens added to the pleasure of this journey.

Excerpts from Wallace Stevens' *Collected Poems,* © 1954 by

Contents

Introduction

Irony is a central concept in the poetry of Wallace Stevens, and it has attracted commentary from critics as different as Conrad Aiken, Lewis Untermeyer, Frank Lentricchia, and J. Hillis Miller.[1] Despite the attention the concept has received, the expression of romantic irony in Stevens' work has not been explored. The term itself may have contributed to this critical oversight. As Lilian Furst writes, "Partly because of the misleading implications of its name, romantic irony has acquired the reputation of being a peculiar caprice of a few esoteric writers at the turn of the eighteenth into the nineteenth century, resistant to common comprehension and of slight relevance anyway."[2] Its importance to the modern period, though, has been succinctly stated by D. C. Muecke: "To study Romantic Irony is to discover how modern Romanticism could be, or, if you like, how Romantic Modernism is."[3]

The first theorist of romantic irony, Friedrich Schlegel, described the concept for the most part in aphorisms scattered throughout three collections of fragments, *Lyceum Fragments* (1797), *Athenaeum Fragments* (1799), and *Ideas* (1800). As Schlegel conceives it, romantic irony rejects Newton's orderly universe of immutable laws. In its place, it posits a chaotic universe of becoming and change. While romantic irony affirms a chaotic universe, it also affirms the power of the mind to construct a world out of chaos. Aware that these constructs are finite patterns imposed by the mind on an infinite and dynamic universe and hence have no final validity, the ironist adopts a deeply skeptical attitude toward them. But skepticism is not the only attitude expressed by the ironist toward the mind's patterning of experience. Though aware that all structuring concepts are, ultimately, fictions, the ironist also accepts and is committed to these concepts. This dual stance of the ironist—at once skeptically free from and deeply committed to a particular order, structure, or system—engenders a never-ending process. Skeptical reduction leads to the creation of a new structure, a new way of ordering experience. This pattern is subjected in turn to critical scrutiny, which again leads to creation, and so on endlessly. The ironist's experience of the world, then, continues to broaden and to become ever more fragmented in the never-ending process of reduction and creation.

The theory was vigorously attacked by Hegel and Kierkegaard, who view romantic irony as an unjustified and dangerous glorification of the subjective. In romantic irony, as Kierkegaard puts it, subjectivity is "raised to the second power."[4] To Hegel and Kierkegaard, the great creative power of the ironist is, finally, enclosing and isolating. The Fichtean ego of the ironist negates the world of time and circumstance and replaces it, again in Kierkegaard's words, with a "self-created actuality" (CI 292). The aesthetic world the ironist devises is in their view sport for the reflective consciousness of the ironist.

Both of these views of romantic irony, one that gestures toward engagement, the other toward transcendence and enclosure, were inherited by the moderns. Hegel's and Kierkegaard's emphasis on the subjectivity and caprice of the ironist was echoed, for example, early in the century by Irving Babbitt in Rousseau and Romanticism (1919).[5] A similar view of the concept can be seen in Charles Glicksberg's later study, The Ironic Vision in Modern Literature (1969). Glicksberg writes that John Davidson, a contributor to the Yellow Book and member of the Rhymers' Club, "gave expression to romantic irony at its blaspheming best and worst, a form of irony that Irving Babbitt, in Rousseau and Romanticism, had condemned as a species of literary perversion, a cult of irresponsibility and egocentric insolence."[6] Candace Lang's more recent study of irony also views romantic irony only in Kierkegaardian terms. "[T]he romantic irony to which I refer and from which I sharply distinguish the spirit animating such recent trends in literary and critical practice as the *nouveau roman* or deconstruction is the romanticism that Kierkegaard sees, rightly or wrongly, in Schlegel and Tieck . . . and which remains today the prevalent conception of romanticism."[7]

Other critics have found a Schlegelian sense of irony in modern literature. Lilian Furst, for instance, finds this irony in Joyce, Italo Svevo, Borges, and Beckett, as well as in later writers such as Gil Sorrentino and Italo Calvino.[8] Gary Handwerk, who criticizes Hegel and Kierkegaard for reducing romantic irony to an "untrammeled subjective willfulness, a taking of the self at its most immediate and naive level as absolute[,] . . . cut off from both historical actuality and objective reality,"[9] argues that in romantic irony the subject moves away from isolation and toward intersubjectivity. Irony "establishes the dependence of the subject's identity on the web of social relations within which it exists."[10] For him, romantic irony is an exploration of the subject's situation in the world as it relates to the Other, and he discusses this "ethical irony" in the work of Meredith, Beckett, and Lacan. The expression of a Schlegelian sense of irony has been described by other critics in modern poets such as Frost and Yeats.[11]

Numerous cultural, political, and literary factors affected the reception and influence of each of these senses of irony in the twentieth century. Though this study does not investigate these factors (indeed, such an investigation would make a lengthy study in itself), I wish to mention three that are of particular importance. The First World War had an extremely negative impact on romantic irony as conceived by Schlegel. Anne Mellor, whose study of romantic irony takes its theoretical direction from Schlegel, writes, "After such devastation, the romantic ironist's enthusiastic celebration of process and change seemed callow or philosophically absurd. . . . [The First World War] sabotaged the romantic ironist's sense of exuberant freedom in an infinitely various and infinitely possible world."[12] The strongly antiromantic character of early literary modernism also had a negative influence on the Schlegelian sense of irony. Babbitt's attack on romantic irony, for instance, was only part of a larger campaign he waged against romanticism in its broadest conception. (Kierkegaard, too, makes clear in *The*

Concept of Irony that his attack on romantic irony should be seen as an attack on romanticism itself and not on just one aspect of it. "Throughout this discussion [of irony after Fichte] I use the expressions: *irony* and the *ironist,* but I could as easily say: *romanticism* and the *romanticist.* Both expressions designate the same thing" [*CI* 292 n. 2].) Attacks on romanticism were also undertaken with enthusiasm by Eliot, Pound, Hulme, and, in France, Pierre Lassere.[13] A third factor, and one that relates to both senses of romantic irony, is the cultural response to industrialism. T. J. Jackson Lears writes that the early modern period is marked by a desire to withdraw from industrial society. "Antimodern dissenters recoiled from this ethic [capitalism] and groped for alternatives in medieval, Oriental, and other 'primitive' cultures."[14] This expression of what Samuel Hays in *The Response to Industrialism* calls a "nostalgia for a calmer, less perplexed, pre-industrial life"[15] coexisted with another impulse. In Lears' words, "Antimodernism was not simply escapism; it was ambivalent, often coexisting with enthusiasm for material progress."[16] The opposing senses of romantic irony seen in the modern period reflect in a literary context this cultural dialectic between engagement and transcendence.

And it is a dialectic that lies at the center of Stevens' poetry. James Longenbach writes that "Stevens began his career torn between an overripe *fin de siècle* desire to transcend things as they are and a rough-hewn urge to tackle the world of politics and economics head on."[17] Longenbach has explored the "tension between conflicting desires for engagement and transcendence"[18] that runs through all of Stevens' poetry in the context of the great economic and political events of Stevens' lifetime: the First World War, the Great Depression, the Second World War. These conflicting desires have also been discussed by biographical critics such as George Lensing, who writes that Stevens' "1899 concern with ideal versus fact anticipated . . . his absorption in the claims on him by the inner life of imagination and the outer world of the real. . . . The pull of both . . . set forth the scope of his future art."[19]

In looking at Stevens through the lens(es) of romantic irony, I also explore this central aspect of his art. Before turning to Stevens, though, I discuss the Schlegelian and the Hegelian and Kierkegaardian senses of romantic irony, and I explore their expression in late-nineteenth- and early-twentieth-century writers—the Hegelian and Kierkegaardian senses in J. K. Huysmans and the early T. S. Eliot, the Schlegelian sense in Nietzsche. Of course, these are not the only writers from whom Stevens could have learned of romantic irony. He might also have known of the concept from its expression in Byron, Shelley, and Keats, in Victorian authors such as Carlyle, Thackeray, Browning, Arnold, Dickens, and Tennyson, or in French writers such as Diderot, Musset, Stendhal, Gautier, Baudelaire, and Flaubert.[20] Though Stevens could have known of romantic irony from a number of sources, I discuss Eliot, Huysmans, and Nietzsche in part because of their importance to Stevens. Eliot is the modern against whom Stevens perhaps most defined himself. Five years before his death in 1955, Stevens wrote to William Van O'Connor that he and Eliot were "dead opposites" and that he had "been doing about everything that [Eliot] would not be likely to do" (L 677). Huysmans, particularly in *A Rebours,* expresses the "*fin de siècle* desire to transcend things as they are" that so attracted Stevens. (In a journal entry from 1906 Stevens wrote that "Arthur Symons has great weight with several fellows I know" [*SP* 163], and Stevens may have been led to Huysmans by Symons' comments on him in *The Symbolist Movement in Literature* [1899].) Though Stevens in his letters distances himself from Nietzsche (see, for example, L 431–32), this philosopher, as B. J. Leggett, Milton Bates, and Leonard and Wharton have shown, deeply influenced the content and style of Stevens' work.[21]

The remainder of my study is devoted to exploring the expression of these opposing senses of irony in Stevens' poetry, and I look first at his relation to Schlegel. Numerous aspects of Schlegel's theory, for instance, his view of the ironist as endlessly creative, as simultaneously committed to and detached from all patternings of experience, and as engaged in a never-ending process of self-creation and self-destruction, are echoed in Stevens' work. But Stevens also differs from Schlegel. Though he does express a sense of endless and effortless creativity, Stevens also writes of the difficulty of creating. And though, like Schlegel, Stevens affirms a chaotic world of process and change, he at times asks to be released from what he calls, in a very late poem, "facts." I take up next Stevens' affiliation with Hegel and Kierkegaard, and the relation between the Schlegelian and the Hegelian and Kierkegaardian senses of irony in his poetry. This relation is not limited to simple opposition. Though either sense of irony can predominate in individual poems, Stevens does not just oscillate from one ironic stance in one poem to the other stance in another poem. The two ironies are often present in, and can be the subject of, a single lyric. Nor does Stevens always choose one ironic stance over the other. Some of his bitterest poems are those in which he is situated *between* the two ironies. I turn in the following chapter to the issue of irony and the structure of Stevens' poetry. Schlegel felt that romantic irony could be expressed through a number of forms, including the dialogue, aphorisms, and the novel, which he considered the best vehicle for romantic irony. These forms, however, are not the only ones through which romantic irony can be expressed, and I look at three of the ironic forms that Stevens uses and modifies throughout his poetry. My final chapter is devoted to a discussion of irony in Stevens' late poetry, that is, *The Auroras of Autumn* (1950) and *The Rock* (1954). Here Stevens expresses an irony that, while recognizably romantic, is different from the irony seen in the earlier work. In a brief afterword, I suggest that the conflict between the Schlegelian and the Hegelian and Kierkegaardian senses of romantic irony is also part of the matrix of postmodern literature, and I describe the expression of this conflict in writers such as Barthelme, Ashbery, Sukenick, and Federman.

Though both the Schlegelian and the Hegelian and Kierkegaardian senses of romantic irony are expressed in twentieth-century literature, Stevens may be the modern heir who is most burdened by this aspect of his romantic inheritance. His poetry shows us not only both senses of irony, but the unresolved, indeed, unresolvable tension between them. It exemplifies, perhaps more fully and subtly than the work of any other modern

British or American poet, what Albert Gelpi describes as the "tension within poetic Modernism [between engagement and transcendence] which makes it as much a Janus-face as the Romanticism from which it evolved."[22]

Chapter 1

Antithetic Views of Romantic Irony: Schlegel, Hegel, and Kierkegaard

> Tieck and others of these distinguished people are indeed familiar with such expressions as "irony," but without telling us what they mean.
>
> —Hegel

> To the extent that one seeks a complete and coherent discussion of this concept [irony], one will soon convince himself that it has a problematic history, or to be more precise, no history at all. In the period after Fichte where it was particularly important, one finds it mentioned again and again, suggested again and again, presupposed again and again. But if one searches for a lucid discussion one searches in vain. Solgar complains that A. W. Schlegel in his *Vorlesungen über dramatische Kunst und Literatur,* where one would certainly expect to find an adequate exposition of it, mentions it only briefly in a single passage. Hegel complains that the same is true of Solgar, and finds it no better with Tieck. And now since all complain why should not I also complain?
>
> —Kierkegaard

Neoclassical writers, following medieval and classical custom, used the word *irony* most frequently to refer to a rhetorical device that meant "blame-by-praise." The term was also used, though less often, to mean "praise-by-blame." As Norman Knox writes, "By far the most frequently used meaning of *irony* was, during the English classical period as during the preceding eighteen or nineteen centuries, 'censure through counterfeited praise.' . . . The stock definitions always linked blame-by-praise with 'praise through counterfeited blame,' but this sense was much less frequently invoked in actual use of the word."[1] Blame-by-praise irony was particularly favored in the satiric literature of the period.[2] Some neoclassical polemicists, ingeniously exploiting irony's double nature, used it as both sword and shield. The attacker would claim that praise which was actually insincere was meant to be seen through.[3] For the most part, neoclassical irony is characterized by what Wayne Booth has termed stability. Once the meaning of an ironic work or passage has been reconstructed, the reader is not invited to undermine the reconstructed meaning.[4] Both the sense of indirection and the sense of stability in rhetorical irony are nicely captured in Kierkegaard's description of it as "a riddle and its solution possessed simultaneously" (*CI* 265). Around the end of the eighteenth century, though, irony began to take on a new meaning, a specifically philosophical one, and those who articulated this sense of irony sharply distinguished it from irony understood as a verbal device associated with satire and polemic. "Nothing is more unlike than satire, polemic and irony," writes Friedrich Schlegel.[5] Elsewhere he states, "Philosophy is the real homeland of irony."[6]

Romantic irony (a phrase that gained currency after its use by the German scholar Hermann Hettner in 1850 and was not commonly used by those who wrote about the concept)[7] rejects the world of Newton's *Principia Mathematica,* a world not only ordered by immutable laws but one whose order is able to be comprehended by the reason. Irony posits instead a universe that is infinite, abundant, and chaotic. As Schlegel writes, "Irony is the clear consciousness of eternal agility, of an infinitely teeming chaos" (*LF* 247, no. 69). This "teeming chaos" is inexhaustibly vital. New forms are created and older ones die away in a never-ending process that has no goal, purpose, or design. The *absence* of order, though, is not seen as a *loss* of order. If the Newtonian world had deliquesced into fragments, these fragments were not seen as parts of a preexisting order. Nor is the mind's inability to comprehend a chaotic universe a cause for despair. The romantic ironist celebrates the universe of becoming and change and warns against a universe that is completely available to rational comprehension. "Verily," Schlegel writes, "it would fare badly with you if, as you demand, the whole world were ever to become wholly comprehensible in earnest" (*LF* 268).

In addition to affirming a chaotic and abundant universe, romantic irony also affirms the power of the mind to construct a world out of chaos. "And isn't this entire, unending world constructed by the understanding out of incomprehensibility or chaos?" Schlegel asks rhetorically in his essay "On Incomprehensibility" (*LF* 268). Aware that the order the mind perceives is a finite pattern imposed by it on an infinite and dynamic universe and hence is, ultimately, false, a fiction, the ironist adopts a deeply skeptical attitude toward all structurings of experience. This skeptical attitude allows the ironist to transcend any particular patterning of experience. Irony, Schlegel writes, is "the mood that surveys everything and rises infinitely above all limitations" (*LF* 148, no. 42). Freedom from limitation is for Schlegel an escape from egocentrism and self-love. To see the universe only through the patterns the self imposes on it is to turn the universe into a mirror image of the self. Skeptical reduction shatters this mirror and leaves the self confronting a universe that no longer reflects its image. The displacement of the world as self-image does not for Schlegel result in feelings of isolation or alienation. Freed from its narrow focus on itself, the self can turn to the universe at large. "We must rise above our own love," Schlegel writes, "and be able to destroy in our thoughts what we adore; if we cannot do this, we lack . . . the feeling for the universe."[8]

Skepticism, however, is not the only attitude expressed by the ironist toward the mind's patterning of experience. Though aware that all structuring concepts are, ultimately, fictions, the ironist also accepts and is committed to these fictions. This dual stance of the ironist—at once skeptically free from and deeply committed to a particular order, structure, or system—is described by Schlegel in an *Athenaeum* fragment. "It's equally fatal for the mind to have a system and to have none. It will simply have to decide to combine the two" (*LF* 167, no. 53). Schlegel elsewhere describes this ironic attitude of the mind as one that combines playfulness and seriousness. "In this sort of irony," he writes, "everything should be playful and serious" (LF 156, no. 108). That is, the mind is sincerely committed to its creations even as it indicates its awareness of their limitations through its playful attitude toward them. Not only are the attitudes of commitment and detachment held simultaneously, but for Schlegel both attitudes are equally necessary. Skepticism alone would leave the mind detached and isolated while commitment alone would blind the mind to its finite limitations.

The relation between commitment and skeptical detachment is not one of static opposition or balance. Rather, the two attitudes are mutually enlivening and engender a never-ending process. Skeptical reduction leads to the creation of a new structure, a new way of ordering experience. This new structure is subjected in turn to skeptical analysis, which again leads to creation, then to reduction, to more creation, and so on endlessly. Schlegel points to the dynamic quality of romantic irony when he writes that it is "an absolute synthesis of absolute antitheses, the continual self-creating interchange of two conflicting thoughts" (LF 176, no. 121). In Schlegel, two conflicting thoughts do not lead, as they do in Hegel, to a final synthesis, but remain in creative opposition. As Ernst Behler writes, Schlegel's irony "lacks the teleology and goal-oriented drive of Hegel's dialectical thought process."[9] The process of creation and destruction without goal or design repeats in miniature a similar pattern in the universe at large.

The ironist's simultaneous commitment to and detachment from the structures the mind creates results in an endless broadening and fragmenting of experience. The skeptical stance of the ironist leads to the destruction of older concepts and the creation of new ones. These new concepts are sincerely accepted even as they are critically examined, and so on. The ironist's experience of the world is thus continually changing and enlarging in the process of reduction and creation. The more the ironist reconceives the world, the richer and more diverse the experience of it becomes. From this perspective, romantic irony can be contrasted with the secularized Judeo-Christian pattern of experience that, as M. H. Abrams argues in Natural Supernaturalism, is presented in many German and English romantic works.[10] Experience in this pattern is seen as being initially unified, becomes fragmented, and then moves toward a final unity.

It is not just the world that continually changes in romantic irony. In Schlegel's view, the ironist is engaged in a never-ending process of "self-destruction" and "self-creation" (*LF* 147, no. 37). Self-destruction occurs when the mind skeptically examines existing concepts of the self; self-creation takes place when it creates and commits itself to new ones. Because the process of self-destruction and self-creation is continual, the self can never acquire a sense of identity that is fixed and unchanging. Rather, the self develops through this process an ever-expanding, ever-more-complex sense of itself. As Anne Mellor writes, "For Schlegel, this self-becoming is a process of enlargement: one develops from conceptions of the self as a unity to ever-clearer conceptions of the self as flowing into a rich and manifold chaos."[11]

Schlegel's concept of irony was vigorously attacked by both Hegel and Kierkegaard. Hegel's most detailed analysis of the concept, particularly as it relates to Schlegel, is made in the *Aesthetics*.[12] Volleys are also fired in *Lectures on the History of Philosophy, The Philosophy of Right, Lectures on the Philosophy of Religion,* and *The Philosophy of Mind*.[13] Kierkegaard presses the attack in *The Concept of Irony* and in volume 1 of *Either/Or*. Since Kierkegaard's criticism of romantic irony, particularly in *The Concept of Irony,* owes so much to Hegel, I consider first Hegel's treatment of the concept. This irony, Hegel writes, "had its deeper root" (*A* 64) in Fichte's philosophy. "F[riedrich] von Schlegel, like Schelling, started from Fichte's standpoint, Schelling to go beyond it altogether, Schlegel to develop it in his own way" (*A* 64). Though Hegel adds that Schlegel was later to "tear himself loose" (*A* 64) from Fichte's philosophy, Hegel limits himself in the *Aesthetics* to describing Schlegel's debt to Fichte.

Hegel's attack on romantic irony is conducted through an analysis of the Fichtean concept of the ego.[14] Hegel argues that the world generated by the Fichtean ego has no substantial reality since it is only a product of the ego. "[N]othing is treated *in and for itself* and as valuable in itself, but only as produced by the subjectivity of the *ego*. . . . Consequently everything genuinely and independently real becomes only a show, not true and genuine on its own account or through itself" (*A* 64, 65). Hegel is also critical of the capricious and whimsical nature of the Fichtean ego, which can create and destroy at its pleasure. The world is "a mere appearance due to the *ego* in whose power and caprice and at whose free disposal it remains. To admit or cancel it depends wholly on the pleasure of the *ego*, already absolute in itself simply as *ego*" (*A* 65).

Hegel's third point concerns the ego as "a *living*, active individual . . . making its individuality real in its own eyes and in those of others. . . . Now in relation to beauty and art, this acquires the meaning of living as an artist and forming one's life *artistically*" (*A* 65). While the individual ego can create a self and world for itself, this creative activity encloses the ego and isolates it from any actuality external to it. Though enclosed, the ego has two kinds of freedom. First, it is not bound to its own creations. The "virtuosity of an ironical artistic life apprehends itself as a divine creative genius for which anything and everything is only an unsubstantial creature, to which the creator . . . is not bound, because he is just as able to destroy it as to create it" (*A* 66). Second, in enclosing itself in its own world, the ego negates the validity of the external world and no longer recognizes the claims of the world on it. Hegel portrays the ironical artist as looking down in lordly fashion on those who *do* feel bound by the legal and moral obligations of life. "[H]e who has reached this standpoint of divine genius looks down from his high rank on all other men, for they are pronounced dull and limited, inasmuch as law, morals, etc., still count for them as fixed, essential, and obligatory" (*A* 66). Even when the ego "does give [itself] relations to others," that is, "lives with friends, mistresses, etc.," because of its divine ironical standpoint, these relations are "null" (*A* 66), a characterization that looks forward to Kierkegaard's portrait of the romantic ironist in "Diary of the Seducer." The seducer has a relation to another, Cordelia, but his relation to her is completely "null" by virtue of his ironic stance.

Hegel has three other criticisms of the Fichtean ego. First,

Hegel writes of the narcissistic component of the ego. He describes "the divine irony of genius" as "this concentration of the *ego* into itself, for which all bonds are snapped and which can live only in the bliss of self-enjoyment" (*A* 66). Second, he writes of the moment in which the ego may "fail to find satisfaction in this self-enjoyment," recognize that it is cut off from reality, and feel a longing, a "craving for the solid and the substantial" (*A* 66). Finally, Hegel deftly identifies the sense of paralysis that the "divine creative genius" can experience. On the one hand, "the subject does want to penetrate into truth and longs for objectivity, but, on the other hand, cannot renounce his isolation and withdrawal into himself or tear himself free from this unsatisfied abstract inwardness" (*A* 66). This paralysis, Hegel suggests, results not from a lack of self-knowledge, but from a lack of will. The subject "lacks the strength to escape from this vanity and fill himself with a content of substance" (*A* 67).

Hegel's view of the romantic ego strongly influenced Kierkegaard, who offers a highly critical analysis of it in *The Concept of Irony,* which was completed three years after the first edition of the *Aesthetics* (1835–38). Kierkegaard's attack on romantic irony in *The Concept of Irony,* though, is not conducted solely through a formal analysis of the ego. He writes in *The Concept of Irony* that "one cannot overrate Hegel's great contribution to the conception of the historical past" (*CI* 295), and it is the romantic ego understood within a fundamentally Hegelian conception of history that underlies Kierkegaard's criticism of Schlegel's concept of irony. For Hegel, history is the gradual unfolding or dialectical actualization of Mind or Spirit. Each historical epoch both embodies Mind and yet is only a partial and limited expression of Mind as it progresses toward complete, self-conscious actualization. Central to this view of history is the idea of negation or displacement. As Kierkegaard puts it, "With every such turning point in history there are two movements to be observed. On the one hand, the new shall come forth; on the other, the old must be displaced" (*CI* 277). Because irony is the movement that negates a given actuality, it is at the turning point between one age and another that "we meet the ironic subject" (*CI* 278). Irony in the "eminent sense," or what Kierkegaard also terms absolute irony, "directs itself not against this or that particular existence but against the whole given actuality of a certain time and situation" (*CI* 271). Absolute irony is the "determination of subjectivity" (*CI* 279); they arise simultaneously. "[W]hen subjectivity asserts itself, irony appears. Subjectivity feels itself confronted by the given actuality, feels its own power, its own validity and significance" (*CI* 280). The subject asserts its own "validity" against the given actuality and destroys this actuality. In doing so, it negatively frees itself from the world. "With irony the subject is negatively free. The actuality which shall give him content is not, hence he is free from the restraint in which the given actuality binds him, yet negatively free and as such hovering, because there nothing is which binds him" (*CI* 279).

Kierkegaard views Socrates as an ironist in the eminent sense. He destroyed Hellas, and as he destroyed it, he became "ever lighter and lighter, always more negatively free" (*CI* 287). Though Socratic irony is "infinite absolute negativity" (*CI* 287), a phrase Kierkegaard borrows from Hegel's *Aesthetics,* Kierkegaard limits what this irony destroys, a limitation that he will later use in distinguishing between Socratic irony and romantic irony. It is not "actuality altogether that [Socrates] negated, but the given actuality of a certain age, of substantiality as embodied in Hellas" (*CI* 287–88). It is because Socrates only destroys the Hellenic world that Kierkegaard judges Socrates' irony to be "world historically warranted" (*CI* 288). Essentially, it "takes place in the service of the Idea" (*CI* 280). "This," Kierkegaard writes, "is the genial quality of an irony that is warranted" (*CI* 280).

There is no genial quality in Kierkegaard's description of romantic irony. He writes that "such an irony was wholly unwarranted, and . . . Hegel's efforts to oppose it were quite in order" (*CI* 292). While Socratic irony is the determination of subjectivity, yet "subjectivity was already given by the conditions of the world" (*CI* 292). Irony arises within, though it negates, a given actuality, and it is in the service of Mind. This is not so in romantic irony. Kierkegaard argues that Schlegel and Tieck accept the Fichtean principle that the infinite ego "has constitutive validity, that it alone is the almighty" (*CI* 292). In accepting this Fichtean view of the ego, they raise subjectivity "to the second power," and they negate not just a given actuality but "all historical actuality" (*CI* 292). Hence, Kierkegaard writes, "it is evident that this irony was not in the service of the world spirit" (*CI* 292). What takes the place of the given actuality is a "self-created actuality" (*CI* 292), which the ironist can posit and abrogate at will.

> Now [irony] took its choice, had its own way, and did exactly as it pleased. . . . At one moment it dwelt in Greece beneath the beautiful Hellenic sky, lost in the presentational enjoyment of the harmonious Hellenic life, dwelt there in such a way that it had its actuality in this. But when it grew tired of this arbitrarily posited actuality it thrust it away so far that it wholly disappeared. Hellenism had no validity for it as a world historical moment, but it had validity, even absolute validity, because irony was pleased to have it so. At the next moment it concealed itself in the virgin forests of the Middle Ages. . . . But no sooner had this love affair lost its validity than the Middle Ages were spirited away back into infinity, dying away in ever weakening contours on the undercloth of consciousness. (*CI* 294–95)

True history has been negated by the absolute subjectivity of the romantic ironist. Historical epochs are simply aesthetic creations of the ego and demonstrate the ego's complete freedom from history. "With a twist of the wrist all history became myth, poetry, saga, fairy tale—irony was free once more" (*CI* 294).

The ironic ego enjoys and changes identities with the same ease that it creates and dispenses with various environments.

> For irony, as for the Pythagorean doctrine, the soul is constantly on a pilgrimage, except irony does not require such a long time to complete it. But if irony is a little skimpy with time, it doubtless excels in the multiplicity of determinations. And there is many an ironist who . . . has traversed a far more extraordinary fate than the cock in Lucian, which had first

been Pythagoras himself, then Aspasia the ambiguous beauty
from Miletus, Crates the Cynic, a king, a beggar, a satrap, a
horse, a jackdaw, a frog, and a thousand other things. . . . All
things are possible for the ironist. (*CI* 298–99)

Kierkegaard's description of the ironic ego as whimsically sporting
with a world it creates and then destroys, as inhabiting and then
discarding various personalities, and as enjoying a "divine freedom
acknowledging no bonds, no chains, but, abandoning itself heed-
lessly to reckless play, romps like a leviathan in the deep" (*CI* 296),
recalls Hegel's description of the romantic ironist as a capricious
ego, creating and destroying the world at its pleasure.

It is from the point of view of "ethics and morals" that
Kierkegaard's portrait of the romantic ironist recalls Hegel in
two other respects. Even though the ego can enjoy its self-created
world, it comes to recognize the emptiness of this world and to
long for reality. In a striking oxymoron, Kierkegaard describes the
ironist's bored existence as a "hungry satiety" (*CI* 302), a figure
that brilliantly conveys the sense of the fullness of the ego that,
godlike, can create its own reality, the utter emptiness of this com-
plete subjectivity, and the ego's "hunger" for actuality. Second, in
Hegel's view there can be no ethical life without a recognition of
the substantiality of the world apart from the ego. Hence, in
negating actuality, the romantic ego sets itself above the ethical.
Kierkegaard makes a similar point. "When the given actuality loses
its validity for the ironist, therefore, this is not because it is an out-
lived actuality which shall be displaced by a truer, but because the
ironist is the eternal ego for whom no actuality is adequate. Hence
it is evident how this relates to the fact that the ironist sets himself
above ethics and morals" (*CI* 300).

It is from the point of view of "ethics and morals" that
Kierkegaard attacks Schlegel's *Lucinde*, which he describes as "a
very obscene book" (*CI* 303). Kierkegaard does not object to
Schlegel's ironic treatment of love and marriage. "There is a moral
prudishness, a strait-jacket in which no rational human being can
move. In God's name let it be sundered! There is, on the other
hand, the moonlit kind of theatre marriages of an overwrought
romanticism for which nature, at least, has no purpose. . . . Against

all these let irony rage!" (*CI* 304). What Kierkegaard objects to is that Schlegel does not limit his attack to "untruths such as these" (*CI* 304) but "seeks to abrogate all ethics" (*CI* 306), which he does by virtue of the "special pursuit of irony: to cancel all actuality and set in its place an actuality that is no actuality" (*CI* 306). That is, the ironist substitutes a self-created actuality for a true actuality, a self-created actuality being for Kierkegaard "no actuality" at all.

In "Diary of the Seducer" Kierkegaard dramatizes the way in which the creativity and enclosure of the ironist abrogates the ethical. The seducer is another guise for the romantic ironist. The identification is made early in the essay when Kierkegaard writes of the seducer, "His life had been an attempt to realize the task of living poetically."[15] Living poetically, or as he sometimes puts it, poetically to produce oneself, has a special meaning for Kierkegaard. In *The Concept of Irony* he describes the concept along with its opposite, to let oneself be poetically produced. "The man who allows himself to be poetically produced also has a specific given context to which he must accommodate himself, and hence is not a word without meaning for having been divested of connection and context. But for the ironist this context . . . has no validity, and as he is not inclined to fashion himself to suit his environment, so his environment must be fashioned to suit him, that is, he not only poetically produces himself but his environment as well" (*CI* 299–300). To produce oneself poetically is to substitute a self-created actuality for actuality itself. In doing so, the ironist raises himself above the actual world, his true "context," which now "has no validity." To live poetically is to abrogate the ethical since the ethical rests on the ego's recognition of a substantial and concrete reality external to it. This kind of recognition is made when the ego allows itself to be poetically produced. Here, the ego acknowledges that it can to some extent shape reality, but it equally acknowledges that it must accommodate itself to reality, that is, be produced by it.

Because the ego poetically produces itself and its environment, life becomes for the ironist a kind of internal drama, a performance of the self for the self. As Kierkegaard puts it, "Life is for him [the ironist] a drama, and what engrosses him is the ingenious

unfolding of the drama. He is himself a spectator even when per-
forming some act" (*CI* 300). The "Diary of the Seducer" can be
thought of as a record of this kind of performance. The seducer
poetically produces himself through the role he plays in public
with Cordelia, and Cordelia and the people around her are part of
the environment that the seducer is poetically producing. Hegel
had written that because the ironic self exists in a world of its own
making, it has no true relations with others. This observation is
borne out in a late passage in the "Diary." "Now she lets drop
numerous remarks. . . . They do not pass my ear unheeded, they
are the scouts of my operation in the domain of her soul, who give
me enlightening hints; they are the ends of the thread by which I
weave her into my plan" (*E/O* 420). To the seducer, these
remarks are seen only as indications of how far he has progressed
in his artistic "plan," that is, how far he has poetically produced
Cordelia. Apart from this plan, she has no reality for the seducer.
Yet even as he is poetically producing himself and his environ-
ment, in writing the diary he is also watching the entire perfor-
mance.

When the seduction is complete, the seducer breaks off with
Cordelia. He feels no remorse. The end of the affair is for him
only the starting point of another dramatic performance, and the
"Diary" ends with these chilling words:

> It would, however, really be worth while to know whether or
> not one might be able to poetize himself out of a girl, so that
> one could make her so proud that she would imagine that it
> was she who tired of the relationship. It could become a very
> interesting epilogue, which, in its own right, might have psy-
> chological interest, and along with that, enrich one with many
> erotic observations. (*E/O* 440)

Despite the power over events that his own enclosure seems
to offer him, the seducer may not be the victor in this relationship.
In the introduction to the "Diary," Kierkegaard acknowledges
that Cordelia has suffered, but he also writes that the suffering of
the seducer will be even more terrible than Cordelia's. "[A]t the

moment his anxious soul believes that it already sees daylight breaking through, it turns out to be a new entrance, and like a startled deer, pursued by despair, he constantly seeks a way out, and finds only a way in, through which he goes back into himself" (*E/O* 304). Kierkegaard is describing here the ironist's painful recognition of his absolute isolation and of his inability to break out of this isolation. Every way out of the self turns out to be another entrance into the self. In poetically producing himself and his environment, the ironist completely encloses himself, an enclosure that renders "null" the ironist's relation to any other person and thereby eliminates the possibility of overcoming isolation through the bond of human sympathy or love.

Kierkegaard ends his discussion of irony in *The Concept of Irony* by contrasting romantic irony and Socratic irony to "mastered irony." This concept rests on the idea that every "segment" of history has "validity," but that the validity of the segment is only a "relative validity" (*CI* 296). Because each segment of history has validity, Kierkegaard describes mastered irony as a return to the actual. "When irony has first been mastered it undertakes a movement directly opposed to that wherein it proclaimed its life as unmastered. Irony now limits, renders finite, defines, and thereby yields truth, actuality, and content" (*CI* 338). Mastered irony in this respect is unlike Socratic irony, which does not recognize the validity of a given actuality, and is unlike romantic irony, which, in Kierkegaard's view, does not recognize the validity of any actuality. Since mastered irony also recognizes that a given actuality has only relative validity, it "prevents all idolatry with the phenomenon" (*CI* 341). Though the ironist longs for the ideal, the "higher and more perfect," this longing does not "hollow out actuality; on the contrary, the content of life must become a true and meaningful moment in the higher actuality whose fullness the soul desires" (*CI* 341). Paradoxically, the ironist is both in experience since he accepts the validity of a given actuality and yet is above experience since he recognizes that the given actuality is not congruent with the ideal that he seeks.

The view of romantic irony that emerges in Hegel's and Kierkegaard's criticism of it differs from Schlegel's concept in a number of ways. First, Kierkegaard criticizes romantic irony because it is "not in the service of the world spirit" (*CI* 292). To argue, however, that irony is not in the service of the world spirit as it actualizes itself is to presume that there is an ordered, teleological universe in which irony can be of service. But it is exactly this presumption that irony in Schlegel denies. For him, irony posits a universe that has no underlying order or direction. The true point of difference between Kierkegaard and Schlegel here is not whether irony is or is not in the service of an ordered universe but their underlying assumptions about the nature of the universe itself. Is it ordered or is it chaotic? For Kierkegaard, this is not an issue that is open to question. The order is presumed, and he does not debate Schlegel on this point. Perhaps, as Muecke shrewdly speculates, it is Kierkegaard's commitment to a "closed-world" ideology and his inability to take an "open view of the totality of existence," a view that acknowledges the instability of existence, that is the "real basis of his objections to irony."[16]

Second, Kierkegaard and Hegel interpret Fichte as denying content to reality since the world is essentially a manifestation of the ego. Both read this view of Fichte's philosophy into Schlegel, and both see the romantic ironist as a subjective idealist who denies nature positive content in itself. There is no doubt that Schlegel was influenced by Fichte. In an aphorism, Schlegel praises Fichte highly, saying that his philosophy along with Goethe's *Wilhelm Meister* and the French Revolution are the "greatest tendencies of the age" (*LF* 190, no. 216). But Schlegel does not accept Fichte's absolute idealism. Eichner writes, "Whereas to Fichte, Nature was merely the 'non-ego,' a mere obstacle in man's way to Freedom or a mere field for his activity, Schlegel endowed Nature with a life of its own."[17]

Third, because the ironic ego in Schlegel's view is both committed to and also skeptically detached from its own ordering or patterning of experience, it is both in and yet above experience. As Hegel and Kierkegaard present the ironic ego, it remains above experience, enclosed in its self-created actuality. In *The Concept of Irony* Kierkegaard describes the ironic ego in a way that appears to place it back in experience. He writes, "At one moment it [romantic irony] dwelt in Greece beneath the beautiful Hellenic sky, lost in the presentational enjoyment of the harmonious Hellenic life, dwelt there in such a way that it had its actuality in this" (*CI* 294). Though the ironic ego may have its "actuality" in Greece, it remains above experience because its actuality is one that is "arbitrarily posited" by the ego, has no substantiality in itself, and depends for its continued existence upon the ego, which can whisk it away when it pleases. "[W]hen it grew tired of this arbitrarily posited actuality it thrust it away so far that it wholly disappeared" (*CI* 294).

Kierkegaard does describe in *The Concept of Irony* a kind of irony in which the self is both in and above experience, mastered irony. The similarity between this concept of irony and Schlegel's concept of irony, however, is only superficial since the two concepts are based on entirely different assumptions. Mastered irony presumes an ordered, teleological universe. It recognizes that the revelation of Spirit in a particular historical epoch is valid, but only relatively valid. In mastered irony the self accepts the validity of its own historical moment while acknowledging that this reality is *only* a moment in the movement of Spirit toward complete actualization. Thus, the self can both accept reality and seek the ideal without hollowing out reality through this seeking. Irony in Schlegel presumes not that the universe is ordered but that it is chaotic. The self stands above experience because it skeptically acknowledges that all experiential patterns or structures are imposed by the mind on the world and hence are, ultimately, false. However, the self's acknowledgment that no structure or pattern has final validity does not hollow out the experience that the self has through a particular structure since the self is also sincerely committed to the patterns it creates.

Fourth, romantic irony as Schlegel presents it expresses a sense of endless self-creation and self-destruction. The self continually destroys and creates new conceptions of itself and of the world. This aspect of romantic irony can also be seen in Kierkegaard. The ironist creates one actuality and then thrusts "it away so far that it wholly disappear[s]" (*CI* 294) only to create another, and so forth. The same process can be seen in the many selves or "personages" that the ironist creates and then destroys. Goethe writes that "a subjective nature has soon talked out his little internal material,"[18] and since what the ironic ego in Kierkegaard's description experiences through its creative activity is essentially itself, the ego is constantly confronted with the problem of boredom. Boredom might be thought of as the ironist's moment of extreme unction since when the self has completely talked out its little internal material, and boredom signals such a moment, the self becomes nothing. It becomes nothing because it has no existence apart from its self-created actuality. To exist apart from its creations, the self, in Hegel's as well as Kierkegaard's view, must accept reality "as a gift which will not admit of being rejected" (*CI* 293), that is, see itself as part of a particular, concrete reality over which it has no final sovereignty and to which it must accommodate itself. Hegel writes, "I only become essential myself in my own eyes in so far as I have immersed myself in such a content and have brought myself into conformity with it in all my knowing and acting" (*A* 65). And Kierkegaard writes that the individual "must feel himself assimilated into a larger context" (*CI* 296). Because the ironic self does not acknowledge such a context, it cannot be said to exist apart from what it creates. For Kierkegaard, this is tantamount to not existing at all. Commenting in the *Concluding Unscientific Postscript* on the aesthete/ironist A, whom he presents in *Either/Or,* Kierkegaard writes, "[H]e has thought everything possible, and yet he has not existed at all."[19] Because the romantic ironist for Kierkegaard has no existence apart from his self-created world and self, the process of self-creation and self-destruction, celebrated by Schlegel, is presented by Kierkegaard as a constant struggle for self-preservation. Once the ironist runs out of material, he "comes to nothing" (*CI* 298).

Kierkegaard returns to the issue of boredom in *Either/Or* in the short, humorous essay, "The Rotation Method." Here Kierkegaard offers several procedures that the ironist can follow to avoid running out of material and hence becoming bored. Given the lethal implications of boredom, the essay can be thought of as an instruction manual on how to prevent self-annihilation. Kierkegaard suggests that the ironist cultivate the art of remembering and forgetting. This can be done by living in as neutral a way as possible: avoid marrying, having friends, accepting official appointments, or becoming involved in business affairs. Nothing will have so much significance that it cannot be forgotten when convenient, yet everything will have just enough significance to be recalled when needed. Kierkegaard also suggests that the ironist try to live in an arbitrary way. "You go to see the middle of a play, you read the third part of a book" (*E/O* 295). The arbitrary will offer the self continually different and unexpected experiences. "The Rotation Method" was anticipated in *The Concept of Irony*, where Kierkegaard writes that the ironic ego, though it can be anything in an instant, should leisurely select "the proper costume for the poetic personage [it] has poetized [itself] to be. In this matter the ironist has great skill, not to mention a considerable assortment of masquerade costumes from which to make a judicious selection" (*CI* 299). The careful husbanding of material through the art of remembering and forgetting, the novel experiences offered by the arbitrary, and the enormous time that can be expended in carefully selecting a proper costume for the personage the ironist has decided to be should result in a considerable lengthening of the ironist's existence.

Fifth, though the ironic ego as Kierkegaard portrays it faces the constant threat of evaporation should it cease in its creative efforts, anxiety over an untimely demise does not preclude the ego from taking a strong sense of pleasure in its creations. Both Hegel and Kierkegaard describe the ego as immensely enjoying its self-created actuality. Hegel writes of the ego living in "the bliss of self-enjoyment" (*A* 66), and Kierkegaard writes of the pleasure the ironist takes in the environments that he poetically produces, "lost in the presentational enjoyment of the harmonious Hellenic life" (*CI* 294), and in his poetic production of himself. "Now he strolls about with the proud mien of a Roman patrician in trimmed toga, now he is sitting in the *sella curulis* with weighty Roman seriousness, now he disguises himself in the humble cloth of a penitent pilgrim, now he crosses his legs like a Turkish pasha in his harem, flits airily about like a bird, a lovesick cyther player. This is what the ironist means when he maintains that one should live poeti-

cally, and this is what he attains by poetically producing himself"
(*CI* 299). Since what the ego experiences in these creations is an
aspect of itself, the pleasure it takes in its experience is essentially
the pleasure of narcissism. This narcissistic pleasure is not limited
to directly enjoying the world as the self. The ironist can also take
pleasure in reflecting upon the world as the self. Commenting on
the "poetic coloring" of "The Diary of the Seducer," Kierkegaard
comments, "The poetical was the *more* he himself brought with
him. This *more* was the poetical he enjoyed in the poetic situation
of reality; he withdrew this again in the form of poetic reflection.
This afforded him a second enjoyment, and his whole life was
motivated by enjoyment" (*E/O* 301).

Schlegel's concept of irony directly opposes the narcissistic
engagement of the self with itself. By skeptically acknowledging
the limitations of any particular pattern of experience, irony forces
the ego to break away from its own creations. Reflection upon
experience shaped by the self is not, as in Kierkegaard, an act of
narcissistic enclosure, but a critical displacement of the self's ego-
centrism and self-love. In chastising the self's narcissism, irony
forces the self to look away from its own reflection to the universe
at large. Schlegel writes, "We must rise above our own love and
be able to destroy in our thoughts what we adore; if we cannot do
this, we lack . . . the feeling for the universe."[20]

Sixth, Kierkegaard argues in *The Concept of Irony* that authen-
tic history is both temporal and continuous. It is the actualization
of Mind or the Idea in time. "The Idea is concrete and must there-
fore become concrete, but this becoming concrete of the Idea is
the historical actuality" (*CI* 296). In Kierkegaard's view, as I point
out earlier in this chapter, romantic irony negates "all historical
actuality" (*CI* 292). In doing so, it both places itself above the tem-
poral and also loses all continuity. Unencumbered by the past,
irony has the power to begin at will. Irony "knows itself to be in
possession of the power to begin from the beginning whenever it
pleases, for nothing in the past is binding upon it" (*CI* 296). What
replaces historical actuality is an actuality created by the ironist.
But because irony is always at its beginning, whatever the ironist

creates, be it personage or environment, is new, has no link to what came before. It is for this reason that Kierkegaard describes the existence of the ironist as fragmentary, chaotic, lacking in continuity. "Because the ironist poetically produces himself as well as his environment with the greatest possible poetic license . . . his life finally loses all continuity" (*CI* 300–301).

The fragmentary quality of the ironist's existence is a prevalent theme in *Either/Or*. In "Diapsalmata," A comments that his life is "meaningless."

> My life is absolutely meaningless. When I consider the different periods into which it falls, it seems like the word *Schnur* in the dictionary, which means in the first place a string, in the second, a daughter-in-law. The only thing lacking is that the word *Schnur* should mean in the third place a camel, in the fourth, a dust-brush. (*E/O* 35)

His life is meaningless because, like the definitions of the word *Schnur,* the different periods of his life have no relation or connection to each other. Kierkegaard's harshest criticism of the ironist's fragmentary existence, however, may not be in "Diapsalmata" but in "The Ancient Tragical Motif as Reflected in the Modern," "Shadowgraphs," and "The Unhappiest Man." In these essays, Kierkegaard presents the Symparanekromenoi, a Greek word invented by Kierkegaard that means fellowship or society of buried lives or living dead. This society is "devoted to the aphoristical and the accidental" (*E/O* 218), and the lives of the members are characterized by the absence of continuity. As one member explains, "[W]e . . . do not merely think and speak aphoristically but live aphoristically" (*E/O* 218). An aphoristical existence is one that lacks continuity, and for Kierkegaard the lack of continuity implies the absence of the historical and temporal, the context in which existence acquires continuity. These interrelated concepts, fragmentation and the absence of the temporal and historical, suggest one of the reasons that Kierkegaard associates an aphoristical existence with death. The Symparanekromenoi have no existence in the present. Their aphoristical nature denies them that possibility. Unable to have an immediate, present existence, they are truly "living dead."

Kierkegaard's attack on the sense of fragmentation in romantic irony is carried out on a formal as well as a philosophical level. *Either* can be viewed as a parody of what Schlegel saw as "the characteristic form of the great modern tradition in literature,"[21] the *Roman*. Unlike classical literature, in which genres are not mixed, the *Roman* is a mixture of genres, a *Mischgedicte*. It can combine verse, dramatic elements, and narrative, and the same work can include humor, philosophical speculation, and unsophisticated emotion. In constructing such a work, the author recognizes only one law, that his own caprice, "Willkur," is subject to no law. A mélange of genres, capriciously or wittily constructed, the novel reflects Schlegel's view of the universe as an infinite, chaotic plenitude. Schlegel's own novel, *Lucinde,* embodies this theory of romantic form. Julius states at the outset of the novel that he is going to "destroy . . . all that part we call 'order'" (*LF* 45). Rather than present his story systematically and progressively, he "claim[s] explicitly and affirm[s] actually the right to a charming confusion" (*LF* 45). The novel itself is a mixture of genres: letters, verse, allegory, idyll, and narrative prose. It includes philosophical speculation and, in the portrait of three-year-old Wilhelmine, emotions as yet unshaped by social conventions.

Either can be seen as belonging to the *Roman* tradition. The arrangement of the work is deliberately unsystematic. Like Julius, Kierkegaard destroys "that part we call 'order.'" In his guise as Victor Eremita, the editor of A's papers, Kierkegaard writes, "The arranging of A's papers was not so simple. I have therefore let chance determine the order, that is to say, I have left them in the order in which I found them" (*E/O* 7–8). This work, the order of whose parts is arranged by chance, incorporates numerous elements, including aphorisms (the "Diapsalmata" is a kind of structural miniature of the whole), an "ecstatic lecture," a diary, verse, narrative prose in the prefaces to the "Diapsalmata" and the "Diary of the Seducer," meditative essays, and a review.

That Kierkegaard regards this form with the utmost antipathy is suggested by a comment he makes in his critique of *Lucinde* in *The Concept of Irony*. The confusion and disorder that *Lucinde* introduces into the ethical sphere "it illustrates itself by means of the most perfect confusion in its design and structure" (*CI* 308), and Kierkegaard quotes in support of his point Julius' declaration of his right to a "charming confusion." The correlation between the ethical and the formal here is a bit of Kierkegaardian short-hand. Ultimately, the two concepts rest on the same foundation, Kierkegaard's view of the romantic ego. As I discussed earlier in the chapter, the ethical life for Kierkegaard at least begins with the acceptance of an actuality that is not created by the ego and over which the ego has no final power. The ironist abrogates the ethical by denying this actuality. A second implication of Kierkegaard's view of the ego is that in denying historical actual-ity, the ironist acquires the power to begin, and in continually beginning, the ironist loses all continuity. As a consequence, irony for Kierkegaard must be expressed in a mode that is formally dis-continuous. Both concepts, formal discontinuity and the denial of the ethical, are mutually implicating: formal discontinuity implies the denial of historical actuality, which is the foundation of the ethical, while the denial of the ethical, as Kierkegaard says about *Lucinde,* is "illustrated" by the absence of any formal order. Kierkegaard's attitude toward the *Roman*-tic structure of *Either,* then, could hardly be said to be one of ringing endorsement.

Irony as Schlegel presents it also repetitively begins. As the ironist repeats the process of self-creation and self-destruction, older conceptions of self and world are destroyed and new ones are continually created. These concepts may have a relation to, but are not necessarily conditioned by, what came before. Hence the ironist's existence, as Schlegel describes it, is, finally, aphoristical— lacking in order and continuity. For Schlegel, unlike Kierkegaard, irony's ongoing beginnings do not negate the present. Rather, in always being at its beginning, irony continually situates itself in the present. As Paul de Man writes, "The dialectic of self-destruction and self-invention which for him [Friedrich Schlegel] . . . charac-terizes the ironic mind is an endless process that leads to no syn-thesis. . . . In temporal terms it designates the fact that irony engenders a temporal sequence of acts of consciousness which is endless."[22] Because the ironist's experience of the world is unordered, the sense of the present expressed by irony cannot be conceived as being progressive, linear, or teleological. As the ironist repetitively begins, he locates himself within and experiences a present that expands without direction or goal. For both Kierkegaard and Schlegel, to be an ironist is "to think . . . speak . . . and live aphoristically." For Schlegel, however, to do so is not to become a member of the fellowship of the living dead, but to join the living in an ever-expanding present, an endless temporal sequence of acts of consciousness.

Finally, romantic irony for Kierkegaard is the mode of existence in which the self, out of time, enclosed within itself, stripped of historical context, has no identity and cannot acquire an identity. The mode of existence in which the self first begins to acquire an identity is the ethical. Here the self becomes inextricably bound in historical actuality. But the ethical is not the mode of existence in which the self most fully realizes itself. This occurs in a religious, and specifically Christian, mode of existence. In "the Christian stage of existence," Mark Taylor writes, "there is the fullest realization of individual selfhood."[23] In an aphorism in "Diapsalmata," A appears to express a Christian view of the self.

> I seem destined to have to suffer every possible mood, to acquire experience in every direction. Every moment I lie like a child, who must learn to swim, out in the middle of the sea. I scream (which I have learned from the Greeks, from whom one can learn everything which is purely human); for I have indeed a harness about my waist, but the pole that holds me up I do not see. It is a fearful way in which to get experience. (*E/O* 31)

As in many of the aphorisms in "Diapsalmata," A complains that his life lacks continuity. (That the complaint is often repeated should come as no surprise; diapsalmata means "refrain" [*E/O*

443 n. 4].) He says that he lies like a child out in the middle of the sea. The image suggests the chaotic nature of his existence. Floating in the middle of the sea, he changes direction with each passing wind or current. Yet A also believes that there is something apart from the self that sustains his existence, the unseen pole that holds him up. Every individual in Kierkegaard's view is dependent upon God, whether or not the individual recognizes this dependence. As Taylor writes, the "concrete self . . . is constituted by another—by God. This is a given in the self's being that, though it might be denied, cannot be negated. If the self is to accept itself, it must constantly acknowledge its ontological dependence on God."[24] But A cannot acknowledge his ontological dependence on God. Confined by the conceptual limitations of his own mode of existence, he cannot "even raise the question of God and of the self's relation to God."[25] One result of this limitation is that A cannot comprehend the religious implications of his own meditation. He simply does not "see" what "holds [him] up," and hence his existence continues to be chaotic, meaningless, enclosed, and so on. Though it is here only gestured toward and, given what Kierkegaard sees as the limitations of an ironic mode of existence, certainly could not be enacted, the turn to religion will be a prominent feature in later presentations of the ironic/aesthetic consciousness.

In contrast to Kierkegaard, Schlegel views romantic irony as the mode of existence in which the self acquires an ever richer sense of itself. In the continuing process of self-creation and self-destruction, the self experiences itself and the world in ever more differentiated ways and hence gains an increasingly complex sense of its own identity. In Kierkegaard's view the self develops through various stages of existence and reaches its fullest and final sense of itself in the Christian stage. For Schlegel, the self does not realize itself in this way. Since the process of self-creation and self-destruction is never ending, the self as Schlegel conceives it can never *be* a self; it never acquires a sense of identity that is final and unchanging. It can only continue to *become* a self.

Both the Schlegelian and the Hegelian and Kierkegaardian con-
cepts of romantic irony are part, in Sanford Schwartz's phrase, of
the matrix of modernism. To describe in detail the historical trans-
mission of these concepts would take us far beyond the limits of
this essay. The more modest goal of the remainder of this chapter
is to discuss, in admittedly selective fashion, several of the major
ways in which these opposing concepts entered into twentieth-
century thought.

Hegel was not well known in America before the second half
of the nineteenth century,[26] and early commentary on him is often
negative. James Murdoch, for example, in his *Sketches of Modern
Philosophy Among the Germans* (1842), the "first American
overview of German thought," judged Hegel to be " 'the most
unintelligible writer' [he] had ever read."[27] Three years later,
Hegel was attacked by Asa Maher, president of Oberlin College,
as a pantheist.[28] Hegel's cause, however, was taken up after the
Civil War by one of the most influential philosophical societies in
nineteenth-century America, the St. Louis Philosophical Soci-
ety.[29] Its president, Henry Brokmeyer, emigrated to America in
1844 from Westphalia, worked his way from New York to Missis-
sippi, attended Georgetown College in Kentucky and Brown
University, and then retreated from society into the Missouri
woods in 1854. In St. Louis in 1858, Brokmeyer met W. T. Har-
ris, who was later to become the society's secretary and United
States commissioner of education. Harris paid Brokmeyer's
expenses for a year while he worked on a translation of Hegel's
Logic. In January of 1867 the society began to publish its influen-
tial *Journal of Speculative Philosophy.* The St. Louis Hegelians came
into contact with the New England transcendentalists in part
through Bronson Alcott, who spent January and part of February
1859 in St. Louis and, while there, had daily contact with
Brokmeyer and Harris.[30] In 1865 Harris spent two days in Con-
cord with Emerson and Alcott and eventually moved to Con-
cord.[31] A second group, organized in midcentury in Cincinnati,

also promulgated Hegel's ideas. This group, whose members included J. B. Stallo, Peter Kaufman, Moncure Conway, and August Willich, did not publish a journal, and their influence was felt more in the realm of public affairs than in higher education.[32]

Whitman was also influential in disseminating and popularizing Hegel. He writes in *Specimen Days* of having a "pleasant chat" with "W. T. Harris, the Hegelian,"[33] and he comments in "Carlyle from American Points of View" that Hegel's system "beams forth to-day, in its entirety, illuminating the thought of the universe, and satisfying the mystery thereof to the human mind, with a more consoling scientific assurance than any yet."[34] Whitman also comments on Hegel in *Democratic Vistas*. He writes that "there must, for future and democratic purposes, appear poets" who are "possess'd of the religious fire and abandon of Isaiah, luxuriant in the epic talent of Homer" and who can create "proud characters as in Shakspere." Their creative activity, however, must be "consistent with the Hegelian formulas."[35] A short poem added to the 1881 edition of *Leaves of Grass* offers a very positive interpretation of these formulas.

Roaming in Thought
(*After reading* Hegel)

Roaming in thought over the Universe, I saw the little
    that is
Good steadily hastening towards immortality,
And the vast all that is call'd Evil I saw hastening to
    merge itself and become lost and dead.[36]

In addition to Whitman and the St. Louis and Cincinnati Hegelians, the regular instruction in German philosophy at colleges and universities that began in the 1870s also brought Hegel's ideas to a larger audience. Professor Bowen at Harvard, for instance, conducted his first course in German philosophy in 1873–74.[37] W. T. Harris taught a course at Holyoke in 1882, and in 1886 the University of Michigan offered a seminar in Hegel's *Logic*.[38] Interest in Hegel continued to develop through the work of Josiah Royce at Harvard and Brand Blanschard at Yale.[39]

A very specific aspect of Hegel's thought, his attack on romantic irony, was indirectly, but very forcefully, expressed early in the twentieth century by Irving Babbitt, who begins his famous blast of the concept in *Rousseau and Romanticism* (1919) with the words, "Hegel . . . repudiates [romantic] irony" (*RR* 240). Like Hegel, Babbitt views the creativity of the ironist as both capricious and as isolating and enclosing. "The Schlegelian irony in particular merely pushes to an extreme the doctrine that nothing must interfere with the imagination in its creative play. 'The caprice of the poet,' as Friedrich Schlegel says, 'suffers no law above itself.' Why indeed should the poet allow any restriction to be placed upon his caprice in a universe that is after all only a projection of himself?" (*RR* 241). Babbitt also points to what he calls the ironist's aloofness, which results from a continual movement of self-transcendence. The ironist first stands aloof from his ordinary ego, then stands aloof from the ego that stands aloof, and so on. "But there is in him something that may stand aloof even from this aloofness and so on indefinitely" (*RR* 241). At the very least, this aloofness leaves the ironist in a state of "homeless hovering" (*RR* 249). The romantic ironist "lays hold imaginatively upon the infinite only by expanding beyond what his age holds to be normal and central" (*RR* 242), and he opposes his "unique and private self" to the conventions of his age. To the romantic ironist, Babbitt contrasts Socrates. Although the irony of Socrates also "implies a certain degree of detachment from the received beliefs and conventions of his time" (*RR* 244), unlike the romantic ironist, Socrates opposes to these conventions "his universal and ethical self" (*RR* 245). In doing so, he experiences and helps his age to recognize that which is "more profoundly representative" (*RR* 246), a "deeper centre of experience" (*RR* 247). Babbitt's view of the ironist as one whose continual self-transcendence separates him from reality recalls Hegel's and Kierkegaard's view of the ironist as detached, "hovering" over the actual. In *The Concept of Irony* Kierkegaard also contrasts Socratic and romantic irony. Though Kierkegaard and Babbitt differ on what they believe Socratic irony helps bring to light, both view Socratic irony as having a positive historical role and see romantic irony as a negative force in history. And Babbitt's view that for the ironist the universe is only a "projection of himself" recalls Hegel's and Kierkegaard's characterization of the ironist as Fichtean ego. In their interpretation, the world is both a creation of the ironist's ego and a plaything for his reflective consciousness. It has no "validity" in itself.

Philosophy and academic criticism were not the only ways in which the Hegelian and Kierkegaardian senses of romantic irony were transmitted to the twentieth century. This consciousness is also seen in the aesthetic literature of the 1880s and 1890s. J. K. Huysmans' *A Rebours* is a representative example. Early in *A Rebours,* Des Esseintes describes the way in which an imaginary world can be substituted for the real one. "In fact it appeared to him a futile waste of energy to travel when, so he believed, imagination was perfectly competent to fill the place of the vulgar reality of actual prosaic facts. . . . The whole secret is to know how to set about it, to be able to concentrate the mind on a single point, to attain to a sufficient degree of self-abstraction to produce the necessary hallucination and so substitute the vision of the reality for the reality itself."[40] Certainly, Des Esseintes' comment is not meant to imply that Huysmans holds a Fichtean view of the ego. But Des Esseintes' creative act has the same result that the ironist's creative act has in Kierkegaard and Hegel. In creating a world that he substitutes for reality, Des Esseintes frees himself "from the restraint in which the given actuality binds him" (*CI* 279). He "hovers" over reality, enclosed in his "self-created actuality."

As Hegel and Kierkegaard present it, life for the ironist is a solitary aesthetic event, a drama that is shaped for the ironist's own amusement and is devoid of true relations with others. Hegel writes that even when the ironist does have a relationship with another, the relationship is "null," and we noted earlier in this chapter that Cordelia in "Diary of the Seducer" exists to the seducer only as aesthetic material. The reduction of life by the ironist/aesthete to a well-made play is illustrated in *A Rebours* in two episodes. The first is the marriage of Des Esseintes' friend, D'Aigurande. Though all of D'Aigurande's other friends oppose his intention to marry, Des Esseintes encourages him to marry, but only after learning that the couple intend to live in an apartment built on a circular floor plan. Des Esseintes foresees that they will eventually tire of the apartment, that they will move to one built on more traditional lines, that none of their old furniture will fit in their new quarters, and that, bereft of the money that would eliminate this problem, they will have endless squabbles and eventually separate. He sees in their marriage and in their subsequent misery only endless entertainment for himself—"an indefinite vista of ludicrous miseries to come" (*AR* 66). They follow his advice, marry, and everything that Des Esseintes predicted comes true. His final comment on the episode is reminiscent of the seducer, who sets a plot in motion and then compliments himself on his own artistic genius. "'Yes, my plan of campaign was quite correct,' Des Esseintes had told himself on hearing the news [that the couple had separated]; he enjoyed the same satisfaction a strategist feels when his manoeuvres, planned long beforehand, end in victory" (*AR* 66).

Des Esseintes' second "campaign" is more ambitious than his first. Quite by accident (and the aesthete/ironist's life, as Kierkegaard points out, is ruled by chance), Des Esseintes meets a young boy and decides to take him to a bordello. While the boy is enjoying the company of one of the women, Des Esseintes explains to the madam that he is trying to train a murderer. Once again, he sets a plot in motion. He pays for the boy's entertainment at the bordello for three months in advance, hoping the boy will "acquire the habit of these pleasures" (*AR* 68). Since the boy is poor and has no way to pay for this entertainment, Des Esseintes anticipates that the boy will turn to crime to support his habit. During a robbery, so Des Esseintes hopes, the boy will be surprised by a householder, whom he will murder. Unlike the episode with D'Aigurande, Des Esseintes does not know whether his plan has been successful. He has not read of the boy's arrest, and he chides himself for not becoming more involved in the drama. In neither episode are the individuals understood as more than dramatic characters in Des Esseintes' play. The reduction of the individuals to "characters" effectively nullifies any true relationship between them and Des Esseintes. Both episodes are to

Des Esseintes artistic events alone and are evaluated by an aesthetic standard. The first episode is a successful play; the second is a not so successful play.

As Des Esseintes retreats further and further into his self-made world, he, like his aesthete/ironist predecessors, faces the problem of running out of material. He resolves this problem in several ingenious ways. In a passage that almost could have come from "The Rotation Method," Des Esseintes recounts how he has mastered the art of remembering and forgetting. The difficulty, as A explained, is in being able to recall the experience when it is needed and yet be able to forget it until it is needed. Des Esseintes brilliantly meets this challenge. He takes a special bonbon made of "a drop of sarcanthus scent, a drop of essence of woman, crystallized in a piece of sugar" and lets it "melt in his mouth" (*AR* 97). Its effect is to bring back memories of his former liaisons. "[T]hen, in a moment, would recur with an infinite tenderness recollections, almost effaced, altogether soft and languishing, of the lascivious doings of other days" (*AR* 97). By means of these bonbons, the "lascivious doings of other days" can be forgotten and then recalled as need requires.

Another way of getting material is to stimulate a physical sense and then fashion that sense into a work of art. One example of this technique is Des Esseintes' compositions on his "mouth organ," a collection of casks of various liquors. Through a clever mechanical device, Des Esseintes is able to fill simultaneously tiny cups arranged beneath the casks. The organ is then "open," and it provides Des Esseintes with almost endless synaesthetic pleasure. Each liquor, so he holds, corresponds in taste to the sound of a particular instrument or voice, and by imbibing a drop here a drop there, Des Esseintes is able to "execute on his tongue a succession of voiceless melodies; noiseless funeral marches, solemn and stately; could hear in his mouth solos of crème de menthe, duets of vespetro and rum" (*AR* 45). He can transfer "to his palate selections of real music, following the composer's *motif* step by step . . . by combinations and contrasts of allied liquors, by approximations and cunning mixtures of beverages" (*AR* 45). And he even composes a pastoral symphony "with the gentle blackcurrent ratafia that set his throat resounding with the mellow notes of warbling nightingales" (*AR* 45). As long as Des Esseintes remains musically inventive, this sense will provide him with new material. Similar works of art are created with the sense of smell (chap. 10). Oscar Wilde alludes to *A Rebours* in *The Picture of Dorian Gray,* and perhaps Des Esseintes' fashioning of himself into a work of art was the inspiration for Wilde's epigram in "Phrases and Philosophies for the Use of the Young": "One should either be a work of art, or wear a work of art."[41]

The narrator in *A Rebours* remarks at one point that Des Esseintes had "lived on himself, fed on his own substance, like those hibernating animals that lie torpid in a hole all the winter" (*AR* 71), and Des Esseintes' third technique for replenishing his "substance" is one that is not explored by Kierkegaard, whose aesthete/ironist is so clever that he seems to create enough material for himself through his own intellectual acrobatics. As the self exhausts its ordinary range of experience, it can turn to bizarre or forbidden subjects for fresh material. Such subjects are available to Des Esseintes in part through the works of art that he collects. The Luyken prints are representative of this aspect of his collection.

> The works he possessed of this artist, at once fantastic and depressing, vigorous and brutal, included the series of his *Religious Persecutions,* a collection of appalling plates representing all the tortures which the savagery of religious intolerance has invented, plates exhibiting all the horrors of human agony,— men roasted over braziers, skulls laid open by sword cuts, pierced with nails, riven asunder with saws, bowels drawn out of the belly, and twisted round rollers, finger-nails torn out one by one with pincers, eyes put out, eyelids turned back and transfixed with pins, limbs dislocated or carefully broken bones laid bare and scraped for hours with knives. (*AR* 58)

Des Esseintes testifies to the effectiveness of these prints in sustaining a self that would otherwise be depleted. "These prints were mines of curious information; a man could look at them for hours and never weary; profoundly suggestive of ideas, they often helped

Des Esseintes to kill the time on days when books refused to inter-
est him" (*AR* 58).

Certainly, a great deal of Des Esseintes' isolated existence is to
him very enjoyable. His libidinal relation to his own bodily senses
clearly brings him exquisite narcissistic pleasure. Both Hegel and
Kierkegaard write of the enjoyment that the aesthete/ironist takes
in his self-created world. They also write of the ironist's recogni-
tion that the world made up of the self is hollow and insubstantial.
Isolated and enclosed in a self-created actuality, the ironist longs
for the external and objective. Des Esseintes, too, suffers from his
isolation. "[T]his solitude he had so ardently desired and won at
last had resulted in poignant distress; this silence that had once
appealed to him . . . now weighed upon him with an intolerable
burden. One morning, he had awoke as frenzied in mind as a man
who finds himself locked up in a prison cell" (*AR* 119). He yearns
to experience the objective world and "so escape the divagations
of a mind dizzied with grinding, grinding at nothing" (*AR* 120).
He plans a trip to London, goes to Paris to catch a train and then,
in a tavern, just before the train leaves, he falls "into a dream" (*AR*
125) and in his imagination peoples the tavern with a set of cus-
tomers he derives from Dickens. Des Esseintes loiters "idly in this
London of the imagination, happy to be under shelter, seeming to
hear on the Thames the hideous whistles of the tugs at work
behind the Tuileries, near the bridge" (*AR* 125). He decides not
to go to London, preferring, once again, the vision of reality for
reality itself. "Was he not in London, whose odours and atmos-
phere, whose denizens and viands and table furniture were all
about him?" (*AR* 130). He chides himself for having attempted to
"repudiate [his] old settled convictions, to have condemned the
obedient figment of [his] imagination" (*AR* 130). This canceled
trip to London seems to bear out Hegel's observation that the iro-
nist longs for objectivity but "cannot renounce his isolation and
withdrawal into himself" (*A* 66). Des Esseintes clearly desires the
objective world and yet turns away from it, retreating once more
into himself.

Eventually, Des Esseintes completely uses up his little internal
material and suffers a total collapse. His doctor orders him to

return to society or contemplate an immediate end to his earthly existence. Des Esseintes agrees to go back to Paris, but he loathes and despises the commercialism, the baseness, the Americanism (the ultimate insult) of French society. "It was the vast, foul bagnio of America transported to our Continent; it was, in a word, the limitless, unfathomable, incommensurable firmament of black-guardism of the financier and the self-made man" (*AR* 205). So it is not society to which Des Esseintes turns emotionally to end his isolation. Like his aesthete/ironist predecessors, Des Esseintes turns to religion to escape from his crushing subjectivism. "Lord," he says at the very end of the novel, "take pity on the Christian who doubts" (*AR* 206).

The philosophical and literary expressions of the Hegelian and Kierkegaardian senses of romantic irony swirl in an almost uncanny way around the writer who has painted perhaps the most famous negative portrait of the romantic ironist in the modern period, T. S. Eliot. He was born and received his early education in St. Louis. While Eliot was studying at Harvard for his master's degree in English literature, he attended Irving Babbitt's course, Literary Criticism in France,[42] and Eliot has remarked on the deep influence Babbitt exerted on him.[43] Eliot spent the 1910–11 academic year in Paris. Lyndall Gordon writes that "Eliot looked for the decadent Paris of *Bubu de Montparnasse*. . . . He hunted down decadence, and allowed lust and drunkenness to circle round him."[44] In his essay on Baudelaire, Eliot mentions *A Rebours,* and perhaps his interest in Huysmans began with Eliot's Parisian search for decadence. Or he might have learned of him from Jean Verdenal, the French medical student to whom "The Love Song of J. Alfred Prufrock" is dedicated. Eliot and Verdenal shared lodgings in Paris, and Verdenal writes of Huysmans in a 1911 letter to Eliot.[45] And by 1911 Eliot had begun to read Hegel.[46]

"The Love Song of J. Alfred Prufrock" may be Eliot's most subtle characterization of the romantic ironist. In Kierkegaard's view, the romantic ironist has the ability to begin again whenever he pleases because he is detached from the actual. These beginnings, though, are not true beginnings because true beginnings for

Kierkegaard cannot be divorced from the self's acceptance of and engagement with the actual and temporal. To begin is to accept limitation. The absence of a beginning in Kierkegaard's sense and the disengagement that this lack of a beginning implies are expressed in "Prufrock" in the opening verse paragraph.

> Let us go then, you and I,
> When the evening is spread out against the sky
> Like a patient etherised upon a table;
> Let us go, through certain half-deserted streets,
> The muttering retreats
> Of restless nights in one-night cheap hotels
> And sawdust restaurants with oyster-shells:
> Streets that follow like a tedious argument
> Of insidious intent
> To lead you to an overwhelming question . . .
> Oh, do not ask, "What is it?"
> Let us go and make our visit.[47]

The poem begins at the moment when, apparently, debate is finished, a resolution has been made, the journey is about to begin. "Let us go *then*, you and I" (emphasis added). The actual beginning of this journey, however, is immediately delayed by the prepositional phrase that follows. "Let us go then, you and I / *When* . . ." (emphasis added). The effect of the phrase is to push an act that is about to occur (let us go, now) into the future (let us go, when). The opening words of line 4 repeat the first words of the poem, but "Let us go" in line 4 lacks the sense of urgency, resolution, and immediate action that characterizes these words in line 1. Rather, they continue to express the future-oriented direction of thought that was suggested by the "when" of line 2. Let us go (when we do go) through certain half-deserted streets, the muttering retreats, and so on. The long description that follows functions as a digression and pushes back even further the moment of actual beginning. Huysmans writes in *A Rebours* that "a man can undertake long voyages of exploration sitting in his armchair by the fireside" (*AR* 21), and the entire first verse paragraph of

"Prufrock" can be thought of as a kind of elaborate, circular, *faux voyage*. It starts with an intention to begin and continues to delay this beginning until it circles back in the final line of the verse paragraph to where it started, with an intention to begin, "Let us go and make our visit" (l. 12). The experience that is recounted in the opening of "Prufrock" is both richly detailed and yet never actually seems to take place. But, as Hegel and Kierkegaard write, the disengagement from reality, the lack of true content and substantiality, is precisely what characterizes the existence of the ironist/aesthete.

Prufrock's detachment and disengagement is again expressed in the meditation on time that follows the opening verse paragraph (ll. 23–48). He notes the seemingly endless amount of time available for acting. "There will be time, there will be time," he repeats over and again. There will be time to wonder, "'Do I dare,'" time to prepare a face to meet the faces that you meet, time to turn back and descend the stair, and so on. Yet all the events for which Prufrock imagines there will be time remain only possible or potential events because the entire section is written in the actual or implied future tense. Envisioned as taking place in the future, these events have only "the validity of possibility," not the validity of actuality. And even their validity as possibility is attenuated by the sense of reversal. "In a minute there is time / For decisions and revisions which a minute will reverse" (ll. 47–48). An event contemplated as taking place in the future is canceled, reversed, prior to its actual occurrence. Prufrock's meditation on events that have not yet happened and, though they have not happened, may be "reversed" or canceled, robs his immediate existence of content and leaves him, as in the opening verse paragraph, hovering and disengaged. Like A, he "keeps existence away by the most subtle of deceptions, by thinking."

Prufrock's time is chiefly taken up in meditating about whether, as he puts it later in the poem, he will have the "strength to force the moment to its crisis" (l. 80). Whether he actually does or does not remains a mystery. Certainly, he often seems to be on the verge of forcing the moment. He first approaches this precipice in the opening verse paragraph, where we are led up to an "overwhelming question" and then led away from it, "Oh, do not ask, 'What is it?'" He returns to this moment in line 54, where he asks, "So how should I presume?" and then immediately turns away from the issue to reflect upon the "eyes" he has known, and he has "known them all." Like the opening argument of insidious intent, his thoughts on the eyes lead him back to the issue of forcing the moment, "And how should I presume?" (l. 61). This question starts the process of approaching the moment of crisis and then backing away from it all over again. This time round (ll. 62–69) Prufrock deflects the issue by meditating not on eyes but on arms, and he has known them all already, too. Once again, these thoughts lead him to the issue of presuming. But the question Prufrock now asks differs slightly from the two previous questions. Instead of asking, "And *how* should I presume?" (ll. 54, 61; emphasis added), he asks, "And *should* I then presume?" (l. 68; emphasis added). The second is a more urgent question than the first. It calls for a decision. And should I then presume? Yes, I should presume, or, no, I should not presume. The first question, *how* should I presume, only asks about the means or method of presuming. It sidesteps the issue of any actual presuming since deciding *how* to presume is not at all to decide *to* presume. Prufrock carefully slips away from the call for an immediate decision in line 68 by reverting in the next line to the more evasive "how" phrasing, "And how should I begin?" And he proceeds to tell us how. "Shall I say, I have gone at dusk through narrow streets," and so forth. Not (at least by now) surprisingly, these reflections lead once again to the moment of decision. "Should I, after tea and cakes and ices, / Have the strength to force the moment to its crisis?" (ll. 79–80). The ices-crisis rhyme beautifully deflates the emotional intensity of the moment by linking the crisis to a social setting whose most distinguishing feature, at least in this poem, may be what used to be called polite conversation.

Up to this moment in the poem, Prufrock has been referring to the moment of decision as a future event. The streets "lead you to an overwhelming question." He asks, "how should I presume" (twice) and "how should I begin" (once), questions that ask about the means of going about an as yet undecided upon future course

of action. "And should I then presume," though calling for an
immediate decision, still refers to an event in the future. "Should"
in the "crisis" couplet expresses a strong sense of the future.
"Should I, after tea and cakes and ices, / Have the strength to force
the moment" (ll. 79–80) means *will* I, after tea and cakes and ices,
have the strength to force the moment. At line 87 Prufrock begins
to look on this moment of decision as if it were a past event. "And
would it have been worth it, after all," he asks repeatedly (ll. 87,
99), if he had forced the moment to its crisis and she had said, also
repeatedly, "That is not what I meant at all" (ll. 97, 110).
Prufrock's backward glance, though, is not directed at an actual
past, but at a hypothetical past. The conditional tense of the ques-
tion, "would it have been worth it" if he had forced the moment,
allows Prufrock to look back upon and evaluate an action before
the action takes place. That is, he imagines what his reaction to
forcing the moment would be if, upon doing so, she were to reject
his advances. Though it is contemplated as a future event and
looked back upon as a conditional past event, the actual event
itself, forcing the moment to its crisis, is never directly presented.
Prufrock's world of linguistic obfuscation, indirection, and eva-
sion, his world of possible, perhaps, would it have been, if one
should say, how should I, shall I say, should I then, and so on,
leaves him, once again, disengaged from the actual and recalls
Kierkegaard's description of the romantic ironist as one who "lives
completely hypothetically and subjunctively" (*CI* 301).

Hegel and Kierkegaard write of the ironist/aesthete's desire to
give up a painfully isolated existence and of his inability to do so.
Both attribute this inability to the "vanity" (Hegel's word) of the
ironist/aesthete, the vanity of a gigantic, creative self, puffed up
and in love with itself and its creations. Prufrock also suffers deeply
from his isolation, and like his ironist/aesthete predecessors, he,
too, cannot give up his isolation. Yet his inability to do so does not
seem to be the result of vanity. Prufrock is not a Fichtean ego but
a small, scared (extremely nimble but scared nonetheless) ego. His
isolation seems to be a kind of much needed self-protection, not
self-projection. He comments at the end of the poem, "We have
lingered in the chambers of the sea / . . . / Till human voices wake

us, and we drown" (ll. 129, 131). Though isolation may be a cause of suffering, it protects Prufrock against the Other, "human voices," whose intrusion upon the ego's reflective and enclosing relation with itself is seen as annihilating to the ego—"we drown." Peter Ackroyd describes these same opposing psychic needs—protection against and desire for intimacy with or openness to an other—in Eliot at the time he wrote "Prufrock." In the summer of 1911 (Eliot had completed "Prufrock" that summer), he was, Ackroyd writes, "evincing a kind of narcissistic vulnerability."[48] Given these irreconcilable and paralyzing needs, perhaps Eliot's own psychic drowning, his breakdown ten years later, was inevitable.

Prufrock is not the only character in early Eliot who has affinities with Hegel's and Kierkegaard's ironist/aesthete. The Young Man in "Portrait of a Lady" and Gerontion also experience the ironist's negative freedom from the temporal and the actual and the sense of isolation, enclosure, and despair that accompanies this freedom.[49] And *The Waste Land,* because of its extreme fragmentation, "I can connect / Nothing with nothing" (ll. 301–2), and its repeated evocation of death-in-life, might be considered an extended oration from one of the Symparanekromenoi, those for whom fragmentation is the defining condition of their existence as "buried lives" or living dead. Given the overwhelming sense of isolation, despair, and nonexistence that Eliot expresses in the early work, it is perhaps not surprising that he should turn to religion. In 1927 he officially accepted the Anglican faith.

Four years prior to his conversion, Eliot had written of the need to give "allegiance to something outside" the self.

> Mr. Murry makes his issue perfectly clear. "Catholicism," he says, "stands for the principle of unquestioned spiritual authority outside the individual; that is also the principle of Classicism in literature." . . . Those of us who find ourselves supporting what Mr. Murry calls Classicism believe that men cannot get on without giving allegiance to something outside themselves.[50]

Eliot's embrace of religion can be seen as fulfilling his own need to give allegiance to something outside the self. As such, religion serves the same purpose for him that it does for his aesthete/ironist predecessors; it allows the self to turn to the "outer" and hence escape from a suffocating subjectivism. To give allegiance to something outside the self has for Eliot political and literary as well as religious implications. He writes in the same essay:

> I am aware that "outside" and "inside" are terms which provide unlimited opportunity for quibbling . . . but I will presume that Mr. Murry and myself can agree that for our purpose these counters are adequate. . . . If, then, a man's interest is political, he must, I presume, profess an allegiance to principles, or to a form of government, or to a monarch; and if he is interested in religion, and has one, to a Church; and if he happens to be interested in literature, he must acknowledge, it seems to me, just that sort of allegiance which I endeavoured to put forth in the preceding section. (*SE* 15)

For Eliot, Anglicism is the religious expression, while Toryism and classicism are the political and literary expressions of his allegiance to something outside the self. All can be viewed as a complex and intertwined expression of Eliot's rejection of the reflective, ironic consciousness that he portrays in his early verse.[51]

The moderns inherited not just the Hegelian and Kierkegaardian interpretations of romantic irony, but also Schlegel's sense of the concept. Some of Schlegel's writings were available in English as early as 1818. An abridged version of *Lucinde* was published in 1913. As I suggest in my introduction, twentieth-century writers might also have known of Schlegel's concept of irony from its expression in the second generation of English romantic poets, in French writers such as Diderot, Musset, Flaubert, and Stendhal, and in Victorian writers such as Carlyle, Thackeray, Arnold, and Browning. A Schlegelian sense of irony is also expressed in the writings of a late-nineteenth-century philosopher who was to have a profound effect on twentieth-century culture, Friedrich Nietzsche. In Nietzsche's work, the great creative power of the mind does not lead to self-enclosure, nor does the skeptical recognition of the limitations of what the mind creates lead either to paralysis or to nihilism. Rather, the mind accepts the patterns it imposes on experience even as it acknowledges that these patterns are fictions. They are structures imposed on a universe that Nietzsche describes as a chaotic "sea of forces" and have no ultimate validity. A discussion of the points of contact between Nietzsche and Schlegel must be postponed, however, until Nietzsche's views on creativity and on the mind's stance toward what it creates have been more fully described.

For Nietzsche, the woorld we perceive is a construct of the human intellect. "[T]his world has gradually *become* so strangely colorful, frightful, profound, soulful; it has acquired color, but we have been the painters: the human intellect allowed [the world of appearances] to appear."[52] The world of appearance appears in part by means of concepts, through which the intellect structures reality. These concepts, however, tell us absolutely nothing of the world as it is in itself. Even our most literal descriptions of the world are only figures that do not disclose anything about the actual nature of reality. "It is this way with all of us concerning language: we believe that we know something about the things themselves when we speak of trees, colors, snow, and flowers; and yet we possess nothing but metaphors for things—metaphors which correspond in no way to the original entities."[53] Nietzsche is here rejecting the correspondence view of knowledge, which holds that knowledge results from the correspondence between an independently real world and our descriptions of it. He goes on to argue that even if we assume that some of our descriptions do correspond to reality as it is, we could not know that the two correspond. Only if we had what Nietzsche calls "absolute knowledge"[54] of reality would we be able to compare our descriptions of reality with reality itself and to judge whether there is a correspondence between the two. Such absolute knowledge is not available to our "nook-perspective of consciousness" (*WP* 474).

To argue that there is or is not a correspondence between things-in-themselves and our descriptions of them is to presume that there are things-in-themselves to which our descriptions do or do not correspond. As Nietzsche writes, the "capacity to know would be revealed only in the presence of 'true reality.' . . . This presupposes that, distinct from every perspective kind of outlook . . . something exists, an 'in-itself'" (*WP* 473). Nietzsche attacks the concept of the in-itself that is presumed in the correspondence theory of knowledge by arguing first that the "reality of things" is only an image of or modeled after the subject. "It is only after the model of the subject that we have invented the reality of things and projected them into the medley of sensations" (*WP* 552b). He then argues that the subject itself is an invention, a fabrication, a fiction. "The 'subject' is not something given, it is something added and invented and projected behind what there is" (*WP* 481). The inner world and the outer world, then, can be thought of as reflecting the false image of the other. Danto writes that for Nietzsche, "The inner and outer worlds are images of each other, projections and reflections, each of each. . . . The perspective which the latter imposes is only an exportation of false ideas concerning ourselves."[55] Nietzsche observes that "When one has grasped that the 'subject' is not something that creates effects, but only a fiction, much follows" (*WP* 552b).

> If we no longer believe in the effective subject, then belief also disappears in effective things, in reciprocation, cause and effect between those phenomena that we call things.
>
> There also disappears, of course, the world of effective atoms: the assumption of which always depended on the supposition that one needed subjects. At last, the "thing-in-itself" also disappears, because this is fundamentally the conception of a "subject-in-itself." But we have grasped that the subject is a fiction. The antithesis "thing-in-itself" and "appearance" is untenable; with that, however, the concept "appearance" also disappears. (*WP* 552b)

Once Nietzsche dismantles the concept of the subject, then all of the entities and relationships implied by the subject are equally undermined—things, reciprocation, cause and effect, thing-in-itself, antithesis of thing-in-itself and appearance, and so on.

Nietzsche's attack on the correspondence theory of knowledge here is very different from his earlier attack. He is arguing not that our descriptions do not correspond to things-in-themselves (and even if they did we could never know it), but that there are no things-in-themselves to which our descriptions can correspond. This latter argument can be seen as an implicit criticism of his earlier analysis of the correspondence theory of knowledge, which, however damaging it is to the theory, remains circumscribed by the concept of the in-itself which is presumed by it.

Nietzsche's analysis, though, seems to liberate him from more than the in-itself. At first glance it seems to liberate him from existence altogether. The thing-in-itself "disappears" (he uses the word four times in the passage quoted above) because it is fundamentally the idea of the subject-in-itself, and he argues that the subject is a fiction. With the disappearance of the thing-in-itself, appearance also disappears. Nietzsche's analysis, though, is not intended to vaporize existence but to embed us in it. When he says that appearance disappears, he does not mean that the phenomenal world vanishes, but that appearance understood as an oppositional term—appearance versus thing-in-itself—no longer has any meaning. To give up the idea of the in-itself is to give up the idea that there are two worlds, the world of appearance and the world of reality, things-in-themselves, hidden behind it. Without the in-itself, we are left with only one world, the phenomenal world of becoming and change that we inhabit.

Nietzsche writes that the world of appearance has been devalued or "defamed" by virtue of the idea of the true world of the in-itself. "[O]ne realizes that this hypothesis of beings is the source of all world-defamation (—the 'better world,' the 'true world,' the 'world beyond,' the 'thing-in-itself')" (*WP* 708). One expression of this defamation is the view that the world of appearance has a lesser ontological status than the world of the in-itself. Plato, for example, places the world of appearance between the completely real world of being, the world of the forms, and the utterly unreal (*The Republic*, bks. 5 and 6). By eliminating the world of the in-itself, Nietzsche does away with the basis on which this ontological defamation has been made and restores to the world of appearance the sense of ontological plenitude or fullness. (To anticipate briefly, it is the ontological fullness of the world of appearance that

Stevens so movingly affirms in the late poem, "The River of Rivers in Connecticut." "There is a great river this side of Stygia, / . . . / It is not to be seen beneath the appearances / That tell of it" [*CP* 533].)

If language does not mirror an independently existing world, what is the function of language? Nietzsche writes, "Life is founded upon the premise of a belief in enduring and regularly recurring things" (*WP* 552), and language gives us a world that is stable, orderly, regular. "One should not understand this compulsion to construct concepts, species, forms, purposes, laws ('a world of identical cases') as if they enabled us to fix the *real world;* but as a compulsion to arrange a world for ourselves in which our existence is made possible:—we thereby create a world which is calculable, simplified, comprehensible, etc., for us" (*WP* 521). Concepts, laws, and purposes are linguistic arrangements of reality, fictions by means of which we organize reality and thereby make existence possible for ourselves. Among the conceptual fictions that are necessary for our existence are "time, space, and motion" (*WP* 487), the "I" (this is "indispensable" [*WP* 483]), and the "law of causality," which, Nietzsche says, is "so much a part of us that not to believe in it would destroy the race" (*WP* 497). It is not only our fictional concepts, the products of the intellect, that arise in response to the conditions of life; the intellect itself comes into being as a "consequence of [the] conditions of existence" (*WP* 498). Even consciousness, which Nietzsche, anticipating Freud, describes as a faculty that mediates between the self and the outer world, is "present" only to the extent that it is "useful" (*WP* 505). This interpretive activity of the mind is supported by the senses. They do not report experience indiscriminately; rather, they too organize experience in a way that is useful for life. "This same compulsion [to arrange a world] exists in the sense activities that support reason—by simplification, coarsening, emphasizing, and elaborating, upon which all 'recognition,' all ability to make oneself intelligible rests. Our needs have made our senses so precise that the 'same apparent world' always reappears and has thus acquired the semblance of reality" (*WP* 521).

Given that through our descriptions of reality we create a

world in which life is possible for us, how did we come to see these descriptions as referring to another world, the real world of the in-itself? Believing that our descriptions refer to the "real" world further organized and schematized existence and hence was useful for life. As Nietzsche writes, "The intention was to deceive ourselves in a useful way" (*WP* 584). Our "naïveté" was to take an "anthropocentric idiosyncrasy as the *measure of things,* as the rule for determining 'real' and 'unreal': in short, to make absolute something conditioned" (*WP* 584). As a result of this naïveté, the world became divided into "true" and "apparent" worlds. The world of appearance that "man's reason had devised for him to live and settle in was discredited" (*WP* 584). Ironically, our linguistic arrangements of reality, whose original purpose was to preserve life, to make life possible, now became the means by which human beings attempted to "assassinate life" (*WP* 583b).

Nietzsche writes that it is of "cardinal importance that one should abolish the *true* world" (*WP* 583b) and turn back to the world of appearance. But how are we to do this? We cannot simply give up those linguistic orderings of reality, those concepts, laws, and purposes that the intellect has created and that we have naively taken to be "true." To do so, he believes, would threaten our very existence. "Our salvation," Nietzsche writes, "lies not in *knowing,* but in *creating*" (*PT* 33, no. 84). In asking us to create, Nietzsche is not asking us to do anything that we have not done before. In his view human beings are by their very nature creative. What he is asking us to do is to understand ourselves *as* creators, or, as he often puts it, as artists, and not as knowers. It is *how* we view ourselves that determines to a great extent whether our creative activity situates us in existence or removes us from it. If we understand ourselves as knowers and look upon our creations as "fixing" the "true world," then they separate us from existence. If we understand ourselves as artists and look upon our creations as useful shapings of reality, then they become the means by which we "live and settle in" the world.

Though Nietzsche's view that human beings are by their nature artists suggests that all of our structurings of reality, our laws, purposes, concepts, and so on are artistic products whose purpose is to make life possible, it is in art understood in the narrower sense that Nietzsche finds the strongest affirmation of our existence. "[A]rt is essentially *affirmation, blessing, deification of existence. . . .* Art and nothing but art! It is the great means of making life possible, the great seduction to life, the great stimulant of life" (*WP* 821, 853 II). One of the ways in which the artist seduces us to life is by offering new interpretations of the world, a process Nietzsche sees as both destructive and creative. In creating a new way of organizing experience, the artist first destroys the concepts by which the mind has stabilized existence. "That immense framework and planking of concepts to which the needy man clings . . . is nothing but a scaffolding and toy" for the artistic intelligence, which "smashes this framework to pieces" (*PT* 90). "With creative pleasure it throws metaphors into confusion and displaces the boundary stones of abstractions" (*PT* 90). The artist then puts this "framework" together "in an ironic fashion, pairing the most alien things and separating the closest" (*PT* 90). The purpose of this creative activity is to "refashion the world which presents itself to waking man," and the result of this refashioning is to give us a sense of pleasure and delight in a world that is "eternally new" (*PT* 89). The reimagined world is "colorful, irregular, lacking in results and coherence, charming, and eternally new as the world of dreams" (*PT* 89). So strong is "the intense and manifold joy in life which art implants in us" that it would "still demand satisfaction were art to disappear" (*H* 222). And Nietzsche views this artistic activity as potentially limitless: "No limit to the ways in which the world can be interpreted" (*WP* 600).

The ongoing artistic process of destruction and creation replicates the "eternally self-creating" and "eternally self-destroying" activity of a chaotic and dynamic universe. That humanity's artistic activity does replicate the activity of the universe at large is perhaps not so surprising given Nietzsche's view that the artistic ability of man is something "he has . . . in common with everything that is. He is himself after all a piece of reality, truth, nature" (*WP* 853).

And do you know what "the world" is to me? . . . This world: a monster of energy, without beginning, without end . . . a sea of forces flowing and rushing together, eternally changing, eternally flooding back, . . . out of the simplest forms striving toward the most complex, out of the stillest, most rigid, coldest forms toward the hottest, most turbulent, most self-contradictory, and then again returning home to the simple out of this abundance, out of the play of contradictions back to the joy of concord, still affirming itself in this uniformity of its courses and its years, blessing itself as that which must return eternally, as a becoming that knows no satiety, no disgust, no weariness: this, my *Dionysian* world of the eternally self-creating, the eternally self-destroying, this mystery world of the twofold voluptuous delight. (*WP* 1067)

In addition to criticizing the theory that language mirrors a world of independently real entities, Nietzsche also subjects to critical scrutiny the theory that human beings can create entities through language. In *Allegories of Reading,* Paul de Man argues that Nietzsche criticizes both the view of language as "constative," that is, as giving knowledge of independently real entities, and the view of language as "performative," that is, as creating or predicating entities. For de Man, though, Nietzsche's critical undermining of the two models of language leaves him in the *aporia* between them. He can only turn from one to the other without embracing either. "The differentiation between performative and constative language (which Nietzsche anticipates) is undecidable; the deconstruction leading from the one model to the other is irreversible but it always remains suspended, regardless of how often it is repeated."[56] De Man is correct, I believe, in his view that Nietzsche is as skeptical of a performative model of language as he is of a constative one. But de Man's way of framing the issue makes the two models of language equivalent. In de Man's analysis, the two models have a conceptual equivalence. That is, the models are equivalent because they are approached and evaluated cognitively. Seen from a cognitive point of view, each is equally false, and the difference between the two is undecidable. But Nietzsche does not ask us to evaluate concepts on cognitive or rational grounds alone. Once having acknowledged that all concepts are false when subjected to rational analysis, he revalues them on the basis of their utility for life. "Truth is the kind of error without which a certain species of life could not live. The value for *life* is ultimately decisive" (*WP* 493). Approached from the perspective of their utility for life, the two models of language lose their equivalence and the difference between them is quite definitely decidable. The fiction of performative language is preferable to the fiction of constative language. The former embeds the self in existence; the latter leads the self away from it.

The issue suggests one of the affiliations between Nietzsche and Schlegel. It is not that Nietzsche, knowing that both performative and constative models of language are fictions, "remains suspended" between them. Rather, he continues to create, to invent, to posit, and to be committed to his creations based on their utility for life, while being fully aware that neither a performative nor a constative concept of language has any final validity. This sense of commitment and of continuing on, of movement even as the mind simultaneously expresses its skepticism toward all of its concepts, is close to the sense of skepticism and commitment, of ongoing activity in the absence of all certainty, that is one characteristic of Schlegel's irony.

There are other points of contact between Schlegel and Nietzsche. While both writers see the mind as having great creative power, in neither writer does the exercise of that power enclose the world within the mind. Both view reality as essentially chaotic, "a monster of energy . . . eternally changing" (*WP* 1067). In both, the mind "live[s] and settle[s] in" the world through the patterns it imposes on reality. And in both the mind is also skeptically aware that all patternings of experience are, ultimately, fictions. This skeptical detachment subverts the sense of self-enclosure that results from the mind gazing at a world that "reflects" the patterns the mind imposes on it. It redirects the gaze of the mind from the inner to the outer, however "'unknowable' for us," as Nietzsche puts it, the outer may be once it no longer reflects our image. This disruption equally criticizes the self's narcissistic attachment to its own creations and can be thought of as an ongoing rejection of the kind of self-love that for Hegel and Kierkegaard is characteristic of the romantic ironist. In detaching the mind from its own creations, skepticism frees the mind to create new patterns through which it can experience the world.

Nietzsche's view that the artist destroys old relationships and creates new ones between seemingly unlike things, "pairing the most alien things and separating the closest," parallels Schlegel's view that the creative activity of the artist is an expression of *Witz*.[57] Wit both destroys old relationships, "A witty idea is a disintegration of spiritual substances which, before being suddenly separated, must have been thoroughly mixed" (*LF* 146, no. 34), and brings together apparently disparate ideas, "Many witty ideas are like the sudden meeting of two friendly thoughts after a long separation" (*LF* 166, no. 37). Both writers view this witty artistic activity as ongoing, and in both the artistic process of creation and destruction replicates a similar process in the universe at large. In addition, both Schlegel and Nietzsche view the creative act as one of *beginning*. Each time the artist destroys old concepts and creates new ones, he or she gives us a world that, in Nietzsche's words, is "eternally new." Hegel and Kierkegaard argue that the act of beginning separates the ironist from the world. In Schlegel and Nietzsche, however, beginning does not separate the mind from the actual and temporal. Rather, it repeatedly turns the mind toward and situates it in the actual. For Nietzsche, there is no world except the phenomenal one that the intellect repeatedly reinterprets. Since the creation of new patterns, new structures, is an ongoing activity, the self's experience of the world, in Schlegel and in Nietzsche, both continually expands and becomes increasingly fragmented.

Stevens could have known of the Schlegelian and the Hegelian and Kierkegaardian interpretations of romantic irony from a number of sources. At Harvard (1897–1900) he took a course in English literature that covered the romantic poets (*SP* 61) and a course in French literature where he read, among other authors, Musset.[58] He knew German well enough to take a course taught in German on Goethe and his time,[59] and both Schlegel and Hegel may have been discussed there. Stevens' friendship with Santayana is well known, and Hegel could have been the subject of some of their conversations. Royce, the leading idealist philosopher at Harvard at that time, was Santayana's dissertation advisor, and, as I noted earlier in this chapter, Royce was influential in stimulating interest in Hegel in the United States. Though Babbitt is listed as one of the instructors of two courses Stevens took (French 2-C and French 6-C), he did not have Babbitt as a teacher.[60] But Stevens need not have taken a course with Babbitt to be aware of his antipathy to romanticism. Richardson notes that Stevens knew of the work of other Harvard professors through his classmates. From talks with Russell Loines, for example, he learned of Charles Eliot Norton's views on Dante and the Middle Ages,[61] and Stevens may have become acquainted in a similar way with Babbitt's ideas. In a letter to Henry Church, Stevens comments that when he was a young man he read Nietzsche (*L* 409), and, as Milton Bates points out, Nietzsche "was much in the air during the first decades of this century. His impact on England and America was remarkable, despite the handicap of poor translations and expensive editions."[62]

Unlike Eliot's work, Stevens' poetry expresses opposed senses of romantic irony. In poems such as "Tea at the Palaz of Hoon," for instance, he explores what Hegel calls the "bliss of self-enjoyment" that comes from "the concentration of the ego into itself." In other poems he examines, as does Eliot, the negative side of this sense of irony: the self's sense of isolation from reality, its desire, not always realized, to return to the real, and its recognition that, cut off from the actual, its own identity is in jeopardy. Again unlike Eliot, Stevens does not turn from this irony to religion.[63] His poetry offers instead a countering ironic vision, one that is affiliated with Schlegel. Here, the creative power of the mind does not lead to self-enclosure, nor does the skeptical recognition of the limits of what the mind creates lead to paralysis or nihilism.

Critics such as Alan Wilde have argued that modernism is characterized by an irony that is Kierkegaardian in orientation. Wilde writes that "disjunctive irony," at its extreme point "absolute irony," "is the characteristic form of modernism."[64] The absolute ironist, and here Wilde quotes from Kierkegaard, "elevates himself higher and higher, becoming ever lighter and lighter as he rises, seeing all things disappear beneath him from his ironical bird's eye perspective."[65] Wilde finds this irony expressed in the work of, among others, Gide, Kafka, Faulkner, and Woolf. A similar assessment is offered by Paul Bové in his "Kierkegaardian Critique" of New Criticism. Irony is the central concept of New Criticism, and Bové argues that the fundamental goal of New Critical irony is to "become negatively free of all restrictions, to stand or hover above actuality."[66] The withdrawal from the world that is effected through New Critical irony exemplifies the "modern temperament as a turning to the aesthetic as a means to . . . 'absolute freedom' and as a movement away from time, finitude, and the world."[67] An opposing sense of irony can also be seen in the period. As I have discussed in my introduction, Yeats, Joyce, Frost, Italo Svevo, Borges, Meredith, and Beckett express an irony that has an affiliation with Schlegel. Modernism, then, can be seen as being characterized less by one or the other of these concepts of irony than by their copresence. In expressing these antithetical senses of romantic irony, Stevens' poetry, at least from this perspective, offers a portrait in miniature of the modern period.

Chapter 2

The Never-Resting Mind:
Stevens and Schlegel

It's equally fatal for the mind to have a system and to have
none. It will simply have to decide to combine the two.
—Friedrich Schlegel

In "Yours, O Youth" (1919), William Carlos Williams describes
the artist's relation to the external world. The artist, he writes,

> is limited to the range of his contact with the objective world.
> True, in begetting his poem he takes parts from the imagina-
> tion but it is simply that working among stored memories his
> mind has drawn parallels, completed progressions, transferred
> units from one category to another, clipped here, modified
> there. But it is inconceivable that, no matter how circuitously,
> contact with an immediate objective world of actual experi-
> ence has not been rigorously maintained. By "artist" is meant
> this thing alone.[1]

Williams is in part setting himself here against symbolist aesthetics.
Mallarmé, for instance, writes, "To create is to conceive an ob-
ject . . . in its absence."[2] He comments in another essay, "When I
say: 'a flower!' then from that forgetfulness to which my voice
consigns all floral form, something different from the usual calyces
arises, something all music, essence, and softness: the flower which
is absent from all bouquets."[3] In insisting on maintaining contact
with the objective world of actual experience, Williams is not
arguing that the artist passively record experience. But note that
the activity of the mind in creation—clipping, modifying, trans-
ferring, completing—is limited to its modification of experience.

The mind, that is, is not to add to experience. It is to follow experience in its shaping of it.

A similar point was made by Pound in 1914 in his account of the process of writing what may be his best-known imagist poem, "In a Station of the Metro."

> Three years ago in Paris I got out of a "metro" train at La Concorde, and saw suddenly a beautiful face, and then another and another, and then a beautiful child's face, and then another beautiful woman, and I tried all that day to find words for what this had meant to me, and I could not find any words that seemed to me worthy, or as lovely as that sudden emotion. . . . I wrote a thirty-line poem, and destroyed it because it was what we call work "of second intensity." Six months later I made a poem half that length; a year later I made the following *hokku*-like sentence: —"The apparition of these faces in the crowd: / Petals, on a wet, black bough."[4]

Like Williams, Pound does not passively record experience. The activity of the mind here is expressed in metaphor, the favorite trope of imagism. But again as in Williams, the mind's activity does not add to experience. Rather, the creation of metaphor is intended to render precisely the contours of Pound's experience.

Seen against this current of modernism, Stevens' words, published two years after Williams published "Yours, O Youth," must have seemed hopelessly retrograde: "The imagination, the one reality / In this imagined world" (*CP* 25).[5] Huysmans had suggested in *A Rebours* that the mind could replace the actual world with a reality of its own devising. The imagination can "substitute the vision of the reality for the reality itself" (*AR* 22). Stevens' lines go further and suggest that there may be nothing but mind. The artist as Fichtean creator is the subject of the next chapter, where I discuss not only the narcissistic pleasure the mind can take in the creation and contemplation of a world that is only a reflection of itself, but also the dark side of this creative activity, the mind's sense of isolation and loneliness, its fear that it has no identity, and, perhaps most painful of all, its inability to return to the world when it deeply desires to do so. In this chapter I focus on a different sense of creativity, one that lies between the modern desire to limit the mind to the actual world and the Fichtean exuberance of the lines quoted above. This sense of creativity draws Stevens close to Schlegel, though creative activity in the two writers is by no means identical. Affiliations as well as differences can begin to be discerned in the wintery reductions of "The Snow Man."

The poem opens on a landscape that seems to be devoid of any human presence. The self, already reduced to an impersonal "one," merely observes the winter scene.

> One must have a mind of winter
> To regard the frost and the boughs
> Of the pine-trees crusted with snow;
>
> And have been cold a long time
> To behold the junipers shagged with ice,
> The spruces rough in the distant glitter
>
> Of the January sun.
>
> $\qquad\qquad\qquad$ (CP 9–10)

The opening lines could almost be an imagist exercise. At the least, they avoid the "don'ts" that Pound laid down in his 1913 essay on imagism: "Use no superfluous word," "Go in fear of abstractions," "Don't be 'viewy.'"[6] The landscape depicted in these lines, however, is far from being stripped bare of the self. The highly decorative language used to describe the landscape suggests that sight itself is a mode of self-projection. The pine trees are *crusted* with snow; the junipers are *shagged* with ice, and the spruces are *rough* in the distant *glitter*. The landscape that is seen is the landscape that the mind beautifully "decorates" with language.

This self-projection is stripped away in the next six lines, which shift from a visual to an aural mode:

> $\qquad\qquad$ and not to think
> Of any misery in the sound of the wind,

In the sound of a few leaves,

Which is the sound of the land
Full of the same wind
That is blowing in the same bare place.

(*CP* 10)

The shift from sight to sound is telling. Stevens often opposes human language to the language or speech of nature, which, being inhuman, is to us pure sound. In "The Idea of Order at Key West," for example, Stevens writes,

Whose spirit is this?

.   .   .   .   .   .

If it was only the outer voice of sky
And cloud, of the sunken coral water-walled,
However clear, it would have been deep air,
The heaving speech of air, a summer sound
Repeated in a summer without end
And sound alone.

(*CP* 129)

We hear the "speech" of nature again in "Notes toward a Supreme Fiction," and there, as in "The Idea of Order at Key West," the language spoken by the "fluent mundo" is pure sound, what Stevens calls "gibberish" (*CP* 396). The sound of the wind "blowing in the same bare place" in "The Snow Man" anticipates, however, not the "summer sound" of "Key West" but the "desolate sound" that is heard "beneath / The stillness of everything gone" in "Autumn Refrain" (*CP* 160) and "the cry of the leaves" that "concerns no one at all" in "The Course of a Particular" (*OP* 123, 124). The movement in "The Snow Man" from a visual mode to an aural one, then, signals a further reduction of the mind's presence in the landscape. By stripping away its decorative projections onto the landscape through the language of sight, the mind is left with the sound of bare nature.

Yet even sound in "The Snow Man" can be a vehicle for self-projection. Stevens does not directly attribute misery to the sound of the wind. He says that one must be cold a long time *not* to think of any misery in the sound of the wind. What Stevens is asking is whether one can be cold enough to hear the language of nature and not turn it into human language by attributing misery to it. The final lines of the poem suggest that this degree of cold can be reached.

> For the listener, who listens in the snow,
> And, nothing himself, beholds
> Nothing that is not there and the nothing that is.
>
> (*CP* 10)

To behold nothing that is not there is to behold reality stripped of all that the self attributes to it. Since misery is not part of nature but something that the self adds to it, to behold nothing that is not there suggests that it is possible not to think of any misery in the sound of the wind.

The reduction of all concepts from nature in "The Snow Man" turns the mind's attention from the world created by the self to the larger universe. This redirection of the mind's gaze is expressed in part through the subtle change in perspective from the particular and located to the unspecified and vast that occurs in the poem. Stevens begins this shift in perspective with the change from the very close detail of the "pine-trees *crusted* with snow" (*CP* 9; emphasis added) to the particular but more remote "spruces rough in the *distant* glitter" (*CP* 10; emphasis added). In lines 7–12, Stevens drops spatial metaphors altogether, and he shifts from the *distant* glitter of the spruces to the unlocated though particularized "sound of a few leaves" (*CP* 10). The particularity of the "few leaves" is dropped for the less specified "sound of the land," which in turn gives way to a "bare place" (*CP* 10). And even this bare place threatens to evaporate in the repeated "nothing"'s of the final two lines.

Stevens' use of the word "behold" also contributes to the sense that the mind is apprehending the larger universe at the end of "The Snow Man." "Behold" suggests in addition that Stevens

views this apprehension as an extraordinary moment of height-
ened intensity. As well as expressing a sense of possession, the
word "behold" also expresses a sense of revelation, in the biblical
sense of the revelation of extraordinary things. We "behold" acts
of God, miracles, mysteries. "Behold," God said after creating the
world, "I have given you every herb bearing seed, which *is* upon
the face of all the earth, and every tree" (Gen. 1:29). As "The
Snow Man" moves toward its reductive extreme, the perspective
widens and the tone of the poem becomes elevated and more seri-
ous. At the poem's conclusion, "the nothing that is," pure being,
is *beheld,* magisterially "revealed" and "possessed."

The skeptical reduction that leads to a profound beholding of
the universe in "The Snow Man" echoes one aspect of irony as
Schlegel conceives it. Irony, Schlegel writes, is "the mood that
surveys everything and rises infinitely above all limitations" (*LF*
148, no. 42). This freedom from limitation is for Schlegel an
escape from egocentrism and self-love. To see the universe only
through the patterns the self imposes on it is to turn the universe
into a mirror image of the self. Skeptical reduction frees the self
from its narrow focus on itself and allows it to turn to the universe
at large. As Schlegel writes, "We must rise above our own love
and be able to destroy in our thoughts what we adore; if we can-
not do this, we lack . . . the feeling for the universe."[7] In "The
Snow Man," as in Schlegel, the reduction of all concepts the mind
imposes on reality allows the mind to behold or to gain a feeling
for the universe at large.

"The Snow Man" also points to the need for creative activity.
It sets itself against the modernist impulse, seen in Pound and
Williams, that would restrict the mind's activity to selecting and
arranging experience but not adding to it by showing that without
the active contribution of the mind, the world can only be appre-
hended as "the nothing that is." It is a point that Stevens will
return to thirty years later in his discussion of "modern reality" in
"The Relations between Poetry and Painting." "She [Simone
Weil] says that decreation is making pass from the created to the
uncreated, but that destruction is making pass from the created to
nothingness. Modern reality is a reality of decreation, in which our

revelations are not the revelations of belief, but the precious por-
tents of our own powers" (NA 174–75). In Stevens' usage, decre-
ation has two aspects. The first, seen at perhaps its most extreme in
"The Snow Man," is "making pass from the created to the uncre-
ated." By decreating its projections on to the world, the mind
beholds not "nothingness" but "the nothing that is." This reduc-
tive process leads to a recognition of our creative power, that is,
our power to create what Stevens says painters such as Cézanne
and Klee create, "a new reality" (NA 174).

This second issue, creativity, both relates Stevens to Schlegel
and points to one of the differences between them. For Schlegel,
the ironic mind is endlessly creative. Reduction leads to a new
patterning of experience. This patterning is in turn subjected to
skeptical reduction, which again leads to creation, and so on. But
creative activity in Stevens is a problematic issue, and he often
writes of the difficulty of creating. Poetic fluency can be inhibited
by the magnitude of nature. In canto VI of "The Auroras of
Autumn," for example, he writes that "The scholar of one candle
sees / An Arctic effulgence flaring on the frame / Of everything
he is. And he feels afraid" (CP 417). What he fears is that his own
creative power, the "one candle" of the imagination, will be over-
whelmed by nature's greater light, the aurora borealis. In addition
to the magnitude of nature, the absence of change can also silence
the poet. Stevens writes in "The Man Whose Pharynx Was Bad"
that

> The time of year has grown indifferent.
> Mildew of summer and the deepening snow
> Are both alike in the routine I know.
> I am too dumbly in my being pent.
>   (CP 96)

A third way the poetic process can be inhibited is expressed in
"Metaphors of a Magnifico." Stevens writes in The Necessary Angel
that "For all the reasons stated by William James, and for many
more . . . we do not want to be metaphysicians" (NA 59). James
stated some of these reasons in Pragmatism (1907).

The world of concrete personal experiences to which the street belongs is multitudinous beyond imagination, tangled, muddy, painful and perplexed. The world to which your philosophy-professor introduces you is simple, clean and noble. The contradictions of real life are absent from it. Its architecture is classic. Principles of reason trace its outlines, logical necessities cement its parts. Purity and dignity are what it most expresses. It is a kind of marble temple shining on a hill.

In point of fact it is far less an account of this actual world than a clear addition built upon it, a classic sanctuary in which the rationalist fancy may take refuge from the intolerably confused and gothic character which mere facts present.[8]

The pragmatist "turns away from abstraction and insufficiency" and "turns towards concreteness and adequacy, towards facts, towards action, and towards power."[9] He looks *"away from first things, principles, 'categories,' supposed necessities"* and looks *"towards last things, fruits, consequences, facts."*[10]

Stevens' early poem, "Metaphors of a Magnifico," echoes the spirit of this passage.[11] The poem begins with a criticism of idealism's lack of contact with reality.

> Twenty men crossing a bridge,
> Into a village,
> Are twenty men crossing twenty bridges,
> Into twenty villages,
> Or one man
> Crossing a single bridge into a village.
>
> This is old song
> That will not declare itself . . .
>
> (CP 19)

The first description plays with the idea of universals and the particular. If every person's experience is unique, then twenty men crossing a bridge into a village are twenty men crossing twenty bridges into twenty villages. If the experience is universal, then each crossing is identical with every other crossing and twenty men crossing a bridge into a village can be thought of as one man crossing a single bridge into a village. Because the experience has been cast in a philosophical formulation, nothing in the experience can "declare itself."

The critique of idealism continues in the second description of reality.

> Twenty men crossing a bridge,
> Into a village,
> Are
> Twenty men crossing a bridge
> Into a village.
>
> That will not declare itself
> Yet is certain as meaning . . .
>   (CP 19)

The statement will not declare itself because the tautological form of the statement will not allow any aspect of the experience to stand forth, even though the statement seems to follow the contours of the experience, "is certain as meaning."

In his third description of the experience, the magnifico abandons his propositional form and begins describing twenty men crossing a bridge into a village as an unfolding event.

> The boots of the men clump
> On the boards of the bridge.
> The first white wall of the village
> Rises through fruit-trees.
> Of what was it I was thinking?
> So the meaning escapes.
>   (CP 19)

In his prior descriptions, men, bridge, and village had no specifiers. In this description, the magnifico uses qualifiers to particularize and locate the experience. He specifies the "first white wall of the village." These men wear boots. They clump. The village has fruit trees. The magnifico asks, "Of what was it I was thinking? / So the meaning escapes." The meaning that escapes is the meaning of the experience that is yielded by rational analysis.

Up to this point in the poem, Stevens seems to accept pragmatism without reservation. But the last two lines of the poem swerve sharply away from James.

> The first white wall of the village . . .
> The fruit-trees. . . .
>
> (CP 19)

For James, the turn from abstraction to facts is a moment of liberation, "towards action . . . towards power." This is not the case with the magnifico. His escape from abstraction, the ellipses suggest, leaves him in a state of bewilderment. He haltingly uses his newly acquired language of fact and then falls silent. A comment by Eleanor Cook on "Metaphors of a Magnifico" suggests the reason for this silence. "[T]he point about the magnifico's metaphors seems to be that he has none."[12] The first two descriptions of twenty men crossing a bridge into a village establish an identity between terms, while the third offers only particulars. These isolated facts are not *like* anything. Without metaphor, the magnifico is overwhelmed, silenced, by the presence of reality. Stevens makes the point explicitly twenty-four years later in "Motive for Metaphor," where he describes the motive for metaphor as a need to escape from the poetically fatal presence of reality: "The motive for metaphor, shrinking from / The weight of primary noon, / The ABC of being," the "vital" yet "fatal, dominant X" (CP 288).[13] Because the magnifico cannot create any metaphors, the vital world of facts, celebrated by James, is to him poetically fatal. As Stevens writes in an aphorism, "It is only au pays de la métaphore / Qu'on est poète" (OP 204).

Though Stevens writes of the difficulty of creating, he also, like Schlegel, writes of the moment in which the spirit is endlessly and effortlessly creative. One such moment is described in section II, canto VIII of "Notes toward a Supreme Fiction."

On her trip around the world, Nanzia Nunzio
Confronted Ozymandias. She went
Alone and like a vestal long-prepared.

I am the spouse. She took her necklace off
And laid it in the sand. As I am, I am
The spouse. She opened her stone-studded belt.

I am the spouse, divested of bright gold,
The spouse beyond emerald or amethyst,
Beyond the burning body that I bear.

I am the woman stripped more nakedly
Than nakedness, standing before an inflexible
Order, saying I am the contemplated spouse.

Speak to me that, which spoken, will array me
In its own only precious ornament.
Set on me the spirit's diamond coronal.

Clothe me entire in the final filament,
So that I tremble with such love so known
And myself am precious for your perfecting.

Then Ozymandias said the spouse, the bride
Is never naked. A fictive covering
Weaves always glistening from the heart and mind.

(CP 395–96)

The canto expresses two opposed activities of the mind. In the
first, familiar to us from "The Snow Man," the mind strips away
its own concepts. But in this canto Stevens does not leave us con-
templating the "nothing that is." The second activity of the mind
expressed here is creation. Ozymandias says, "A fictive covering /
Weaves always glistening from the heart and mind" (CP 396). The
two activities are simultaneous and engender a never-ending
process. The mind continues to reduce its concepts even as it end-
lessly creates new ones. ("Always" modifies both "weaves," a
word Stevens often uses to designate poetic creation, and "glisten-
ing.")

The endless creation of fiction after fiction in the canto can be seen as a rejection of the modernist view of creativity, which would limit the mind to arranging experience but would not allow it to add to experience. But does creative activity in the canto take place at the expense of reality? Are these fictions only Hoon-like creations of the self? The issue is one of art's contents, and it is an issue that Stevens takes up in "Three Academic Pieces."

The images in Ecclesiastes:

> *or ever*
> *the silver cord be loosed, or the golden bowl*
> *be broken, or the pitcher be broken at the*
> *fountain, or the wheel broken at the cistern—*

these images are not the language of reality, they are the symbolic language of metamorphosis, or resemblance, of poetry, but they relate to reality and they intensify our sense of it and they give us the pleasure of "lentor and solemnity" in respect to the most commonplace objects. (*NA* 77–78)

How can images that are "not the language of reality . . . intensify our sense of it"? How can art give the mind a sense of the real when art makes no pretense of being mimetic? Stevens, as Carl Woodring writes, refuses to make a final decision regarding the content of art. When he stirs creatively, Stevens "hesitates to seek language that would say whether . . . the jar to contain [these stirrings] would hold reason, sensation, feeling, or aesthetic intuition."[14] Do the images in Ecclesiastes intensify our sense of reality because they express sensation? Nature? Stevens does not even speculate in the essay on this question. He simply says that art can intensify our sense of reality and leaves open the basis on which art does this.

In the Ozymandias canto, Stevens suggests that art can offer the mind a sense of engagement with reality even as the mind skeptically questions the basis of that engagement. The ongoing process of reduction and creation leads in the canto to a deep feeling of intimacy with the world. This sense of intimacy is expressed in part through the association of the creative process with sexual consummation and marriage. The opening movement of reduction is depicted as an erotic act of disrobing. "She took her necklace off / And laid it in the sand. / . . . / She opened her stone-studded belt. / . . . / I am the woman stripped more nakedly / Than nakedness" (CP 395–96). Naked, Nanzia Nunzio asks Ozymandias to consummate their love by clothing or covering her. "Clothe me entire in the final filament, / So that I tremble with such love so known" (CP 396). Ozymandias readily obliges. "A fictive covering / Weaves always glistening from the heart and mind" (CP 396). Through the creative act, Nanzia Nunzio becomes Ozymandias' "spouse," a word used six times in the canto to describe her. (She is also, once, termed a "bride.") The union of Ozymandias and Nanzia Nunzio through the fictions created by Ozymandias symbolizes a deep commitment by the mind to its creations. Stevens suggests that through them the mind "marries" the world it contemplates. But even as the mind expresses its commitment to its fictions, it also acknowledges that these fictions *are* fictions, "a *fictive* covering / Weaves" (emphasis added). Here, as in Schlegel, the mind expresses a dual attitude toward its creations. Because it is aware that each covering is a fiction, the mind skeptically transcends its creations. Yet the mind's marriage to the world through these fictions suggests that it is at the same time sincerely committed to them. This dual attitude of detachment and commitment is described by Stevens in his well-known aphorism: "The final belief is to believe in a fiction, which you know to be a fiction, there being nothing else. The exquisite truth is to know that it is a fiction and that you believe in it willingly" (OP 189). Since the process of creation in the canto is continual, and since the mind marries the world through its creations, the mind's experience of the world in this canto is seen as becoming ever richer and more diverse. With each new fiction, the world is experienced in a different way. As in Schlegel, creative activity here "Increases the aspects of experience" (CP 447).

This same broadening and fragmenting of experience can be

seen in numerous other poems by Stevens. In still-life poems such as "Someone Puts a Pineapple Together," where Stevens describes a pineapple in twelve different ways, and "Thirteen Ways of Looking at a Blackbird," the various perspectives fragment our view of the object and offer ever more diverse senses of it. A similar technique is used in "Sea Surface Full of Clouds," where Stevens describes a single setting, the sea off the coast of Tehuantepec in November, in five different ways. The technique is reversed in "Six Significant Landscapes," which presents six different settings rather than multiple views of one setting. This perspectivizing can be seen again in "New England Verses," where Stevens looks at various subjects from opposing points of view. A similar impulse is expressed in "Like Decorations in a Nigger Cemetery." Here, Stevens examines a limited number of subjects—poetry, nature, the idea of decay, for instance—in the casually repetitive manner that looks forward to longer poems such as "The Man with the Blue Guitar," "Esthétique du Mal," "Notes toward a Supreme Fiction," "The Auroras of Autumn," and "An Ordinary Evening in New Haven," where the mind explores unsystematically and without limits divergent and sometimes contradictory views of its subject. All of these poems, still life to longer meditation, express the kind of restless, self-questioning mobility that is characteristic of romantic irony[15] and that Stevens describes in "The Poems of Our Climate" as "the never-resting mind" (*CP* 194).

The simultaneous expression of commitment and skepticism in the Ozymandias canto is linked to the sense of repetition that Stevens describes later in "Notes toward a Supreme Fiction." In section III, canto IX he writes of

> vast repetitions final in
> Themselves and, therefore, good, the going round
>
> And round and round, the merely going round,
> Until merely going round is a final good,
> The way wine comes at a table in a wood.
>
>   (*CP* 405)

Because the mind is both skeptically aware of the fictive nature of what it creates and is also committed to these fictions, each act of creation is both "final" and leads to the creation of new fictions. To create is to go "round / And round and round" as the mind continues to seek what it endlessly finds.

The never-ending process of creation and decreation that is exemplified in the Ozymandias canto has been described by Frank Lentricchia, who sees Stevens as the "culmination and summary representative of . . . the conservative fictionalist tradition in modern poetics and philosophy" (*ANC* 31). In this tradition, a "horrible" reality drives the poet to create a pleasing fictional world. However, the poet, "with his prized faculty of self-consciousness, knows his fictions not to be 'true'" (*ANC* 56), that is, knows that they do not give mimetic access to the real. This knowledge leads to an endless cycle of reduction and creation. "[A]s a mature and sane individual (who will not dwell in fantasy) the poet is forced to 'open up' his fictions to reality and to face the hard truth. Once he has done *that,* his sense of the real is renewed, but such renewal is (how could it be otherwise?) a terror-inspiring occasion. The poet is driven back to fiction-making—and so on and so forth" (*ANC* 56). The creative process as it is expressed in the Ozymandias canto differs from this description in at least two respects. First, reality is not seen as "horrible" but as the beloved. Ozymandias is "un *amoureux perpetuel* of the world that he contemplates" (*NA* 30). Barbara Fisher argues that "the presence of eros and the transformations of eros"[16] are at the center of Stevens' poetry, and Ozymandias tells us that his fictions come not just from the mind but also from the heart. And the canto's central device, the address to the beloved, a device that Stevens uses in the early "To the One of Fictive Music" and the late "The Final Soliloquy of the Interior Paramour," links this canto to the tradition of erotic love poetry. Of course, Stevens does not always look at the world the way a lover looks at the beloved. As Lentricchia points out, Stevens does describe reality in "The Noble Rider and the Sound of Words" as a "violence." But Stevens is not using the word in that essay to describe reality at all times and in all places. "Violence" refers instead to a specific historical moment, the Second World War.

"[O]ne is trying to think of a whole generation and of a world at war" (*NA* 20).[17] Stevens' final description in the essay of the mind's response to a violent reality does not suggest that it retreats from this "hard truth." "The mind has added nothing to human nature. It is a violence from within that protects us from a violence without. It is the imagination pressing back against the pressure of reality" (*NA* 36). To "press back" points less to a withdrawal from reality than to an engagement with it.

Second, Lentricchia's analysis pushes Stevens into an either/or position that his poetry does not support. Either the poet gives up his fictions and engages with reality or he creates fictions and withdraws from the world. The assumption is that art and reality are mutually exclusive. But in essays such as "Three Academic Pieces" and in poems such as "Notes toward a Supreme Fiction," Stevens questions this assumption. Both explore the way in which the mind might engage with the world through art, however open to question the basis of the engagement is. The mind's knowledge in the Ozymandias canto of the fictive status of its creations does not lead to the sense of guilty isolation that initiates the cycle of reluctant turn to the world and hasty retreat from it. It signals rather the beginning of a never-ending process in which the mind's desire for reality is both satisfied and perpetuated. With each fiction the mind "marries" the world it contemplates, and yet it knows that its fictions are fictions, a skeptical stance that leads to the creation of new fictions through which mind and world marry, and so forth. The fictions created by Ozymandias might be thought of as epithalamions that are their own prothalamions as the mind perpetually weds that which it endlessly desires.

The Ozymandias canto points to another way in which Stevens differs from Lentricchia's portrait of him as a conservative fictionalist. Stevens writes in an aphorism, "The relation of art to life is of the first importance especially in a skeptical age since, in the absence of a belief in God, the mind turns to its own creations and examines them, not alone from the aesthetic point of view, but for what they reveal, for what they validate and invalidate, for the support that they give" (*OP* 186). The sense of intimacy that the mind feels with the world in the Ozymandias canto is one example of the kind of support the mind can take in its creations. The supportive role art can play in human life is not limited, though, to a sense of intimacy with the world. Stevens writes in *The Necessary Angel* that the role of the poet "is to help people to live their lives" (*NA* 29). He felt strongly enough about this role to repeat later in the essay that the poet's "role is to help people to live their lives" (*NA* 30) and to end the essay by reminding us again that poetry "helps us to live our lives" (*NA* 36). Stevens offers an example of how the poet helps people live their lives by contrasting two conceptions of reality.

If we go back to the collection of solid, static objects extended in space, which Dr. Joad posited, and if we say that the space is blank space, nowhere, without color, and that the objects, though solid, have no shadows and, though static, exert a mournful power, and, without elaborating this complete poverty, if suddenly we hear a different and familiar description of the place:

This City now doth, like a garment, wear
The beauty of the morning, silent bare,
Ships, towers, domes, theatres, and temples lie
Open unto the fields, and to the sky;
All bright and glittering in the smokeless air;

if we have this experience, we know how poets help people to live their lives. (*NA* 31)

The passage from Wordsworth helps us to live our lives because through it the mind experiences a sense of pleasure in reality. The sense of pleasure the mind takes in reality through the fictions created by the poet stands in contrast to the sense of the "complete poverty" of existence that is evoked by the Joad passage.

The view of art expressed in "The Noble Rider and the Sound of Words" had been explored five years earlier in canto XXIV of "The Man with the Blue Guitar."

A poem like a missal found
In the mud, a missal for that young man,

That scholar hungriest for that book,
The very book, or, less, a page

Or, at the least, a phrase, that phrase,
A hawk of life, that latined phrase.

(CP 177–78)

As a "missal found / In the mud," the poem is sacred words (the missal is the book containing the prayers used in the Catholic Church to celebrate Mass) of the natural world, "mud." These sacred secular words are a "hawk of life"; they seize and grasp life. When the "young man" finds the "latined phrase," he flinches "at the joy of it"; that is, he experiences pleasure in the world through art. In Lentricchia's reading of Stevens, art could never play the kind of pragmatic, humanistic, affective role that is expressed in the Ozymandias canto and in "The Man with the Blue Guitar" and is described in "The Noble Rider and the Sound of Words." The only role art can play in his reading, the only "support" it can give, is to allow the mind to escape from reality. The guilty knowledge that the mind is estranged from the world is the price that it pays for this support.

The Ozymandias canto also points to one of the differences between Stevens and his portrait as painted by deconstructive critics such as J. Hillis Miller, whose essay "Stevens' Rock and Criticism as Cure" is perhaps the single most influential deconstructive reading of Stevens.[18] Miller argues that all language in Stevens is fictive. "As the reader tries to rest on each element in the poem or on a chain of elements forming a single scene, as he seeks a solid literal ground which is the curiological basis of the other figurative meanings, that element or chain gives way, becomes itself a verbal fiction, an illusion, an icon (in the sense of similitude and not in the sense of mimetic copy)" (*SR* 18). Miller's analysis, though, only addresses one half of Stevens' ironic stance, skeptical detachment. The poem in Miller's reading is restricted to disclosing repeatedly the fictive nature of all of its elements. But even as

Miller argues that there is no final ground on which "The Rock," or any other poem, rests, he also argues that the reader must continue to search for this ground. "The reader is forced then to shift sideways again seeking to find somewhere else in the poem the solid ground of that figure, seeking, or failing or falling, and seeking again" (*SR* 18). While Lentricchia would push Stevens into an either/or choice between fiction and reality, Miller would deny Stevens the choice of the real, except as an irresistible nostalgia. Like Lentricchia, Miller will not allow the mind to be committed to fictions it knows are fictions. In his reading, the mind could never enjoy a sense of intimacy with the world through the fictions it creates. As a result, his analysis ends where Lentricchia's ends, by denying that art can play a supportive role in human life.

In the Ozymandias canto, as in many of Stevens' poems, the emphasis is on the transformations of the world that take place in the creative process. But Stevens also looks at the effect creation and decreation have on the self. I noted earlier in this chapter that reduction led in "The Snow Man" to a sublime experience of the universe at large. A similar turning to the outer can be seen in "How to Live. What to Do."

> There was neither voice nor crested image,
> No chorister, nor priest. There was
> Only the great height of the rock
> And the two of them standing still to rest.
>
> There was the cold wind and the sound
> It made, away from the muck of the land
> That they had left, heroic sound
> Joyous and jubilant and sure.
>
> (*CP* 126)

The "cold wind" is the same wind that blew through the land in "The Snow Man," and in "How to Live. What to Do" it leaves the man and his companion in a bare world. "How to Live. What to Do," however, has an overt political dimension that "The Snow Man" does not have. What the reducing wind of the poem turns the self away from is the political "muck" of the Great Depression. James Longenbach suggests that this poem, like its companion piece, "A Fading of the Sun," dramatizes "the private self's victory over public adversity."[19] But in "A Fading of the Sun," this victory is accomplished by turning inward. If people will "look / Within themselves," they will find "joy" (*CP* 139). In "How to Live. What to Do," in contrast, the sense of joy, "Joyous and jubilant and sure," comes from the self's turn outward. The man and his companion move "away from the muck of the land" to "the great height of the rock" (*CP* 126).

Reduction does not always turn the self away from the limited and finite. In "The Latest Freed Man," the reduction of all descriptions of the world allows the self to enjoy a fuller sense of reality. "It was how the sun came shining into his room: / To be without a description of to be, / . . . / It was everything bulging and blazing and big in itself" (*CP* 205). This encounter with a larger reality through reduction has a reciprocal effect on the self. "To have the ant of the self changed to an ox / . . . / It was how he was free. It was how his freedom came. / It was being without description, being an ox" (*CP* 205).

"The Latest Freed Man" had been anticipated in the more tentative musings of the botanist in "Botanist on Alp (No. 1)." As in "The Latest Freed Man," the old descriptions of the world have been set aside. "Claude has been dead a long time / And . . . / Marx has ruined Nature, / For the moment" (*CP* 134). Instead of being "tired" of these descriptions, as the latest freed man is, the botanist yearns after at least one of them. "But in Claude how near one was / . . . / To the central composition, / The essential theme" (*CP* 135). Without Claude, the world seems to lack a sense of order, "What composition is there in all this," and to be shabby: "The pillars are prostrate, the arches are haggard, / The hotel is boarded and bare" (*CP* 135). Yet the absence of a "central composition" also gives the botanist an ecstatic sense of reality. "Yet the panorama of despair / Cannot be the specialty / Of this ecstatic air" (*CP* 135). Almost in spite of himself, he becomes a "freed man," enjoying being "without a description of to be" (*CP* 205).

In "The Latest Freed Man," reduction leads to a new sense of self. In getting rid of all of the old descriptions of the world, the ant of the self is changed into an ox. A sense of self can also be achieved through creative activity. In "Description without Place," for example, Stevens writes,

> It is a world of words to the end of it,
> In which nothing solid is its solid self.
>
> As, men make themselves their speech: the hard hidalgo
> Lives in the mountainous character of his speech.
>
> (CP 345)

The self here takes on the character of the reality that it creates: "the hard hidalgo / Lives in the mountainous character of his speech." (A similar theory had been advanced in the *Harmonium* poem "Theory," where the self defines itself by the reality in which it exists. "I am what is around me" [*CP* 86].) If the self takes on the character of the reality it creates, then, as Stevens suggests in the parable of the mariners in "An Ordinary Evening in New Haven," when reality is redescribed, the self is also transformed. The mariners, who come from the land of the elm trees, arrive in the land of the lemon trees.

> They said, "We are back once more in the land of the elm
>   trees,
>
> But folded over, turned round." It was the same,
> Except for the adjectives, an alteration
> Of words that was a change of nature . . .
> . . . .
> The countrymen were changed and each constant thing.
> Their dark-colored words had redescribed the citrons.
>
> (CP 487)

In changing nature, they change themselves.

In addition to exploring the way in which the creation and decreation of reality can affect the self, Stevens also takes up directly different concepts of the self. Stevens will critically examine a concept by pointing to its limitations. But he will also return to the concept and explore its potential uses. Various personae, that is, are reduced in one poem, only to be reimagined and revitalized in another. In "Of the Surface of Things," for example, a realist rejects his own poetic voice, that of decorous versifier, because this voice obscures his relation to ordinary reality.

I
In my room, the world is beyond my understanding.
But when I walk I see that it consists of three or
four hills and a cloud.

II
From my balcony, I survey the yellow air,
Reading where I have written,
"The spring is like a belle undressing."

III
The gold tree is blue.
The singer has pulled his cloak over his head.
The moon is in the folds of the cloak.

(*CP* 57)

The decorous versifier is a persona who was seen early in "The Comedian as the Letter C." "The spring is like a belle undressing" could have come from the Crispin who "wrote his couplet yearly to the spring" (*CP* 31). That "mythology of self" is "Blotched out beyond unblotching" (*CP* 28) when Crispin first encounters the sea. This persona is seen again in "Floral Decorations for Bananas." Here, it is criticized as being ridiculously out of place in a tropical setting and is summarily dismissed.

You should have had plums tonight,
In an eighteenth-century dish,
And pettifogging buds,
For the women of primrose and purl,

Each one in her decent curl.
Good God! What a precious light!
                (CP 54)

In "Banal Sojourn," however, this decorous voice is looked at
very differently.

Pardie! Summer is like a fat beast, sleepy in mildew,
Our old bane, green and bloated, serene, who cries,
"That bliss of stars, that princox of evening heaven!"
   reminding of seasons,
When radiance came running down, slim through the
   bareness.
                        (CP 62–63)

A princox is a conceited youth, a coxcomb, one who would fit
into the eighteenth-century setting of "Floral Decorations for
Bananas," while "bliss of evening stars" is not inconsistent with
the decorous vocabulary of "spring is like a belle undressing." In
having "bloated" summer utter these words, Stevens may be sug-
gesting that one season desires its opposite, a thought he will later
develop in "Notes toward a Supreme Fiction" in his meditation
on the origin of change (section II, canto IV). Far from rejecting
the decorous because it obscures the mind's relation to the world
or seems out of place in a lush setting, the speaker of "Banal
Sojourn" turns to the decorous vocabulary of summer as he seeks
relief from the suffocating presence of the real. "And who does
not seek the sky unfuzzed, soaring to the princox?" (CP 63).
   "The Plot against the Giant" uses a persona that will be seen
again in "Life Is Motion" and "Ploughing on Sunday," the down-
home, rural, unsophisticated American.[20] The giant is described as
a "yokel" and does not seem to be much of a poet. He "maun-
ders," that is, talks in a rambling, foolish, idiotic way. This hayseed
poet is waylaid by three women. The first, the poet of civility,
checks the giant's progress. The second, the poet of the small, an
aesthetic seen again in "New England Verses," stanzas V and VI,

abashes the poet. The third, who represents European, and
specifically French, poetry (she speaks French), undoes him. In
"Bantams in Pine-Woods" Stevens takes a second look at this per-
sona. Like the giant the bantam is associated with the rural. Unlike
the giant, however, the bantam is not undone by Europe. To the
contrary, he rejects the high European romanticism symbolized by
Chieftain Iffucan.[21] "Begone! An inchling bristles in these pines, /
. . . / And fears not portly Azcan nor his hoos" (*CP* 76). If "The
Plot against the Giant" suggests that the American poet is a
parochial yokel and that European poetry will "undo" him, "Ban-
tams in Pine-Woods" represents the American poet's confident,
Emersonian rejection of European models.

In "Hymn from a Watermelon Pavilion" and "The Revolu-
tionists Stop for Orangeade," Stevens offers two perspectives on
the poet of sunlight. In the former poem, Stevens celebrates a
poetry of sun, "Yes, and the blackbird spread its tail, / So that the
sun may speckle, / While it creaks hail" (*CP* 89), and asks the
"dweller in the dark cabin" to wake up from the world of roman-
tic illusion, "wind and moon" (*CP* 88), and "cry hail" (*CP* 89) to
the vital world illuminated by the sun. In the latter poem, how-
ever, Stevens asks his fellow poetic revolutionaries not to make
him sing in the sun. Without something "false," he argues, poetry
lacks life, "pith."

> Capitán profundo, capitán geloso,
> Ask us not to sing standing in the sun,
> Hairy-backed and hump-armed,
> Flat-ribbed and big-bagged.
> There is no pith in music
> Except in something false.
>   (*CP* 102–3)

Stevens sometimes plays two personae against each other, only
to criticize both. In "Disillusionment of Ten O'Clock," for exam-
ple, both burgher and aesthete come under fire.

> The houses are haunted
> By white night-gowns.

None are green,
Or purple with green rings,
Or green with yellow rings,
Or yellow with blue rings.
None of them are strange,
With socks of lace
And beaded ceintures.
People are not going
To dream of baboons and periwinkles.
Only, here and there, an old sailor,
Drunk and asleep in his boots,
Catches tigers
In red weather.

(CP 66)

The disillusionment in the title refers in part to the poverty
described in the first part of the poem. The middle-class American
goes to bed at ten o'clock and haunts his own house by wearing a
white nightgown. The title may also refer to Whistler's "Ten
O'Clock" lecture. Though Stevens' emphasis on color might
recall poems such as Wilde's "Impression du Matin,"

The Thames nocturne of blue and gold
    Changed to a Harmony in gray:
    A bare with ochre-colored hay
Dropped from the wharf,[22]

the use of color in Stevens' poem does not seem intended to ren-
der a "mood" or "impression." Rather, the contemplation of col-
ors in various combinations seems to be a pleasurable end in itself,
and the poem appears to endorse the pure good of artifice and
decoration ("socks of lace / And beaded ceintures") in a landscape
that would otherwise be blank.

Stevens, though, is not giving another "Ten O'Clock" lecture
in "Disillusionment of Ten O'Clock." In imagining the night-
gowns these Americans might wear, Stevens is envisioning a
meeting of art and life that is unaesthetic in emphasis. In the "Ten
O'Clock" lecture Whistler says that he wants to lift the burden of
art from the shoulders of the middle class.

The boundary line is clear. Far from me to propose to bridge it over—that the pestered people be pushed across. No! I would save them from further fatigue. I would come to their relief, and would lift from their shoulders this incubus of Art.

Why, after centuries of freedom from it, and indifference to it, should it now be thrust upon them by the blind—until wearied and puzzled, they know no longer how they shall eat or drink—how they shall sit or stand—or wherewithal they shall clothe themselves—without afflicting Art.[23]

"Disillusionment of Ten O'Clock" does not seem to follow this separationist policy. It colorfully investigates how the middle class might "clothe" itself with art. The disillusionment of the title, then, refers not only to middle-class lack of illusion, but also to Stevens' disillusionment with "Ten O'Clock" aestheticism.

Aesthete and middle-class burgher are used in "Disillusionment" to point to each other's limitations. Both of these personae, however, are criticized from a third perspective, that of the old drunk sailor, a figure Stevens perhaps borrowed from Baudelaire, who writes in "Le Voyage" of "ce matelot ivrogne." The sailor's dream life sets him apart from the burgher. As Milton Bates writes, "[T]he people who keep regular hours are unlikely to dream of baboons and periwinkles."[24] And his tiger hunting is unlikely to appeal to the aesthete. (Try to imagine Des Esseintes traveling to another continent to go on safari!)

In "Disillusionment of Ten O'Clock" the burgher lacks imagination. Yet in other poems Stevens suggests that this figure is not so one-dimensional. In "The Weeping Burgher," the burgher desires what he was oblivious to in "Disillusionment of Ten O'Clock."

Permit that if as ghost I come
Among the people burning in me still,

I come as belle design
Of foppish line.
        (*CP* 61)

And in "The Doctor of Geneva," the sight of the Pacific Ocean
sets the doctor's mind "Spinning and hissing . . . / Until the
steeples of his city clanked and sprang / In an unburgherly apoca-
lypse" (*CP* 24).

Stevens' examination of various concepts of the self—aes-
thete, burgher, decorous poet—echoes the endless process of self-
creation and self-destruction that is for Schlegel characteristic of
the ironic mind.[25] By pointing to their limitations, Stevens criti-
cizes these concepts. But in exploring their possible uses, Stevens
also reimagines and revitalizes them. If the realist rejects the deco-
rous versifier because this kind of poetry obscures the mind's rela-
tion to reality, yet this same voice can also offer relief from a world
that threatens to overwhelm the self. And if the burgher lacks
imagination, as Stevens shows us in "Disillusionment of Ten
O'Clock," he also suggests in "The Weeping Burgher" and "The
Doctor of Geneva" that the burgher is not immune to the imagi-
nation's call or to the sublime possibilities of the real. In maintain-
ing a critical stance toward these concepts even as he continues to
re-create them, Stevens expresses both a sense of commitment to
and detachment from them. This attitude, which Schlegel
described as "fluctuating" between self-destruction and self-
creation, engenders a process that can have no logical conclusion.
My examples are from *Harmonium,* but Stevens will continue to
examine some of these personae throughout his career. In "An
Ordinary Evening in New Haven," for example, we see again in
slightly different guise the burgher and the aesthete. In canto IV,
Stevens describes the plain man who "fought / Against illusion"
(*CP* 467). This is the same fight against illusion that resulted in the
burgher's white nightgowns in "Disillusionment of Ten
O'Clock." Though the burghers seem unaware of their imagina-
tive poverty, the "Plain men in plain towns" (*CP* 467) in "An

Ordinary Evening in New Haven" seek relief from their bareness. A second voice, a "savage voice," the voice of imagination and illusion, cries and in that cry the plain men are "comforted." If the imagination alleviates the poverty of the plain in canto IV, in canto IX, the imagination seems superfluous as the self turns again and again to ordinary reality.

> We keep coming back and coming back
> To the real: to the hotel instead of the hymns
> That fall upon it out of the wind.
>
> (*CP* 471)

Once again, uses are explored even as limitations are suggested.

While the *Harmonium* poems looked at above show the self constantly changing, the mere fact of change is not the only thing that links Stevens with Schlegel here. The romantic ironist in Kierkegaard's view also continually changes his identity. At one moment the ironist is a Roman patrician, the next a penitent pilgrim, the next a Turkish pasha (*CI* 299). For Kierkegaard, however, transformations of the self are associated with fear and anxiety. In contrast, Stevens, like Schlegel, expresses a positive attitude toward these changes. In "The Man with the Blue Guitar," for example, the decreative and recreative process, "Throw away the lights, the definitions, / And say of what you see in the dark," is associated with a sense of revelry in which the world is transformed and the self takes on various "shapes."

> How should you walk in that space and know
> Nothing of the madness of space,
>
> Nothing of its jocular procreations?
> Throw the lights away. Nothing must stand
>
> Between you and the shapes you take
> When the crust of shape has been destroyed.
>
> (*CP* 183)

Aesthete, burgher, down-home American, decorous poet—these are some of the shapes the self can assume when the crust of shape has been destroyed. The canto ends with the suggestion that the self's identity is defined by this transforming process. The speaker of the canto echoes an unheard interlocutor's question—"You as you are?"—and answers, "You are yourself. / The blue guitar surprises you" (*CP* 183). You as you are, you yourself, is the self as it takes on various shapes through the creative and decreative process, playing the blue guitar.

The ongoing process of creation and decreation is linked in Stevens' poetry to a sense of beginning. He writes in "Notes toward a Supreme Fiction" that "The poem refreshes life so that we share, / For a moment, the first idea . . . It satisfies / Belief in an immaculate beginning" (*CP* 382). Commenting on the first idea in a letter to Henry Church, Stevens writes, "If you take the varnish and dirt of generations off a picture, you see it in its first idea" (*L* 426–27). The first idea, then, is not the thing itself but an artistic conception of reality, a "picture" without dirt or varnish. Stevens also tells Church that "the first poem [of "Notes toward a Supreme Fiction"] bore the caption REFACIMENTO" (*L* 431). *Refacimento* is a term "associated with the practice of rewriting or recasting established works of literature. . . . [T]he practice of *refacimento* simply replaces one artist's representation of reality with another's."[26] The ending of the first canto of "Notes" exemplifies this process.

> Phoebus is dead, ephebe. But Phoebus was
> A name for something that never could be named.
> There was a project for the sun and is.
>
> There is a project for the sun. The sun
> Must bear no name, gold flourisher, but be
> In the difficulty of what it is to be.
>
> (*CP* 381)

To replace "Phoebus" with "gold flourisher" as a name for reality is to replace one artistic conception of reality with another. The same process is implied in Ozymandias' reduction and creation of fictive covering after fictive covering. Each fiction is a new and different artistic conception; each is a "first idea," an "immaculate beginning." The poem refreshes life because through it we experience the world as the "first idea," that is, at its newest, its freshest, its earliest, in short, at its beginning. And since the process of creation is a never-ending one, Stevens' poetry repeatedly offers us a new sense of reality.

This new world, "always beginning, over and over" (*CP* 530), is a world of change without direction or goal. To begin again and again is not to journey from point to point. It is to relocate the point from which all journeys start. Yet each beginning also marks a difference from what came before. Hence, beginning can be thought of in Stevens' work as a process of continual differentiation that cannot be measured directionally. Each fictive covering created by Ozymandias, for example, is a first idea that is different from the previous first idea. But though Ozymandias' creative activity expresses continual change, these changes have no direction because each fiction is a return to the beginning. And with each beginning, the poem discloses a new and different aspect of the world, a first idea. Because to begin in Stevens is to disclose a world of difference and change that has no inherent direction, reality in his work seems to flow continually but, as he puts it in "The River of Rivers in Connecticut," it "flows nowhere, like a sea" (*CP* 533).

Irony in Schlegel is also conceived as *beginning*. The skeptical reduction of existing concepts of self and world "frees the imagination to create a new conception of the self, of society, of nature."[27] These conceptions are in turn subjected to skeptical analysis, which again invites the imagination to create new concepts of self and world, and so on endlessly. This ever-new and ever-different world has no inherent telos or pattern. As discussed in chapter 1, romantic irony posits a chaotic universe. Though the romantic ironist "embraces change and process for their own sake,"[28] Stevens sometimes expresses a desire to escape from a world of unending change. He writes in "This Solitude of Cataracts" of "the flecked river, / Which kept flowing and never the same way twice" and of his desire "to rest / In a permanent realization,"

to know how it would feel, released from destruction,
To be a bronze man breathing under archaic lapis,

Without the oscillations of planetary pass-pass.

                                             (*CP* 424–25)

This desire appears to be satisfied in "Solitaire under the Oaks,"
where he feels "completely released" from "facts" (*OP* 137).

Although Stevens sometimes writes of his desire to escape
from a world of unending change, he also, like Schlegel, celebrates
a reality of process without goal or end. In "The Auroras of
Autumn," for example, he describes the world as a "cloud trans-
formed / To cloud transformed again, idly, the way / A season
changes color to no end, / Except the lavishing of itself in change"
(*CP* 416). But lyrical praise of change is not the only way that
Stevens affirms a chaotic world. M. H. Abrams has described the
Western philosophical tradition, "in the main . . . a long series of
footnotes to Plotinus" (*NS* 146),[29] which associates unity with a
fullness of being and fragmentation with absence and loss. As Plo-
tinus formulates it in the *Enneads,* there is an eternal procession
from the unity of the One into multiplicity and division and a
counterprocession back to the One. This process in Plotinus is
sometimes seen as "the parable of an internal spiritual journey in
quest of a lost home" (*NS* 149). Both the pattern of emanation and
return and the view of the pattern as a quest to overcome frag-
mentation and find the unity of a lost but recoverable home pro-
foundly influenced later philosophers. Abrams writes that Hegel's
Phenomenology of the Spirit, for example, recounts the journey of
the self "from its 'moment' of departure from its own alienated
self, around and up and back, until it finds itself 'at home with
itself in its otherness'" (*NS* 192). In Stevens, this tradition is turned
on its head. Fragmentation is associated not with loss or absence
but with plenitude, and the self's fullest understanding of the
chaotic nature of reality is associated with its most comprehensive
feeling of being at home in the world.

These associations are the subject of Stevens' middle poem,
"On the Road Home."

It was when I said,
"There is no such thing as the truth,"
That the grapes seemed fatter.
The fox ran out of his hole.

You . . . You said,
"There are many truths,
But they are not parts of a truth."
Then the tree, at night, began to change,

Smoking through green and smoking blue.
We were two figures in a wood.
We said we stood alone.

It was when I said,
"Words are not forms of a single word.
In the sum of the parts, there are only the parts.
The world must be measured by eye";

It was when you said,
"The idols have seen lots of poverty,
Snakes and gold and lice,
But not the truth";

It was at that time, that the silence was largest
And longest, the night was roundest,
The fragrance of the autumn warmest,
Closest and strongest.

(*CP* 203–4)

In the poem, as in Plotinus, the journey is associated with fragmentation and division. Rather than overcoming fragmentation and finding a unity that is home, the poem identifies home with fragmentation. Like Schlegel, Stevens rejects the presupposition of an original wholeness or unity. These fragments are not fragments *of* the whole; they are simply fragments. "In the sum of the parts, there are only the parts" (*CP* 204). Multiple truths are not parts of *a* truth; they are just multiple truths. "'There are many truths, / But they are not parts of a truth'" (*CP* 203). In Plotinus, the greater the fragmentation, the greater the separation from the unity and fullness of the One. But in "On the Road Home," the more that Stevens repeats his assertion that the world has no unity, the more he evokes images of warmth, nearness, and plenitude. The first assertion, that "'There is no such thing as the truth'" (*CP* 203), evokes a rather tentative response from the mind. "The grapes seemed fatter" (*CP* 203). The statement is both qualified, "seemed," and in the comparative degree, which suggests a lack of fullness and completion. The grapes may be fatter than they were before the speaker of the poem said, "'There is no such thing as the truth,'" but they are not yet all they can be. There is nothing tentative in the mind's final response to fragmentation. The statement that makes up the concluding stanza is made without qualification, unusual in a poet known for his qualified assertions.[30] The silence did not *seem* largest and longest, it *was* largest and longest. The night *was* roundest; the fragrance of the autumn *was* warmest, closest, strongest. The comparative degree of the first stanza has been replaced in the final stanza by the superlative degree, which connotes fullness and finality. In addition to the superlative degree, the adjectives themselves, "largest," "longest," "roundest," "closest," "warmest," "strongest," and the resonance of Keats' "To Autumn" in the concluding couplet,[31] contribute to the feeling of plenitude that is expressed in the poem's close. In linking the mind's most fully elaborated sense of fragmentation with its strongest sense of fullness, of warmth, of intimacy, Stevens suggests that in the parts themselves we have arrived at our destination. To be *on* the road home is to *be* home.

"On the Road Home" can be considered a companion poem to "The Latest Freed Man." While "On the Road Home" argues that the world is richer and fuller when the self recognizes the chaotic nature of reality, "The Latest Freed Man" shows us that the self grows larger when it puts aside all structuring concepts, all "descriptions" of reality. In the following chapter, we will see that the absence of order can lead to a diminished sense of self and world. It is at these moments that Stevens draws close to Eliot, whose earlier work suggests that without a final sense of order, the self is empty and sterile and the world is a heap of rubble. Though

Stevens rejected this view as early as "Gubbinal," whose speaker ironically agrees with an unheard interlocutor (Eliot?), "Have it your way. / The world is ugly, / And the people are sad" (*CP* 85), only to show us in numerous ways that this is not so, in "Two or Three Ideas," written thirty years later, Stevens describes the sense of diminishment that can accompany the loss of order.

> To see the gods dispelled in mid-air and dissolve like clouds is one of the great human experiences. . . . Since we have always shared all things with them and have always had a part of their strength and, certainly, all of their knowledge, we shared like-wise this experience of annihilation. . . . It left us feeling dis-possessed and alone in a solitude, like children without par-ents, in a home that seemed deserted, in which the amical rooms and halls had taken on a look of hardness and empti-ness. (*OP* 260)

And yet, Stevens continues in a decidedly un-Eliotic turn, there was no "crying out" for the gods to come back. "[N]o man ever muttered a petition in his heart for the restoration of those unreal shapes" (*OP* 260). "On the Road Home" and "The Latest Freed Man" suggest why "no man" wants the gods to return. Though their absence does not automatically lead to the sense of enlarge-ment expressed in these two poems, there are moments when, without the gods, without any sense of order, the self changes into an ox and the world seems warmer, closer, stronger.

Chapter 3

Completely Released: Stevens, Hegel, and Kierkegaard

> Irony now appeared as that . . . which was through with everything, yet at the same time as that which had absolute power to do everything.
>
> —Kierkegaard

In 1950 William Van O'Connor sent a copy of his study *The Shaping Spirit* to Stevens. Though Stevens found the "essential part of the book" to be "very well done," he corrected O'Connor on one point: "on p. 45 I am quoted as saying that I knew [T. S.] Eliot only slightly and principally through correspondence. As a matter of fact, I don't know him at all and have had no correspondence whatever with him. . . . After all, Eliot and I are dead opposites and I have been doing about everything that he would not be likely to do" (*L* 677).[1] The letter to O'Connor is of interest partly because it suggests how Stevens, at age seventy, defines, or at least begins to define, his place in modern poetry—in dead opposition to Eliot. The kind of irony expressed in the two poets seems to bear out Stevens' observation. Eliot's early poetry expresses an irony that negatively frees the self from the world. For Hegel and Kierkegaard, this freedom is a defining characteristic of romantic irony, and in their view it leads ultimately to despair. A similar sense of freedom and despair is expressed in Eliot's early work. Stevens' irony, in contrast, does not isolate the self from the world. Though skeptically aware that all structuring concepts are, finally, fictions imposed by the mind on experience, the mind also "marries" the world through these concepts. In addition, Stevens' irony affirms a world of "patches and pitches." Eliot's irony expresses the opposite response to a chaotic world. Contrast, for example,

93

the extreme spiritual destitution felt in *The Waste Land* by the self when it confronts a world without order with Stevens' response in "On the Road Home" to a world in which "there are only the parts." It is when the world is seen in its fragmentary character that the fragrance of the autumn night is "warmest, / Closest and strongest" (*CP* 204).[2]

The letter to O'Connor is of interest in another respect. Stevens so strongly protests against any similarity with Eliot that the letter raises the question of whether its purpose is not simply to define Stevens in opposition to Eliot but also to turn attention away from the possibility that they may have something in common. The letter, that is, can be seen as indirectly expressing Stevens' anxiety about the distinctiveness of his individual poetic voice. Stevens' need to prevail over his rivals was expressed without ambiguity twenty-seven years before his letter to O'Connor in "The Comedian as the Letter C."

> What was the purpose of his pilgrimage,
> Whatever shape it took in Crispin's mind,
> If not, when all is said, to drive away
> The shadow of his fellows from the skies,
> And, from their stale intelligence released,
> To make a new intelligence prevail?
>
> (*CP* 37)

As I discussed in chapter 2, Stevens' irony sets him against major aspects of modern poetics as defined by Pound and Williams and hence can be seen as an expression of a new poetic intelligence. But Stevens' attempt to drive away the shadow of at least one powerful fellow poet from the skies, to be released from his "stale intelligence," was not as successful as he would have liked or, to judge from the O'Connor letter, as he would like us to believe. Though Stevens' work does express an irony that is opposed to the irony of the early Eliot, it also expresses an irony that, like Eliot's, has a deep affiliation with romantic irony as it is interpreted by Hegel and Kierkegaard. One strand of this interpretation, their

view of the romantic ironist as Fichtean ego, is recalled in Stevens'
early poem, "Tea at the Palaz of Hoon."

> Not less because in purple I descended
> The western day through what you called
> The loneliest air, not less was I myself.
>
> What was the ointment sprinkled on my beard?
> What were the hymns that buzzed beside my ears?
> What was the sea whose tide swept through me there?
>
> Out of my mind the golden ointment rained,
> And my ears made the blowing hymns they heard.
> I was myself the compass of that sea:
>
> I was the world in which I walked, and what I saw
> Or heard or felt came not but from myself;
> And there I found myself more truly and more strange.
>
> (CP 65)

Both Hegel and Kierkegaard view the Fichtean ego as having
absolute creative power. "Whatever is," writes Hegel, "is only by
the instrumentality of the *ego*" (A 64). Kierkegaard expresses a sim-
ilar view when he writes that for Fichte "subjectivity, the ego, has
constitutive validity, that it alone is the almighty" (CI 292). Both
believe that the world that is created by the ego is only an aspect
of the ego. Hegel writes that for the Fichtean ego "nothing is
treated *in and for itself* . . . but only as produced by the subjectivity
of the *ego*. . . . Consequently everything genuinely and indepen-
dently real becomes only a show, . . . a mere appearance due to the
ego in whose power . . . it remains" (A 64–65). Kierkegaard makes
the same point when he writes that the ironist negates the actual
world and replaces it with a "self-created actuality" (CI 292). For
Hoon, as for the Hegelian and Kierkegaardian ironists, the world
is both created by and an aspect of his ego. "I was the world in
which I walked, and what I saw / Or heard or felt came not but
from myself" (CP 65). Nothing, as Bloom observes, is exterior to

Hoon. "Seeing, hearing, and feeling find objects only from his own self, and nothing through which he moves is outside him."[3] The sea sweeps through Hoon, but since he is the "compass" of the sea, its movement has direction only in relation to him. Whatever hymns he hears are hymns he creates. The sprinkling of ointment on his beard is a parody of the ceremony in which God's elect is anointed with oil or ointment. Hoon dissolves the distinction between anointer and anointed, elected and elector. "What was the ointment sprinkled on my beard? / . . . Out of my mind the golden ointment rained" (*CP* 65). There can be no distinction in Hoon's world between himself and what he sees or hears or feels or between himself as anointer or anointed because, finally, everything is an aspect of his ego. Dressed in purple, the color of royalty, Hoon, like the romantic ironist portrayed by Hegel, is "lord and master of everything" (*A* 64).

Stevens describes Hoon in a later poem, "Sad Strains of a Gay Waltz," as

> that mountain-minded Hoon,
> For whom desire was never that of the waltz,
>
> Who found all form and order in solitude,
> For whom the shapes were never the figures of men.
>
> (*CP* 121)

For Hoon the shapes are never the figures of men because it is his will alone that is expressed in his world. Though Stevens describes Hoon as finding "all form and order in solitude," yet Hoon denies at the beginning of the poem that his solitude is a lonely one. "I descended / The western day through what you called / The loneliest air" (*CP* 65). "You" and not Hoon call the air "lonely." Part of the reason that his solitude is not lonely is suggested in Stevens' comment that for Hoon "desire was never that of the waltz." Desire, that is, has no social or interpersonal component.[4] Though it is not directed outward toward another person or toward society at large, yet desire is not unfulfilled. Hoon finds the world as himself, and in doing so, desire is turned back to and finds satisfaction in the self. The air is not lonely to Hoon because the pleasure he takes in himself eliminates the need for anyone but himself. Hoon's enclosure and the sense of pleasure that he takes in discovering the world as the self recall Hegel's description of romantic irony as a "concentration of the *ego* into itself, for which all bonds are snapped and which can live only in the bliss of self-enjoyment" (*A* 66).

Both the sense of creativity and the sense of pleasure expressed in "Tea at the Palaz of Hoon" differ from the kind of creativity and pleasure expressed in the irony of skeptical engagement. In the Ozymandias canto of "Notes toward a Supreme Fiction," for example, the mind marries the world through the fictions it creates. And because the process of creation is ongoing, the mind's experience of the world is seen as becoming richer and more diverse. To create in "Tea at the Palaz of Hoon" is to turn the world into the self and hence negate the world. This narcissism stands in opposition both to poems such as "The Man with the Blue Guitar," canto XXIV, where the self, through art, takes pleasure in reality, and to "The Snow Man," whose reduction of all fictions to "nothing," a reduction in which the self turns away from itself and beholds the universe at large, can be seen as Stevens' most severe criticism of the self-love expressed by Hoon.[5]

The Hoon-like imagination is seen again in "The Man with the Blue Guitar," canto XIII.

> The pale intrusions into blue
> Are corrupting pallors . . . ay di mi,
>
> Blue buds or pitchy blooms. Be content—
> Expansions, diffusions—content to be
>
> The unspotted imbecile revery,
> The heraldic center of the world
>
> Of blue, blue sleek with a hundred chins,
> The amorist Adjective aflame . . .
>
> (*CP* 172)

Writing to Renato Poggioli, Stevens comments that this canto "deals with the intensity of the imagination unmodified by contacts with reality, if such a thing is possible. Intensity becomes something incandescent. . . . The poem has to do with pure imagination" (*L* 785). Though Stevens suggests that the poem "deals with the intensity of the imagination unmodified by contacts with reality," the poem opens at the moment when reality and the imagination do come into contact. When the ego is infinite, Kierkegaard writes, then reality becomes "pale" in relation to it. "[W]hen Fichte rendered the ego infinite . . . all actuality became pale" (*CI* 290). It is the intrusion by "pale" reality into the imagination that is described in lines 1 and 2. Reality is seen as "corrupting pallors," that is, as pale colors that corrupt the pure blue of the imagination. What is Stevens' response to this assault upon isolation? Hegel remarks that the isolated ego "may not do or touch anything for fear of losing its inner harmony" (*A* 66). Far from expressing pleasure that the imagination has been "corrupted" by reality, the canto expresses regret that the inner harmony of the pure imagination has been disturbed by contact with the real—"ay di mi." In the remainder of the canto, Stevens urges the imagination to be more detached, more expansive, more self-absorbed. Be the "unspotted imbecile revery." Be unspotted, that is, by any touch of the real. He calls upon the imagination to be, as in "Tea at the Palaz of Hoon," expansive, large, "expansions, diffusions," to be the center of a world that, again as in "Tea at the Palaz of Hoon," is all imagination, "The heraldic center of the world / Of blue" (*CP* 172). Stevens writes in his letter to Poggioli that the intensity of the imagination unmodified by contacts with reality becomes incandescent. The final line of the canto suggests that the intensity of the imagination in the absence of the real has become more than incandescent; it has burst into flames, "The amorist Adjective aflame" (*CP* 172). The adjective is seen as a lover, an "amorist." But what love does the amorist adjective express? It expresses the love experienced when the imagination is unmodified by contacts with reality; that is, it expresses the love of the imagination in and for itself, a love seen earlier in Hoon's blissful self-enjoyment.

The imagination is again portrayed in Hoon-like terms in "The Man with the Blue Guitar," canto XXV. Instead of seeing reality as a threat to the inner harmony of the expansive imagination, as he does in canto XIII, Stevens describes the imagination in canto XXV as powerful, unfettered, whimsically sporting with a world over which it has complete dominion.

> He held the world upon his nose
> And this-a-way he gave a fling.
>
> His robes and symbols, ai-yi-yi—
> And that-a-way he twirled the thing.
>
> . . . .
>
> And the nose is eternal, that-a-way.
>   (CP 178)

This portrait of the imagination as playfully tossing the world on the end of its nose echoes both Hegel's description of the "capricious" godlike ego and Kierkegaard's description of the ironic ego as sporting with a world that it creates and changes as it wishes. Toss the world up and dwell "in Greece beneath the beautiful Hellenic sky" (CI 294). Toss it up again and the "virgin forests of the Middle Ages" (CI 294) are substituted for the Hellenic world. Another toss and the Middle Ages are "spirited away back into infinity" (CI 295) to be replaced by something else. "All things are possible for the ironist" (CI 299).

While canto XIII of "The Man with the Blue Guitar" focuses on the moment in which the detached imagination is intruded upon by reality and canto XXV of the poem displays the imagination playing with a world that is completely in its power, "A Rabbit as King of the Ghosts" shows us the actual movement of irony itself, the movement by which the self becomes negatively free of reality. What is rejected in "A Rabbit as King of the Ghosts" is not only the real, but also the self that is at home in the real. The poem opens "at the end of day" with the rabbit's recollection of "the cat slopping its milk all day, / Fat cat, red tongue, green mind" (CP 209). The fat cat with the green mind is the self that is fully situated in the real. This self is rejected by the rabbit. "To be, in the grass, in the peacefullest time, / Without that monument of cat, / The cat forgotten in the moon" (*CP* 209). But when the cat is forgotten in the moon, reality begins to exist "not in and for itself" (*A* 64), but only for the rabbit: "Everything is meant for you" (*CP* 209).

The grass is full

And full of yourself. The trees around are for you,
The whole of the wideness of night is for you,
A self that touches all edges,

You become a self that fills the four corners of night.
The red cat hides away in the fur-light
And there you are humped high, humped up,

You are humped higher and higher, black as stone—
You sit with your head like a carving in space
And the little green cat is a bug in the grass.

(*CP* 209–10)

When the world stops being "genuinely and independently real" (*A* 65) and only exists for the self, then the self negatively escapes from reality. The self rises higher and higher, "You are humped higher and higher," until the real and the self that inhabits the real are reduced to insignificance, "the little green cat is a bug in the grass" (*CP* 210). Like Kierkegaard's ironist, the rabbit here seems to "hover" over the real. While the rabbit's expansion, "a self that fills the four corners of night," and its subjectivization of the world, "everything is meant for you," recall the expansive subjectivity of Hoon, the rabbit is not completely enclosed. It at least recognizes a world external to the self, however reduced in significance that world may be.

The self's movement of escape from the real in "A Rabbit as King of the Ghosts" looks forward to Stevens' late meditation on withdrawal, "Solitaire under the Oaks."

In the oblivion of cards
One exists among pure principles.

Neither the cards nor the trees nor the air
Persist as facts. This is an escape

To principium, to meditation.
One knows at last what to think about

And thinks about it without consciousness,
Under the oak trees, completely released.
                                   (OP 137)

The self's "escape" from "facts" in this poem is much more com-
plete than in "A Rabbit as King of the Ghosts." The difference in
the nature of the self's negative freedom from the world is sug-
gested in at least two ways. First, though the rabbit tries to forget
the cat, "The cat forgotten in the moon," the cat is never quite
eliminated from the poem. By the end of the poem it has been
reduced to the significance of a bug, but it remains stubbornly
present. The self in "Solitaire under the Oaks" does what the rab-
bit would like to do. In "Solitaire" the self with the "green mind"
has been forgotten in the moon. Its presence, even as a bug, is
nowhere recorded. The second way in which the two poems dif-
fer is suggested in the penultimate line of "Solitaire," "And thinks
about it without consciousness." Bloom writes that "Stevens
recorded a major battle in the war between being-without-
consciousness and consciousness-without-being" in "A Rabbit as
King of the Ghosts," the rabbit representing the "Transcendental
consciousness-without-being."[6] But in "Solitaire under the Oaks"
Stevens moves beyond consciousness itself. Here, one "thinks . . .
without consciousness." What is the thinking without conscious-
ness that Stevens earlier in the poem calls "meditation"? "Notes
toward a Supreme Fiction," section II, canto VI offers some help
in answering this question. Canon Aspirin's meditation after he
falls asleep seems to be the kind of thinking without consciousness
in the absence of facts that Stevens refers to in "Solitaire under the
Oaks."

When at long midnight the Canon came to sleep
And normal things had yawned themselves away,
The nothingness was a nakedness, a point,

Beyond which fact could not progress as fact.
Thereon the learning of the man conceived
Once more night's pale illuminations.

(*CP* 402)

Though the canon, asleep, thinks without consciousness and without facts, "fact could not progress as fact," Stevens contemplates in the canto an even more complete withdrawal, the escape from thought itself. When the canon flies "Straight to the utmost crown of night," he reaches "a point / Beyond which thought could not progress as thought" (*CP* 403). "Solitaire under the Oaks" does not reach the point at which thought cannot progress as thought. But in escaping from facts and from consciousness and in eliminating the presence of the cat, the poem expresses a much deeper withdrawal into the mind than does "A Rabbit as King of the Ghosts."

What motivates the self to seek the negative freedom offered to it by irony, or at least by one kind of irony? For Hegel, irony expresses the ego's sense of its own importance and power. It regards itself as above society and "looks down" on other men as "dull and limited, inasmuch as law, morals, etc., still count for them as fixed, essential, and obligatory" (*A* 66). Kierkegaard describes the ironist in similar terms. In contrast to the "acting individual," who feels "himself assimilated into a larger context," feels "the seriousness of responsibility," and respects "every rational consequence," the ironist "is free from all this" (*CI* 296). He acknowledges "no bonds, no chains" (*CI* 296). The escape from the world through irony also allows the ego to indulge its narcissistic desires. In withdrawing from reality, it can live in the "bliss of self-enjoyment." Both of these motives are expressed in "Tea at the Palaz of Hoon." For Hoon the "shapes are never the figures of men," and he enjoys in his solitude the pleasure of discovering the world as himself.

But there is another desire that is expressed in the ironist's withdrawal from reality. To escape from the world and time is to escape from death, and all of the poems looked at so far in this chapter have as their implicit theme the refusal of mortality. The implicit argument of these poems looks forward to Stevens' late poem, "This Solitude of Cataracts," where the self openly expresses its wish to deny death by escaping from time and change. The poem opens with the self observing the flux of being.

> He never felt twice the same about the flecked river,
> Which kept flowing and never the same way twice,
>   flowing
>
> Through many places, as if it stood still in one,
> Fixed like a lake on which the wild ducks fluttered,
>
> Ruffling its common reflections, thought-like Monadnocks.
>   (CP 424)

The image of being as a river here anticipates its appearance in "The River of Rivers in Connecticut," where Stevens writes of "The river that flows nowhere, like a sea" (CP 533), and in "Metaphor as Degeneration," where Stevens writes that "The swarthy water / That flows round the earth and through the skies, / Twisting among the universal spaces, / Is not Swatara. It is being" (CP 444). The river in "This Solitude of Cataracts" constantly changes, "flowing . . . never the same way twice," as do his feelings about it. "He never felt twice the same about the flecked river" (CP 424). Stevens views this river as a placid lake in which the ordinary physical world is reflected, "common reflections." Seen as a reflection on the lake's surface, the world takes on an unreal, thoughtlike quality. As Stevens commented to Renato Poggioli, "The image of a mountain [Monadnock is a mountain in New Hampshire] deep in the surface of the lake acquires a secondary character. From the sheen of the surface it becomes slightly unreal: thought-like" (L 823). The thoughtlike quality of reality is also emphasized in the word "Monadnocks." These mountains are half "monad." The placid surface of the lake is broken by the ran-

dom and chaotic motion of being, the fluttering of the wild ducks.
This movement disturbs the common images reflected on the sur-
face of the lake, causing the self to feel that what it perceives as real
is not real at all. "There was so much that was real that was not real
at all" (*CP* 425). The feeling of unreality that results from change
gives rise to a desire for a kind of motion without change. Stevens
wants the river to go on flowing, but instead of flowing "*never* the
same way twice" (*CP* 424), he wants it to "go on flowing the *same*
way" (*CP* 425; emphasis added). He wants to continue to feel, but
instead of "never" feeling "twice the same" about the flecked
river, he wants "to feel the *same* way over and over" (*CP* 425;
emphasis added). Motion without change was the subject of
"Notes toward a Supreme Fiction," section II, canto I, where it
was rejected. "It means the distaste we feel for this withered scene
/ Is that it has not changed enough. It remains, / It is a repetition"
(*CP* 390). But in "This Solitude of Cataracts" motion without
change gives way to a desire for complete stasis. Stevens wants to
reach a "permanent realization" in which the moon does not
move, is "nailed fast," in which his heart stops beating and his
mind rests, in which there are no "wild ducks," no flutterings of
being in motion, no mountains that are not really mountains. He
wants to be "released from destruction," that is, released from the
temporal and the destruction that it brings. Yet in escaping from
time and change, the "oscillations of planetary pass-pass," he
becomes nonhuman, a "bronze man . . . / Breathing his bronzen
breath at the azury centre of time" (*CP* 425).

In addition to their refusals of mortality, "Tea at the Palaz of
Hoon," cantos XIII and XXV of "The Man with the Blue Gui-
tar," "A Rabbit as King of the Ghosts," and "Solitaire under the
Oaks" are also linked by a common attitude toward detachment.
In none is detachment seen in a negative way. Hoon lives in the
"bliss of self-enjoyment" (*A* 66), as does, apparently, his world-
juggling cousin in "The Man with the Blue Guitar," canto XXV.
In "Solitaire under the Oaks" and "A Rabbit as King of the
Ghosts" the self seeks to escape from the real and does so with-
out regret, while in canto XIII of "The Man with the Blue Gui-
tar," the imagination voices its resentment of the intrusion of the
real into its own blue sphere. Both Hegel and Kierkegaard write

that the ironic ego can for a time enjoy its enclosure and seeming self-sufficiency. Yet the world of the ironist in their view is essentially an empty one. As Hegel writes, when the world is the product of the ego, "everything genuinely and independently real becomes only a show, not true and genuine on its own account or through itself, but a mere appearance due to the *ego*" (*A* 65). Hegel goes on to write of the moment in which the ego comes to recognize the emptiness of its world and to seek the actual. "[T]he ego may . . . fail to find satisfaction in this self-enjoyment and instead become inadequate to itself, so that it now feels a craving for the solid and the substantial, for specific and essential interests" (*A* 66). Of the poems discussed so far, only "A Rabbit as King of the Ghosts" offers a hint, in the word "Ghosts" in the title, that the world as ego is an insubstantial world. This recognition, however, is not pursued in the poem. Its focus of attention is on the satisfaction the rabbit takes in filling up the four corners of the sky and not on the realization that the rabbit's kingdom is a ghostly one.

The sense of loss that the self can feel when it is detached from the world is given deeper expression in canto XXVI of "The Man with the Blue Guitar."

The world washed in his imagination,
The world was a shore, whether sound or form

Or light, the relic of farewells,
Rock, of valedictory echoings,

To which his imagination returned,
From which it sped, a bar in space,

Sand heaped in the clouds, giant that fought
Against the murderous alphabet:

The swarm of thoughts, the swarm of dreams
Of inaccessible Utopia.

A mountainous music always seemed
To be falling and to be passing away.

(*CP* 179)

"Murderous alphabet" is a revealing phrase. When the ego creates the world, then everything "genuinely and independently real becomes only a show, not true . . . on its own account" (*A* 65). In this canto of "The Man with the Blue Guitar," the self recognizes that to create is to murder the real. The world is seen as a giant that fights against poetry, the "murderous alphabet." This view of the creative process contrasts sharply with the view of creativity in poems such as "Variations on a Summer Day," where poetry does not murder the real but adds to our sense of the real, "Words add to the senses" (*CP* 234), with "The Man with the Blue Guitar," canto XXIV, where poetry is seen as gripping life, "A hawk of life, that latined phrase" (*CP* 178), and with "Large Red Man Reading," where, far from being a "murderous alphabet," the great blue tabulae are "the poem of life" (*CP* 423). The self in canto XXIV of "Blue Guitar" could respond to its murder of the real as it does in, for example, "Solitaire under the Oaks" and "A Rabbit as King of the Ghosts," by enjoying its release from the world. But in this canto, the self sees the world not as something from which it happily escapes, but as something that it desires and whose absence is felt as a loss. The darkest aspect of the canto is suggested by the word "inaccessible." If creative activity separates the self from reality by destroying the real, if poetry, in other words, is a "murderous alphabet," then to strum the blue guitar is to write poems in which the real can be desired or yearned for but can never be realized. To create locks the self away from the world, which remains an "inaccessible Utopia."

In "The Man with the Blue Guitar," canto XXVI, there is no sense of the satisfaction the self can take in detachment. The self turns toward the world, and the pleasures of withdrawal are nowhere put forward. Stevens' attitude toward detachment is not always so unambiguous. He is sometimes critical of detachment even as he continues to express his attraction to mind alone. The early poem, "The Bird with the Coppery Keen Claws," expresses this emotional ambivalence. The bird, "pure intellect," is mocked, and yet Stevens continues to be drawn to it. He criticizes the bird in part by portraying it not in large, grandiose, Hoon-like terms, but as a small household pet, a parakeet. The bird's blindness to the beautiful particulars of the world is also a criticism of it. "(The rudiments of tropics are around, / Aloe of ivory, pear of rusty rind.) / His lids are white because his eyes are blind" (*CP* 82). Stevens comments that the bird is a "pip of life amid a mort of tails," but he means the opposite. The title of the poem that follows "The Bird with the Coppery Keen Claws" is "Life Is Motion," and this bird "moves not on his coppery, keen claws" (*CP* 82). Yet the bird attracts Stevens. There is no mockery in the tone of, for example, "Panache upon panache, his tails deploy / Upward and outward, in green-vented forms" (*CP* 82). The poem concludes with an ambivalent description of the bird. He "never ceases, perfect cock, / To flare, in the sun-pallor of his rock" (*CP* 82). Though the bird is "perfect" and never ceases to "flare," "sun-pallor" suggests a pale, diminished radiance.

In "The Bird with the Coppery Keen Claws" Stevens neither fully rejects the song of "pure intellect" to embrace the rudiments of tropics nor gives up the tropics for the pleasures of mind. He seems, that is, to be situated between the poles of desire for detachment and desire for the real, and to be unwilling or unable to choose between them. This presentation of the self as caught between the desire for detachment and the desire for the real recalls Hegel's description of the ironist as one who, on the one hand, "does want to penetrate into truth and longs for objectivity, but, on the other hand, cannot renounce his isolation and withdrawal into himself" (*A* 66). What is of interest about this ambivalence in "The Bird with the Coppery Keen Claws" and what makes it different from the ambivalence described by Hegel is the very relaxed way in which the poem presents the conflict. For Hegel, this conflict, or to use his term, "contradiction," is a dark moment for the self. But Stevens in "The Bird with the Coppery Keen Claws" seems quite comfortable in this weightless zone.

There is no sense of ease about this conflict as it is presented in "The Man with the Blue Guitar," canto XII.

The whirling noise

Of a multitude dwindles, all said,
To his breath that lies awake at night.

I know that timid breathing. Where
Do I begin and end? And where,

As I strum the thing, do I pick up
That which momentously declares

Itself not to be I and yet
Must be. It could be nothing else.
                    (*CP* 171)

The noise of the multitude that dwindles to his breath looks back to Hoon, "Who found all form and order in solitude, / For whom the shapes were never the figures of men" (*CP* 121). All noise for Hoon ultimately dwindles down to his own breath. But the gigantic egotism of Hoon, described in "Sad Strains of a Gay Waltz" and celebrated in "Tea at the Palaz of Hoon," is in this canto the source of considerable fear. What Stevens is afraid of is that Hoon is right, that the world does come down to his own breath. In playing the blue guitar, he finds not the external world but the self, "That which momentously declares / Itself not to be I and yet / Must be. It could be nothing else" (*CP* 171).

Stevens had answered the question, "Where / Do I begin and end?" very differently in poems such as "The Latest Freed Man," "Description without Place," and "An Ordinary Evening in New Haven." In these poems, as I discussed in chapter 2, the self is transformed even as it transforms the world around it. And Stevens suggests in canto XXXII of "The Man with the Blue Guitar" that the self's identity is inseparable from this transforming process. There can be no final answer in these poems to the question of where the self begins and ends because the relation of self and world is constantly changing in the creative process. In canto XII of "The Man with the Blue Guitar," however, the underlying assumption about creativity is very different. Here, the self associates the creative process with a radical subjectivity and suffers in consequence the kind of anxiety that both Hegel and Kierkegaard knew would be the fate of the romantic ironist.

The fear of the loss of the real that is expressed in canto XII of

"The Man with the Blue Guitar" is related to another fear—loss of the self. For Hegel and Kierkegaard, the self, to be real, must be "immersed" in and conform to an actuality that exists apart from the self. Hegel writes that "I only become essential myself in my own eyes in so far as I have immersed myself in such a content and have brought myself into conformity with it in all my knowing and acting" (*A* 65). Kierkegaard makes a similar point in *The Concept of Irony* when he writes that historical actuality "relates in a twofold way to the subject: partly as a gift which will not admit of being rejected, and partly as a task to be realized. . . . In order for the acting individual to be able to fulfill his task in realizing actuality, he must feel himself assimilated into a larger context, must feel the seriousness of responsibility, must feel and respect every rational consequence" (*CI* 293, 296). That is, the self must recognize that it has no sovereignty over reality, it cannot be "rejected," and that it must bring itself into conformity with reality, "feel the seriousness of responsibility," and so on. In Hegel's and Kierkegaard's view, when reality exists only for the self and not in itself, then the real is negated, loses "substantiality." But when reality is destroyed, the self is also brought into question because in destroying reality the self destroys the ground of its own actuality. For both Hegel and Kierkegaard, the cost of irony is not less than everything.

The fear that the destruction of reality is also a destruction of the self is expressed in "The Man with the Blue Guitar," canto XV. "[T]his picture of Picasso's, this 'hoard / Of destructions'" (*CP* 173), is the poem's point of departure. The quotation, "hoard of destructions," comes from a conversation Picasso had with Christian Zervos that was published in *Cahiers d'Art* in 1935.[7] "In the old days pictures went forward toward completion by stages. Every day brought something new. A picture used to be a sum of additions. In my case a picture is a sum of destructions."[8] (Stevens translates the phrase "une somme de destructions" as "a hoard of destructions.") The phrase relates this canto to a later one, XXV, where Stevens writes of art's power to destroy reality—the "murderous alphabet." Though the self in canto XXV seems unaware of the deadly logic of irony, the self in canto XV is very much aware that the destruction of the real jeopardizes the existence of the self.

> Things as they are have been destroyed.
> Have I? Am I a man that is dead
>
> At a table on which the food is cold?
> Is my thought a memory, not alive?
> (CP 173)

The tone of the canto belies the interrogative form. Here, the self uses the interrogative as protection against its own fear of destruction, since the question form allows, in opposition to what the self suspects, the issue of destruction to remain an open one.

My focus in this chapter so far has been on the philosophical and psychological affiliations between Stevens' poetry and romantic irony as it is interpreted by Hegel and Kierkegaard. Stevens is not at all ashamed to seek an escape from facts, as he does in "Solitaire under the Oaks," or to hover over the real, as he does in "A Rabbit as King of the Ghosts." Both Hegel and Kierkegaard paint the romantic ironist as a Fichtean ego, and Hoon could almost have been the model for this portrait. In addition to his all-encompassing ego, he expresses all of the vanity and self-love that Hegel and Kierkegaard despise in the ironist. Nor is Stevens, once having escaped from facts, slow to remark on the displeasure he feels when the pallid colors of reality intrude upon the pure blue of the imagination, as they do in "The Man with the Blue Guitar," canto XIII. For Kierkegaard and Hegel, the world as ego is essentially an empty world, and they write of the moment in which the ironist recognizes this fact and longs for reality. In poems such as canto XVI of "Blue Guitar," Stevens, too, expresses not an enjoyment of detachment but a yearning for the real. For both Hegel and Kierkegaard, when the self detaches itself from the world, the reality of the self is brought into question. Stevens' poetry also suggests that in withdrawing from the real the self brings its own existence into question. "Things as they are have been destroyed. /

Have I?" (*CP* 173). Finally, Hegel writes of the moment in which "on the one hand, the subject does want to penetrate into truth and objectivity, but, on the other, cannot renounce his isolation and withdrawal into himself," and in, for example, "The Bird with the Coppery Keen Claws," Stevens expresses these conflicting desires.

In the previous chapter I described an irony in Stevens' work that is opposed to the irony of detachment that I have been discussing in this chapter. Instead of looking at these two ironies in isolation, which I have done so far in order to make each more visible, I wish in the remainder of this chapter to describe the interplay between them. My interest is not so much in the fact of their presence in a single lyric as it is in Stevens' stance toward them. If he rejects one kind of irony, does he necessarily have to accept the other, or can he be situated between the two ironies? If he can be, what is his response to being between them? These questions are addressed in Stevens' late lyric, "Crude Foyer."

> Thought is false happiness: the idea
> That merely by thinking one can,
> Or may, penetrate, not may,
> But can, that one is sure to be able—
>
> That there lies at the end of thought
> A foyer of the spirit in a landscape
> Of the mind, in which we sit
> And wear humanity's bleak crown;
>
> In which we read the critique of paradise
> And say it is the work
> Of a comedian, this critique.
>
> (*CP* 305)

This landscape of the mind is one that we have seen before. It is the landscape created by the Hoon-like imagination as it withdraws into itself. In this landscape "we read the critique of paradise." Stevens scornfully writes in "Sunday Morning" that paradise is modeled after the earth.

> Alas, that they should wear our colors there,
> The silken weavings of our afternoons,
> And pick the strings of our insipid lutes!
> (*CP* 69)

To read the critique of paradise in "Crude Foyer," then, is to read the critique of the only paradise there is, the earth. This work could not be the work of a comedian. As Stevens writes, "Sad men made angels of the sun" (*CP* 137). In rejecting the idea that this critique could be a comedy, Stevens may have had in mind such works as Dante's *Divine Comedy.* But he may also have had in mind another work, Eliot's Dantesque *Four Quartets,* the final one of which appeared five years before the publication of "Crude Foyer."

That we can by thinking "penetrate" to a realm of mind, that we can sit in the landscape of the mind, breathe the "innocence of an absolute," and read the critique of paradise, all these ideas are

> False happiness, since we know that we use
> Only the eye as faculty, that the mind
> Is the eye, and that this landscape of the mind
>
> Is a landscape only of the eye; and that
> We are ignorant men incapable
> Of the least, minor, vital metaphor.
> (*CP* 305)

Earlier, in "Poem Written at Morning," Stevens offered an example of this vital metaphorical activity.

> By metaphor you paint
> A thing. Thus, the pineapple was a leather fruit,
> A fruit for pewter, thorned and palmed and blue,
> To be served by men of ice.
> The senses paint
> By metaphor. The juice was fragranter

Than wettest cinnamon. It was cribled pears
Dripping a morning sap.

(*CP* 219)

The landscape in "Poem Written at Morning" is one that is cre-
ated by the mind as it shapes experience through language. This
creative activity results in the kind of vital fictional world that, for
example, Ozymandias endlessly creates in "Notes toward a
Supreme Fiction." What Stevens denies at the end of "Crude
Foyer" is his ability to create these vital metaphors. The bitterness
of the poem in part results from Stevens' rejection of one ironic
stance even as he confesses that he is unable to adopt the other.
Though he rejects detachment in favor of engagement, he is inca-
pable of the kind of creative activity by which the self situates itself
in the world. The final statement in the poem must be one of the
bitterest in the canon, "content, / At last, there, when it turns out
to be here" (*CP* 305). "Content" is clearly to be read in an anti-
thetical sense. Stevens is extremely discontent "there," apart from
the world, when "it," his true happiness, turns out to be "here,"
in the world that is inaccessible to him.

The bitterness of "Crude Foyer" comes not just from Stevens'
confession of creative failure. It comes also from the expression of
desire that has no focus or direction. In poems such as the Ozy-
mandias canto of "Notes toward a Supreme Fiction," desire is at
once fulfilled and yet never satisfied. In fictions known to be
fictions the mind both finds and yet continues to seek what it
desires. "Tea at the Palaz of Hoon" also expresses the satisfaction
of desire. Hoon finds the world as himself, and in doing so, desire
is turned back to and finds satisfaction in the self. Since Stevens in
"Crude Foyer" both turns away from detachment and acknowl-
edges that he cannot situate himself in the world through his cre-
ative activity, desire has no true object. It cannot be satisfied since
it can turn neither to mind nor to reality.

There is a third reason for the bitter tone of "Crude Foyer."
Stevens refuses in the poem to take solace in perhaps the only
thing left, at least in this poem, for him to take solace in, art. He

acknowledges at the end of "Crude Foyer" that he cannot create those "vital metaphors" through which the mind situates itself in the real, and he refuses to make magnificent music of this failure. The final two lines, almost choppy with their multiple caesuras, turn away from formal elegance. To end "Crude Foyer" with the same music with which he concludes, for example, "Sunday Morning," would allow the mind to take refuge from its harsh insight in the beauty of form. Stevens refuses all such aesthetic palliatives, and the poem ends with his unalleviated recognition of his own imaginative failure.

The bitterness of desire, unleashed, without an object, is seen again in "Chaos in Motion and Not in Motion." There, the mind views the world as an ongoing theatrical spectacle.

> The rain is pouring down. It is July.
> There is lightning and the thickest thunder.
>
> It is a spectacle. Scene 10 becomes scene 11,
> In Series X, Act IV, et cetera.
>
> (CP 357)

These scenes, though, seem to be no more than free-floating mental constructs that spin around and become jumbled up in the mind.

> The air is full of children, statues, roofs
> And snow. The theatre is spinning round,
>
> Colliding with deaf-mute churches and optical trains.
> The most massive sopranos are singing songs of scales.
>
> (CP 357)

The lines look back to "The Glass of Water," where "The *metaphysica,* the plastic parts of poems / Crash in the mind" (CP 197), and anticipate the moment in "Notes toward a Supreme Fiction" where the mind again views the world as a theater of tropes. "A bench was his catalepsy, Theatre / Of Trope. He sat in the park. The water of / The lake was full of artificial things" (CP 397).

Seeing this spectacle in "Chaos in Motion and Not in Motion" evokes a feeling that the self "Has lost the whole in which [it] was contained" (*CP* 358). The relation of the self to the whole here can be contrasted with Hoon's relation to the whole. Hoon is not contained within the whole; the whole is contained within Hoon. Hoon, then, could never feel the sense of loss expressed by the self in "Chaos in Motion and Not in Motion." The self in that poem views itself not in Hoon-like terms, but sees itself as part of a larger whole. To feel that the world is nothing but a theater of the mind is to lose the sense that the self is part of this larger reality. Though Stevens expresses in poems such as "A Rabbit as King of the Ghosts" and canto XIII of "The Man with the Blue Guitar" the pleasure the self can take in withdrawing into the mind, in "Chaos in Motion and Not in Motion," the self takes no satisfaction in its separation from the world. As in "Crude Foyer," the self here rejects a withdrawal into the mind even as it acknowledges its separation from the world. Again as in "Crude Foyer," desire can find satisfaction in neither mind nor reality.[9]

In Stevens' very late poem, "Local Objects," the mind is again situated between the stances of detachment and engagement. But in "Local Objects" Stevens' attitude toward being situated between these two stances is very different from what it was in "Crude Foyer." "Local Objects" begins by acknowledging the central truth of "Crude Foyer," that the mind has no entranceway into the world.

> He knew that he was a spirit without a foyer
> And that, in this knowledge, local objects become
> More precious than the most precious objects of home:
>
> The local objects of a world without a foyer.
>
> (*OP* 137)

These local objects are "made" through the process of naming, and, by being named, are kept from perishing. "Little existed for him but the few things / For which a fresh name always occurred, as if / He wanted to make them, keep them from perishing" (*OP*

137). The lines echo many of the themes of "Notes toward a Supreme Fiction"—that the world is realized through the process of naming, that the process is ongoing, "always occurred," that in finding a fresh name for objects they are rediscovered in a new way, and that, in being new, the renamings are not stultifying re-presentations. Yet the demesne of "Notes toward a Supreme Fiction" has been considerably reduced. The sun is what Stevens renames in "Notes," "The sun / Must bear no name, gold flourisher" (*CP* 381), while in this poem he is confined to a few local objects.

At the end of the poem, the self is still a spirit without a foyer to the world. During the course of the poem not a single local object has been realized. Though he says that a new name always occurs, we do not hear a single fresh name. This is precisely the moment at which "Crude Foyer" ended—with the self turning away from mind and toward a world that it cannot enter because it has not named it. Yet the tone of "Local Objects" is almost the complete opposite of the tone of "Crude Foyer." The self-lacerating bitterness of the latter poem is replaced in "Local Objects" by a calmness and poise that verges on "the classic, the beautiful" (*OP* 138). The difference in tone comes not from the self's creative activity (we see none in either poem), but in how the self views its creative potential. In "Crude Foyer," the self confesses that it has no creative potential. It is incapable of vital metaphorical activity. There is an opposite assumption about the creative power of the self in "Local Objects." Even though no local objects are named, the poem expresses the satisfaction the self feels when they are named. If the self were to express the satisfaction that it takes in naming while knowing that it no longer has the power to name, then "Local Objects" would be a poem about the satisfactions of past creative moments, and Stevens is not a poet who probes the contentments of memory. Implied by the tone of "Local Objects" is the assumption that the self has creative power, that it will again name, and that in doing so the self will again experience the satisfaction it now so beautifully evokes. The sense of pleasure that Stevens takes in the world in the absence of any creative activity in

"Local Objects" must surely be one of his most gossamer satisfactions.

Stevens does not always present the self as being poised between the ironic stances of detachment and engagement. In "An Ordinary Evening in New Haven," he first considers and then rejects as even being possible the detachment from which he turns but cannot escape in "Crude Foyer." In canto XX he writes of

> a man,
> Who sits thinking in the corners of a room.
> In this chamber the pure sphere escapes the impure
>
> Because the thinker himself escapes. And yet
> To have evaded clouds and men leaves him
> A naked being with a naked will
>
> And everything to make. He may evade
> Even his own will and in his nakedness
> Inhabit the hypnosis of that sphere.
>
> (CP 480)

To escape from the impure, "clouds and men," to the "pure sphere" and, once there, to have everything to create is to view the self as the kind of detached ironist that was described earlier in the chapter. In "A Rabbit as King of the Ghosts," the self escapes from the world, while "Tea at the Palaz of Hoon" demonstrates the ego's ability to create "everything." In this canto of "An Ordinary Evening in New Haven," however, Stevens considers a further escape. He contemplates the ego's escape from its own creative will and an existence in a kind of motionless state. Neither Hegel nor Kierkegaard nor Schlegel would have recognized such a state in the ironist. Though they differ on whether irony detaches the self from or engages it in the real, for all of them a fundamental characteristic of irony is motion.

After considering this escape from clouds, men, and even his own creative will, Stevens writes that such an escape is not possible.

But he may not. He may not evade his will,
Nor the wills of other men; and he cannot evade
The will of necessity, the will of wills.

(*CP* 480)

Stevens denies first that the thinker can evade his own creative
will. This assertion of creative fluency recalls Ozymandias' ongo-
ing creative activity in "Notes toward a Supreme Fiction." "A
fictive covering / Weaves always glistening from the heart and
mind" (*CP* 396). Second, Stevens denies that the thinker can
evade the "wills of other men." The statement is a rejection of
Hoon, for whom "the shapes were never the figures of men," and
of the Hegelian and Kierkegaardian view of the ironist as one who
"looks down from his high rank on all other men" (*A* 66), know-
ing that what is binding on them does not bind him. Finally,
Stevens denies that the thinker can evade "the will of wills."
There is only one will of wills, one will to which all must bow,
mortality. Stevens' statement denies the rejection of mortality that,
as I discussed earlier in this chapter, is implied in the irony of
detachment. Instead of seeing the ironist as one who can escape
from the temporal and therefore from mortality, Stevens is
acknowledging the final implication of an ironic stance that does
not turn from the world but turns toward it—death.[10] To say, as
he does in this canto, that "he may not," that is, that the thinker
may not escape from the temporal and actual and create "every-
thing," is one of Stevens' most beautiful lies. As we saw earlier in
this chapter, he not only can escape but does so. What is of inter-
est here is not the obvious contradiction with other poems, but,
given Stevens' strong attraction to both detachment and engage-
ment, what his stance is toward these possibilities. Unlike "Crude
Foyer," where the self is painfully situated between detachment
and engagement, Stevens denies in this canto of "An Ordinary
Evening in New Haven" that the detachment he considers is even
possible. To create is to be inextricably engaged in the real. As he
writes elsewhere in "Ordinary Evening," "The poem is the cry of
its occasion, / Part of the res itself and not about it" (*CP* 473).

In "Crude Foyer" and in "Ordinary Evening," the ironies of

detachment and engagement are brought into high relief. Though the self's relation to these ironies differs in the two poems—in "Crude Foyer" the self rejects detachment and yet cannot engage with the world while in "An Ordinary Evening in New Haven" the self considers and then rejects detachment in light of its assumption of an enduring creative power whose expression is by its very nature an engagement with the real—both lyrics highlight the opposition between the two stances and focus on the self's turn, or attempt to turn, from one to the other. In other poems, the turn itself occurs without fanfare and seemingly without effort. These poems are not so much dramatic presentations of the self's movement from one stance to another as they are lyric expressions of the self's response to a particular stance once it has been adopted. Canto XVIII of "The Man with the Blue Guitar" is an example of this kind of lyric.

> A dream (to call it a dream) in which
> I can believe, in face of the object,
>
> A dream no longer a dream, a thing,
> Of things as they are, as the blue guitar
>
> After long strumming on certain nights
> Gives the touch of the senses, not of the hand,
>
> But the very senses as they touch
> The wind-gloss. Or as daylight comes,
>
> Like light in a mirroring of cliffs,
> Rising upward from a sea of ex.
>
> (CP 174–75)

The irony of detachment is expressed in the opening two lines. The dream, what is created by the mind, stands in opposition to the real, the object. The mind, though it confronts or faces the object, desires a dream in which it can believe. That is, the mind turns its gaze away from the object, which it faces, to a dream, which it creates. Beginning with line 3, detachment gives way to engagement. The mind no longer views its creative activity in opposition to the world. Instead, creative activity is seen as a process of discovering, coming into contact with, reality. "A dream no longer a dream, a thing, / Of things as they are, as the blue guitar / After long strumming on certain nights / Gives the touch of the senses" (*CP* 174). But Stevens is attempting to do more in this canto than give an intellectual expression of art's engagement with the real. The true center of the canto is the next two lines, where Stevens attempts to convey the feeling of extraordinary intimacy between the self and reality that results from strumming the blue guitar. All of the senses are touched, and touched in a way that is even finer, more delicate, than the tactile sensations conveyed by the hand. "[T]he blue guitar / . . . / Gives the touch of the senses, not of the hand, / But the very senses as they touch / The wind-gloss" (*CP* 174–75). The self's turn in the canto from detachment to engagement has been seen in other poems. What is different about this canto of "Blue Guitar" is not the fact of the turn but how Stevens turns from one stance to the other and what is expressed when he does turn. The self here seems to accelerate effortlessly from one ironic stance to the other, to exchange easily detachment for engagement, rather than, as in "Crude Foyer," to narrate the difficulty of making (or not making) the transition from one stance to the other. What is the self's stance toward the irony of engagement? In canto XVIII, Stevens conveys the intense emotion the self feels when it is engaged in the world through art. In "An Ordinary Evening in New Haven," the self also rejects detachment and views creative activity as a process that engages the self in the world. But the self in "An Ordinary Evening in New Haven" seems to feel none of the sensuous intimacy with the world that it does in this canto of "The Man with the Blue Guitar."

Stevens offers a different stance toward detachment and engagement in canto XXII of "The Man with the Blue Guitar." What inspired lyric intensity in canto XVIII is the subject of a mock debate in canto XXII.

> Poetry is the subject of the poem,
> From this the poem issues and

To this returns. Between the two,
Between issue and return, there is

An absence in reality,
Things as they are.

(CP 176)

When the poem explores its subject, itself, then reality, things as
they are, is absent. The countering voice enters the canto in the
second half of line 6, "Or so we say."

But are these separate? Is it
An absence for the poem, which acquires

Its true appearance there, sun's green,
Cloud's red, earth feeling, sky that thinks?

From these it takes. Perhaps it gives,
In the universal intercourse.

(CP 177)

But are poetry and things as they are separate? The poem does take
from the world—sun, cloud, earth, sky. Does it also give to the
world? Surely Stevens is being playful when he writes, "sun's
green, / Cloud's *red,* earth *feeling,* sky that *thinks*" (emphasis added),
all attributes that the mind ascribes to the world, and then muses
that "Perhaps" poetry gives to the world. This understated humor
(is Stevens' humor ever anything else?) adds to the sense of play-
fulness at the end of the canto as the mind apparently leaves open
to debate, "Perhaps it gives," what is clearly answered in the lan-
guage of the canto, "green," "red," "feeling," "thinks." To sug-
gest that there is intercourse between the mind and reality in cre-
ative activity, a suggestion that looks forward to the numerous
unions seen in the late poetry—the "two lovers / That walk away
as one" (CP 392), the central poem and world, "each one the mate
/ Of the other" (CP 441), the "mystic marriage" (CP 401)
between the great captain and Bawda—turns the opening propo-
sition of the canto upside down. When poetry turns "inward"

toward itself, it simultaneously turns "outward" toward the world. In meditating on the separation of poetry and reality, the mind discovers their "universal intercourse" (*CP* 177).

Canto XXII of "The Man with the Blue Guitar" may have been the germ of the second canto of "An Ordinary Evening in New Haven," where the self again discovers that it is not separate from reality but both gives to and takes from it. Stevens begins his meditation by speculating that reality may be composed only of the self.

> Suppose these houses are composed of ourselves,
> So that they become an impalpable town, full of
> Impalpable bells, transparencies of sound,
>
> Sounding in transparent dwellings of the self,
> Impalpable habitations that seem to move
> In the movement of the colors of the mind.
>   (*CP* 466)

If these houses are composed solely of the self, then reality is insubstantial, "impalpable." The houses, though, are not solely constructs of the self. As in "The Man with the Blue Guitar," canto XXII, this canto proposes a kind of universal "intercourse" between self and world.

> Obscure, in colors whether of the sun
> Or mind, uncertain in the clearest bells,
>
> . . . .
> Confused illuminations and sonorities,
> So much ourselves, we cannot tell apart
> The idea and the bearer-being of the idea.
>   (*CP* 466)

These concluding lines reverse the canto's opening proposition. Reality and the self are so intertwined that the self cannot tell apart what it contributes to the scene, "the idea," from what reality contributes to it, "the bearer-being of the idea." Though "The

Man with the Blue Guitar," canto XXII, and this canto of "An Ordinary Evening in New Haven" make similar intellectual discoveries, the two cantos are very different. In canto XXII of "The Man with the Blue Guitar," there is a sense of playfulness in the discovery of the universal intercourse of self and reality, while in the second canto of "An Ordinary Evening in New Haven," this discovery is expressed as a heightened moment of visionary intensity in which the self confesses its enduring love for the real. Sight and sound, "the far-fire flowing and the dim-coned bells," come

> together in a sense in which we are poised,
> Without regard to time or where we are,
>
> In the perpetual reference, object
> Of the perpetual meditation, point
> Of the enduring, visionary love.
>
> (*CP* 466)

Let us return to the letter that Stevens wrote to William Van O'Connor and reconsider the self-definition that Stevens offers in it. It is true that Stevens and Eliot can be considered "dead opposites" in regard to the kind of irony expressed in their poetry. The irony of Eliot's early work and the irony of the Ozymandias canto of "Notes toward a Supreme Fiction," for example, have different purposes. The former detaches the self from the world, while the latter turns the self to the world. But Stevens also expresses an irony whose purpose is to gain a negative freedom from reality and that has an affiliation with the view of romantic irony that is put forward by Hegel and Kierkegaard. Stevens explores with considerable subtlety the implications of this kind of irony. In "Tea at the Palaz of Hoon," he expresses the narcissistic pleasure the self can take in continually finding the world as itself. In "A Rabbit as King of the Ghosts," the self "hovers" over the real, and it does so without any apparent sense of loss. Stevens expresses his desire to escape from "facts" in "Solitaire under the Oaks" and, at the end of the poem, is "completely released" from them. And in "The Man with the Blue Guitar," canto XIII, he expresses the displeasure the imagination feels when the pallid colors of reality intrude upon it. Stevens also explores the darker side of the irony of detachment. The self discovers that its self-created world is an empty one, that it can no longer live in the "bliss of self-enjoyment." It yearns to break out of its enclosure but is unable to do so. The world remains, as Stevens phrases it in "The Man with the Blue Guitar," canto XXVI, an "inaccessible Utopia." The self's feeling that reality is lost to it leads in other poems to the fear of another loss—that of the self. When the ironic ego negates reality it at the same time negates the ground of its own existence.

Given the presence of the irony of detachment in Stevens' work, is his description of himself as one who is to be seen in dead opposition to Eliot a false one? Or is his work truly opposed to Eliot? Stevens' identity, I suggest, is to be discovered less in terms of one ironic stance or another than it is in terms of both stances. The area between the two poles of detachment and engagement is the ground that much of his work explores, and it is extremely varied terrain. He can feel, as he does in "Crude Foyer," that neither ironic stance is available to him. He rejects detachment and yet cannot create the vital metaphors by means of which the self can engage with the real. He can effortlessly accelerate from one stance to another, as he does in canto XVIII of "The Man with the Blue Guitar." He can consider, only to reject as even being possible, the irony of detachment, as he does in "An Ordinary Evening in New Haven," canto XXI. Or he can turn from detachment and with visionary intensity express his sense of the universal intercourse of mind and world. The portrait of Stevens that emerges by looking at his stances toward these two ironies may be a truer likeness than one that is painted solely from the perspective of the irony of engagement or from the perspective of the irony of detachment. Since his feelings about the two ironies continue to change, this portrait is one that can never be completed.

Chapter 4

Artfully Ordered Confusion: Romantic Irony and the Form of Stevens' Poetry

The best explanation of the romantic is perhaps chaos and eros.
—Friedrich Schlegel

For Schlegel, romantic ironic art should express simultaneously a sense of order and disorder, unity and chaos. He writes in the *Dialogue on Poetry* that a work of art must be an "artfully ordered confusion, [a] charming symmetry of contradictions, [a] wonderfully perennial alternation of enthusiasm and irony."[1] "[T]he arabesque," he continues, "is the oldest and most original form of human imagination" (*DP* 86). Arabesque, a term Schlegel borrowed from Goethe's essay, *Die Arabesken*, refers to "delicately drawn, brightly painted, curvilinear designs [that] arbitrarily blend architectural, vegetal, animal, and human motifs in irrational but balanced patterns."[2] This blend of irrationality and balance represented to Schlegel the kind of "artfully ordered confusion" that is expressed in an ironic work of art.

Three forms in Schlegel's view are especially suited to the expression of this artistic principle: the dialogue, the novel, and the aphorism. The dialogue allows an author to present an idea from one perspective and then to comment critically on that perspective from another point of view. Schlegel's own *Dialogue on Poetry* exemplifies this kind of ongoing exploration and critical commentary. He writes that the *Dialogue* "is intended to set against one another quite divergent opinions, each of them capable of shedding new light upon the infinite spirit of poetry from an individual standpoint, each of them striving to penetrate from a different angle into the real heart of the matter" (*DP* 55). Schlegel does not attempt to unify these different perspectives. He views the unresolved diversity of opinion expressed in the work as both liberating and enriching. Antonio remarks to Lodovico, "I hope we shall find in what you are about to offer a contrast to Andrea's 'Epochs of Literature.' Thus we shall be able to use one view and force as lever for the others and discuss both the more freely and incisively" (*DP* 80). And Lodovico comments, "Doubts from all sides and in all directions would be welcome, so that the investigation may become that much more free and rich" (*DP* 82). Though the *Dialogue* does "set against one another quite divergent opinions" (*DP* 55), the work is not a chaotic collection of thoughts. All the opinions in the *Dialogue* are related to the central theme of the work, "the infinite spirit of poetry" (*DP* 55).

A similar sense of unity and diversity is central to the novel, the form Schlegel perhaps most favored for the expression of philosophical irony. In the "Letter about the Novel," Schlegel describes the novel as a *Mischgedichte,* a mixture of genres. He writes, "I can scarcely visualize a novel but as a mixture of story-telling, song, and other forms" (*DP* 102). His novel, *Lucinde,* expresses this generic diversity. It includes letters, a "Dithyrambic Fantasia," an allegory, an idyll, dialogue, autobiography, and a philosophical meditation that "parodies . . . the fashionable philosophical terminology of the day."[3] Though *Lucinde* presents a chaotic mixture of genres, all of them "organically cohere around the sentimental theme of Julius' physical and psychological development as man, lover, father, friend, and self-conscious prophet of love."[4]

Like the dialogue and the novel, aphorisms can be used to view a subject from divergent perspectives. But aphorisms can also be used to explore a wide range of subjects unsystematically, as Schlegel does in his three collections of aphorisms, *Lyceum Fragments, Athenaeum Fragments,* and *Ideas.* If a group of aphorisms examines a single idea, then the idea itself can give the sequence a sense of order. In aphorisms that take up a number of subjects, a sense of unity can be expressed through internal repetition, the repeated return to and reexamination of the various ideas being explored.

The forms that Schlegel uses to express his concept of irony have been used by other writers to express an opposing sense of irony. In *Either,* for example, Kierkegaard brilliantly exploits the aphorism to paint a portrait of the ironist not as skeptically engaged with the world, but as withdrawn from it. As I have discussed in chapter 1, *Either* can also be related to Schlegel's concept of the novel. Like *Lucinde, Either* utilizes a variety of genres: aphorisms, an "ecstatic lecture," a diary, verse, narrative prose, meditative essays, and a review. But *Lucinde* and *Either* embody opposing concepts of irony. Much of Nietzsche's work is aphoristic, and his irony, again as I argued in chapter 1, can be related to Schlegel. In contrast, *The Waste Land,* deeply fragmentary in nature, expresses an irony that is affiliated with Hegel and Kierkegaard.

Stevens uses some of the forms favored by both Schlegel and Kierkegaard. Several critics, for instance, have commented on the aphoristic quality of Stevens' work,[5] and in poems such as "The Man with the Blue Guitar," he explores Schlegelian as well as Hegelian and Kierkegaardian concepts of irony through this form. Other poems use different forms to explore one (or both) of these senses of irony. "Notes toward a Supreme Fiction," for example, can be seen as a kind of Schlegelian dialogue that explores "the infinite spirit of poetry." This chapter, however, is not devoted to cataloging the ironic forms that Stevens uses in his work. Rather, my focus is on the principle that underlies forms such as the aphorism and the dialogue: the simultaneous expression of unity and chaos. Stevens points to this principle in "The Auroras of Autumn," where he writes of "form gulping after formlessness" (*CP* 411). The participle suggests the ongoing nature of the activity. In gulping after formlessness, the poems gesture toward chaos. But they are never, finally, formless. They might be thought of as self-effacing artifacts that are never fully effaced. As Stevens puts it in an aphorism, "Poetry is a pheasant disappearing in the brush" (*OP* 198). There are three major ways Stevens structures his poems to achieve the effect of "artfully ordered confusion": through multiple perspectives, through opposition, and through asymmetrical repetition.

Perhaps Stevens' most well known perspective poem is

"Thirteen Ways of Looking at a Blackbird." Each stanza of the poem looks at the blackbird from a different point of view. In stanza I, the blackbird is contrasted with nature. While there is movement by the blackbird, nature remains motionless. In stanza XIII the roles are reversed; nature is dynamic and the blackbird remains still. In stanza III, the blackbird is part of the autumn pantomime, while in stanza XII it is part of the activity of spring. The blackbird is associated with perceptual limitation in stanza IX and with a plurality of perspectives in stanza II. Both the union of man and woman (stanza IV) and their separation (stanza VII) are linked to the blackbird. The mysterious quality of nature is associated with the blackbird in stanza VI. In at least four stanzas the blackbird is related to aesthetic doctrine. Its shadow frightens the aesthete in stanza XI. In stanza X, the blackbird is related to a natural world that is so beautiful that the "bawds of euphony" "cry out" when they see blackbirds "flying in a green light." The blackbird is associated with elevated themes, "noble accents," in stanza VIII and with minor keys and variations, "inflections" and "innuendoes," in stanza V. Though the increasingly differentiated ways in which Stevens presents the blackbird push the poem toward chaos, "Thirteen Ways of Looking at a Blackbird" expresses more than a sense of fragmentation. Each stanza is related to the other stanzas by the central image of the blackbird itself. The poem, then, can be seen as having both a centrifugal and a centripetal movement. The multiple perspectives express a sense of dispersal and chaos while the repeated image of the blackbird links the stanzas to each other and gives the poem a sense of unity and coherence.[6]

The multiple-perspective structure of "Thirteen Ways of Looking at a Blackbird" is used again in a later poem, "Someone Puts a Pineapple Together," where Stevens offers twelve descriptions of a pineapple. It is varied slightly in "Sea Surface Full of Clouds," where, instead of presenting multiple perspectives on a single object such as a blackbird or a pineapple, Stevens offers multiple perspectives on a single setting—"In that November off Tehuantepec, / The slopping of the sea grew still one night" (CP 98). Each of the five cantos repeats this setting and then each gives a very different description of the scene. The more the poem returns to its unifying point of reference, the setting, the more diverse our sense of that November off Tehuantepec becomes. "Six Significant Landscapes" also uses the multiple-perspective structure. Instead of seeing an object or setting from various points of view, however, "Six Significant Landscapes" offers multiple perspectives on a single subject: landscapes. The structure can also be seen in the early poem, "Gubbinal," where Stevens presents and then subverts a single-minded, reductionist attitude.

> That strange flower, the sun,
> Is just what you say.
> Have it your way.
>
> The world is ugly,
> And the people are sad.
>
> That tuft of jungle feathers,
> That animal eye,
> Is just what you say.
>
> That savage of fire,
> That seed,
> Have it your way.
>
> The world is ugly,
> And the people are sad.
>   (CP 85)

The poem is one half of a dialogue. In the unheard half, someone has obviously proposed that "The world is ugly, / And the people are sad." The response, this poem, is an extended piece of verbal irony. The speaker offers six descriptions of reality, "the sun," "strange flower," "tuft of jungle feathers," "animal eye," "savage of fire," and "seed," all the while ironically agreeing with his companion that "The world is ugly, / And the people are sad." This game could go on, of course, forever. Stevens, deadpan, would continue to agree that the world is ugly while delightful images sprout at every turn.

Stevens undermines a single, reductive point of view again in a later poem, "Study of Two Pears." Unlike "Gubbinal," however, in "Study of Two Pears" the speaker of the poem is the reductionist. The speaker insists that pears are unique natural forms that have no resemblance to anything else. "The pears are not viols, / Nudes or bottles. / They resemble nothing else" (*CP* 196). And the poem ends with the words, "The pears are not seen / As the observer wills" (*CP* 197), which can be read as a final assertion that the pears resist the observer's will to transform them into something else through resemblance. Stevens writes in "Three Academic Pieces" that "as to the resemblance between things in nature, it should be observed that resemblance constitutes a relation between them since, in some sense, all things resemble each other" (*NA* 71). He goes on to discuss resemblances between things in nature and things of the imagination, and he comments that "Poetry is a satisfying of the desire for resemblance" (*NA* 77). In denying that the pears resemble anything else, then, the speaker of "Study of Two Pears" takes a decidedly antipoetic stance. But it is a stance that the speaker unknowingly subverts. In the process of defining what the pears are not, the speaker creates resemblances between them and other things in nature (viols, nudes, bottles), and between them and artistic representations of them.

III
They are not flat surfaces
Having curved outlines.
They are round
Tapering toward the top.

IV
In the way they are modelled
There are bits of blue.
(*CP* 196)

In trying to define the pears by excluding everything else, the speaker shows us that it is impossible *not* to relate the pears to things in nature and to things created by the imagination. Ironically, the speaker's attempt to eliminate resemblances results in a "satisfying of the desire for resemblance."

Though they vary in complexity, both "Gubbinal" and "Study of Two Pears" express simultaneously a sense of order and of chaos. In "Study of Two Pears," the speaker's attempt to describe the pears by denying their resemblance to other things results in showing us how many things they do resemble. The centripetal force of reduction and exclusion becomes the centrifugal force of differentiation and dispersion as, through resemblance, the contexts in which Stevens presents the pear expands. In "Gubbinal," the reductionist point of view, "The world is ugly, / And the people are sad," is countered by the ever-increasing, colorful descriptions of the world, descriptions that push the poem toward greater and greater fragmentation.

The artistic principle that underlies Stevens' multiple perspective poems can also be seen in poems that are structured through opposition, such as his five-finger exercises, "Nudity at the Capital" and "Nudity in the Colonies."

Nudity at the Capital

But nakedness, woolen massa, concerns an innermost atom.
If that remains concealed, what does the bottom matter?

Nudity in the Colonies

Black man, bright nouveautés leave one, at best,
    pseudonymous.
Thus one is most disclosed when one is most anonymous.

(CP 145)

Commenting on the poem to Hi Simons, Stevens writes, "Obviously, the savage and the civilized man agree that nakedness concerns the self, but disagree as to the mode of concealment" (L 347). In "Nudity at the Capital," the inner self is concealed, even though the body is revealed. In "Nudity in the Colonies," a distinctive, novel style of dress, "bright nouveautés," does not reveal the self but hides it. In Stevens' paraphrase, "What I wear disguises me, gives me another self, and if I wore enough I should have no self at all" (*L* 347). By this logic, one is most disclosed when one appears not in a distinctive style of dress but in one that is undistinctive, "anonymous."

The structure of the paired poems "Nudity in the Colonies" and "Nudity at the Capital" is varied in "New England Verses," where Stevens strings together numerous oppositions in a single poem. The entire piece can be thought of as a "symmetry of contradictions" (*DP* 86). It is comprised of twelve pairs of opposites: "The Whole World Including the Speaker," "The Whole World Excluding the Speaker," "Soupe Aux Perles," "Soupe Sans Perles," "Boston with a Note-book," "Boston without a Note-book," "Artist in Tropic," "Artist in Arctic," "Statue against a Clear Sky," "Statue against a Cloudy Sky," "Land of Locust," "Land of Pine and Marble," "The Male Nude," "The Female Nude," "Scène Flétrie," "Scène Fleurie." Each pair expresses the kind of balance between unity and dispersal that was seen in "Nudity at the Capital" and "Nudity in the Colonies"; that is, a common subject unites perspectives that forever resist unification. The first pair of opposites, for instance, take opposing views of the relation of "the Speaker" to reality.

I
The Whole World Including the Speaker
Why nag at the ideas of Hercules, Don Don?
Widen your sense. All things in the sun are sun.

II
The Whole World Excluding the Speaker
I found between moon-rising and moon-setting
The world was round. But not from my begetting.

(*CP* 104)

In stanza I, "Don Don" has apparently been quibbling about the "ideas of Hercules," and the speaker rebukes him. Why "nag" at these ideas? Widen your point of view. All things, including the ideas of Hercules, are part of the totality of reality. Stanza II takes an opposing stance. The speaker observes a natural process and shape and realizes that he is essentially "excluded" from what he observes. Both the process and the shape of nature are independent of the speaker's ideas about them. Stanzas III and IV express opposite perspectives on wealth and poverty.

III
Soupe Aux Perles
Health-o, when ginger and fromage bewitch
The vile antithesis of poor and rich.

IV
Soupe Sans Perles
I crossed in '38 in the *Western Head.*
It depends which way you crossed, the tea-belle said.

(*CP* 104)

Stanza III is spoken by a wealthy person, one who wears pearls while eating soup, and expresses an antipathy to the "vile antithesis of poor and rich." From the perspective of this speaker, "The differences between our standards of living are dissolved in the fact that we are all sustained by the same simple pleasures and staples of life (ginger and cheese)."[7] Stanza IV looks at wealth and poverty from the perspective of one who eats soup without wearing pearls. This aphorism takes the rich/poor dichotomy as a given. It's not *that* one crosses the Atlantic by ship, the *Western Head,* its *how,* "which way," one crosses. That is, does one cross "as immigrant or gentleman."[8]

Stanzas V and VI take opposing views of smaller creations of the imagination.

V
Boston with a Note-book
Lean encyclopaedists, inscribe an Iliad.
There's a weltanschauung of the penny pad.

VI

Boston without a Note-book
Let us erect in the Basin a lofty fountain.
Suckled on ponds, the spirit craves a watery mountain.
(*CP* 104–5)

Stanza V rejects the encyclopedic cataloging of reality for the
smaller construct, the "penny pad," while stanza VI suggests that
the spirit is not satisfied with the contained, "ponds," but "craves"
something large, grand, a "watery mountain."

Each pair of opposites in "New England Verses," as Beverly
Coyle points out, is "self-contained," "separate."[9] The autonomy
of the pairs of poems may give the impression that "New England
Verses" has no overall sense of order. The poem, though, is not a
miscellany or collection of fragments. Though the pairs themselves
may have little thematic relation to each other, they can all be seen
as expressions of the point of view identified in the title, "New
England." The overall sense of unity and fragmentation in the
poem, thoughts that have little internal relation to each other but
that are united by a common perspective, looks back to "Six
Significant Landscapes," whose six cantos also have a minimal
relation to each other but are united by a common subject, land-
scapes.

To treat a subject from only two points of view is not a con-
genial restriction for Stevens, as the longer poems especially sug-
gest. Though this method of organization is not a favored one,
there are poems in addition to the ones looked at so far that are
structured in this way. "Contrary Theses (I)," for example, begins
with an opposition between nature and man at war. "Now grapes
are plush upon the vines. / A soldier walks before my door" (*CP*
266). Neither warfare nor nature has an effect upon the other until
the last stanza, where war invades the natural order: "Blood smears
the oaks" (*CP* 267). Though the two worlds are no longer sepa-
rate, the opposition remains unresolved. "Contrary Theses (II)"
turns on the opposition between the vision of a final, transcen-
dental order of things, "The abstract . . . / The premiss from
which all things were conclusions" (*CP* 270), and the order of

nature. Despite this "concluding" vision, the natural process is unaffected: "The flies / And the bees still sought the chrysanthemums' odor" (CP 270). "Botanist on Alp (No. 1)" and "Botanist on Alp (No. 2)" record opposing reactions to the loss of order. The botanist on Alp number 1 regrets the loss of past harmonies. "Claude has been dead a long time / . . . / But in Claude how near one was / . . . / To the central composition" (CP 134–35). For the botanist on Alp number 2, the loss of a "central composition" is no cause for regret. "What's down below is in the past / . . . / And what's above is in the past / As sure as all the angels are" (CP 135–36). The convent crosses that glitter in the sun are a "mirror" of our "delight" in the natural world. There are similar treatments of a subject from two points of view, though not necessarily strictly opposed ones, in "Two Versions of the Same Poem," "Study of Images I," "Study of Images II," and "Two Illustrations That the World Is What You Make of It." Though the poems structured through opposition examine their subjects from only two points of view, like the multiple perspective poems, they express both a sense of unity and of disorder. The opposing points of view gesture toward dispersal, but both perspectives refer to and are unified by a common theme or subject.

The poem that perhaps expresses the greatest sense of fragmentation in Stevens' canon is "Like Decorations in a Nigger Cemetery." As Helen Vendler writes, "Though the poetry of disconnection is Stevens' most adequate form, and though the gaps from canto to canto in the long poems will always challenge the best efforts of critical articulation, still the discontinuity will never again be so arrogant. . . . [The stanzas of the poem] are fragments of vision seen in the mirror of the mind refusing to reconstruct itself, refusing the attempt to make a whole from the ruses that were shattered by the large."[10] The sense of fragmentation is immediately suggested by the form of the title, an asymmetrical simile. Like metaphor, simile is a relational term. In some way or ways x can be compared with y. Like a ski, like water ruffled by the breeze, like decorations in a nigger cemetery—all are similes that give us the y term and withhold the x term. In none do we know what is being compared to a ski, to water ruffled by the breeze, or to decorations in a nigger cemetery, an absence that points to discontinuity and dispersal.

"Like Decorations in a Nigger Cemetery" may be the most fragmented of Stevens' poems, but it is not a random collection of thoughts. Its ordering principle, though, is different from that of the poems looked at so far. It is not organized around a central image or setting or subject or even perspective, as is "New England Verses." It does not present, only to mock or subvert, a single, reductionist point of view, as do "Gubbinal" and "Study of Two Pears." Nor is the poem organized through opposition, as are "Nudity in the Colonies" and "Nudity at the Capital." In "Like Decorations" Stevens takes up in no logical order various subjects and repeatedly returns to them to examine them from different perspectives. It is this unsystematic repetition, this repeated return to the cluster of ideas that are examined in the poem, that gives "Like Decorations" a sense of order and coherence. For example, in at least nine of the stanzas Stevens meditates on poetry. In four of them he uses a traditional symbol for poetry, birds. In stanza XIII Stevens writes,

> The birds are singing in the yellow patios,
> Pecking at more lascivious rinds than ours,
> From sheer Gemütlichkeit.
>
> (CP 152)

These birds sing of those who, unlike the speaker of this stanza, still feel sexual passion. The underlying bitter tone of the stanza and the speaker's description of himself and his "beloved" as "rinds" look back to "Le Monocle de Mon Oncle," canto VIII.

> Our bloom is gone.
> .   .   .   .
> We hang like warty squashes, streaked and rayed,
> The laughing sky will see the two of us
> Washed into rinds by rotting winter rains.
>
> (CP 16)

In stanza XXV, Stevens invites us to "note the decline / In music" from oriole to crow but refuses to restrict the poetry of reality to the song of the crow. "Crow is realist. But, then, / Oriole, also, may be realist" (*CP* 154). This refusal of limitations echoes "Thirteen Ways of Looking at a Blackbird," where the blackbird is associated with "noble accents / And lucid, inescapable rhythms" (*CP* 94) and also with "inflections" and "innuendoes" (*CP* 93). In stanza XXX Stevens suggests that poetry that is strictly of the imagination, "midnight," or of reality, "day," is sterile. "The hencock crows at midnight and lays no egg, / The cock-hen crows all day" (*CP* 155). Poetic fertility results from the union of opposites. "But cockerel shrieks, / Hen shudders: the copious egg is made and laid" (*CP* 155), a thought that looks forward to "Notes toward a Supreme Fiction," section II, canto IV, in which "the particulars of rapture" result from the "embrace" of opposites. And in stanza XXXIII Stevens writes of the poet as the rare, the "purple bird," which sings to "comfort" itself because of "the gross tedium of being rare" (*CP* 155).

In other stanzas, Stevens' thoughts on poetry are expressed without bird symbolism. In stanza VII he writes of a moment of poetic fluency, "How easily the feelings flow this afternoon / Over the simplest words," and then juxtaposes this moment to an extreme of weather, "It is too cold for work, now, in the fields" (*CP* 151), a juxtaposition that perhaps suggests that the harshness of the weather is a condition that is propitious to the imagination. Stevens expresses in stanza XXXII his sense of poetry as brief and uncertain, "a finikin thing of air / That lives uncertainly and not for long" (*CP* 155). Despite this brevity, it lives "radiantly beyond much lustier blurs" (*CP* 155). In canto XL Stevens writes,

> Always the standard repertoire in line
> And that would be perfection, if each began
> Not by beginning but at the last man's end.
> (*CP* 156)

There is a standard repertoire in poetry, and it would be perfection if poets began their treatment of these perennial themes not by beginning where their predecessors began but by beginning where their predecessors ended, "at the last man's end." Stanza XLV sounds a darker note, as Stevens seems to reject happiness as an appropriate theme for poetry.

> *Encore un instant de bonheur.* The words
> Are a woman's words, unlikely to satisfy
> The taste of even a country connoisseur.
>   (*CP* 157)

These words, these poems of happiness, are unlikely to satisfy even the most untutored reader, a "country connoisseur."

A second subject that Stevens revolves in "Like Decorations" is nature. In stanza II Stevens examines a romantic relationship to nature.

> Sigh for me, night-wind, in the noisy leaves of the oak.
> I am tired. Sleep for me, heaven over the hill.
> Shout for me, loudly and loudly, joyful sun, when you rise.
>   (*CP* 150)

"Make me thy lyre," Shelley writes in "Ode to the West Wind." Stevens reverses this relationship in stanza II. Instead of the poet being an instrument through which nature is expressed, here nature is being asked to express the poet, "sigh for me," "sleep for me," "shout for me." In stanza III the speaker's view of the leafless trees in November leads to a broader conclusion about the order of things; the "eccentric" is "the base of design" (*CP* 151). Stanza XVI takes up the plain sense of things, the sense of "simple space" that emerges when "thinking" is "blown away" (*CP* 153). The sense of "simple space" contrasts with the complex landscape of stanza XVII. The sun rising in winter is seen as a powerful force, a "tiger," but not as all powerful. It is "lamed" by the "haggard and tenuous air" (*CP* 153) of the season. Stevens sometimes suggests that the external world may be most fully disclosed when it seems most incomprehensible to us. That is, it is most itself when it is meaningless, or seen without the meanings that we project on to it. In stanza XX Stevens writes of such a moment. "Ah, but the meaningless, natural effigy! / . . . / The rabbit fat, at last, in glassy grass" (CP 153). In stanza XXXI Stevens invites us to see nature's motion, expressed here through the use of multiple present participles, "teeming millpond," "grasses rolling," "thorn-trees spinning," as a "deft beneficence" (CP 155). To the obvious motion of nature in stanza XXXI, Stevens contrasts in stanza XXXIV the invisible, unseen motion of nature.

> A calm November. Sunday in the fields.
> A reflection stagnant in a stagnant stream.
> Yet invisible currents clearly circulate.
> > (CP 156)

In stanza XLI Stevens looks at seasonal change as a mechanical repetition, disguised but not hidden by the bitter fragrance of the chrysanthemums.

> The chrysanthemums' astringent fragrance comes
> Each year to disguise the clanking mechanism
> Of machine within machine within machine.
> > (CP 157)

Finally, in stanza XLIX, Stevens views nature as a socializing force. "It needed the heavy nights of drenching weather / To make him return to people" (CP 158).

A third theme that Stevens looks at from various perspectives in "Like Decorations in a Nigger Cemetery" is that of decay, loss, winter. Stevens is sometimes seen as expressing a fatalistic acceptance of ruin or decay in "Like Decorations," and in stanza L he does write that the wise man's response to the inevitability of loss is to build his city in snow.

> Can all men, together, avenge
> One of the leaves that have fallen in autumn?
> But the wise man avenges by building his city in snow.
> > (CP 158)

But Stevens' responses in "Like Decorations" to winter and emptiness encompass a wide range of attitudes. In stanza VIII he contemplates the loss of religion; the temples are empty. But the emptiness of the temples is not an emptiness of the spirit. What was once celebrated in public is now celebrated in private. "Out of the spirit of the holy temples, / Empty and grandiose, let us make hymns / And sing them in secrecy as lovers do" (*CP* 151). The sense that celebrations or enjoyments in the midst of ruin are private and hidden affairs is also expressed in stanza XV.

> Serve the rouged fruits in early snow.
> They resemble a page of Toulet
> Read in the ruins of a new society,
> Furtively, by candle and out of need.
> (*CP* 153)

In stanza XV, unlike stanza VIII, the sense of enjoyment is coupled with a sense of furtiveness, as if the taking of pleasure, though done "out of need," were not countenanced by society and had to be hidden from public view, "Furtively, by candle." There is no sense of furtiveness in stanza XXVIII, in which the pleasures of the material world simply beguile the fatalist.

> A pear should come to the table popped with juice,
> Ripened in warmth and served in warmth. On terms
> Like these, autumn beguiles the fatalist.
> (*CP* 155)

Finally, in stanza XXXVIII, Stevens turns to art as a solace in winter.

> The album of Corot is premature.
> A little later when the sky is black.
> Mist that is golden is not wholly mist.
> (*CP* 156)

To show me the reproductions of paintings of summer by Corot when it is still summer is premature. Wait until winter, "when the sky is black," to show me the "album of Corot."

"Like Decorations in a Nigger Cemetery" is most closely related to "The Man with the Blue Guitar," published in 1937, two years after "Like Decorations" was published in a limited edition by the Alcestis Press. Neither poem advances an argument or progresses toward any conclusion. In neither does Stevens examine his subjects in any logical order. Rather, in both poems, Stevens repeatedly loops back to certain subjects and examines them from different perspectives. Cantos VIII and IX of "The Man with the Blue Guitar," for example, take up the idea of the unpredictability of the imagination, how its response to reality cannot be foreseen or calculated. In canto VIII, the setting seems to be one to which the imagination would readily respond.

> The vivid, florid, turgid sky,
> The drenching thunder rolling by,
>
> The morning deluged still by night,
> The clouds tumultuously bright
>
> And the feeling heavy in cold chords
> Struggling toward impassioned choirs,
>
> Crying among the clouds, enraged
> By gold antagonists in air—
>
> I know my lazy, leaden twang
> Is like the reason in a storm;
>
> And yet it brings the storm to bear.
> I twang it out and leave it there.
>   (CP 169)

The imagination, though, is unable to respond to what ought to be congenial to it. Commenting on this canto in a letter to Hi

Simons, Stevens writes, "Where apparently the whole setting is propitious to the imagination, the imagination comes to nothing. What is really propitious (the florid, the tumultuously bright) antagonizes it. Thus, one's chords remain *manqué;* still there they are. They at least state the *milieu,* though they are incapable of doing anything with it" (*L* 362). In canto IX Stevens looks at the issue from the opposite perspective. A setting that appears to be uncongenial to the imagination is responded to readily.

> And the color, the overcast blue
> Of the air, in which the blue guitar
>
> Is a form, described but difficult,
> And I am merely a shadow hunched
>
> Above the arrowy, still strings,
> The maker of a thing yet to be made;
>
> The color like a thought that grows
> Out of a mood, the tragic robe
>
> Of the actor, half his gesture, half
> His speech, the dress of his meaning, silk
>
> Sodden with his melancholy words,
> The weather of the stage, himself.
>   (*CP* 169–70)

"[I]n IX," Stevens writes, "the imagination being confronted with a kind of universal dullness, most unpropitious, the overcast everything, seizes on it and makes use of it, dominates it, takes its place, becomes the world in which we live" (*L* 362–63).

A second idea that Stevens considers from more than one perspective is the imagination's detachment from reality. In canto VII Stevens offers a negative view of detachment.

> It is the sun that shares our works.
> The moon shares nothing. It is a sea.
>
> When shall I come to say of the sun,
> It is a sea; it shares nothing;

. . . .

Detached from us, from things as they are?
Not to be part of the sun? To stand

Remote and call it merciful?
The strings are cold on the blue guitar.
                                                    (*CP* 168)

"[M]y imagination," Stevens writes about this canto, "grows cold
at the thought of such complete detachment. I do not desire to
exist apart from our works and the imagination does not desire to
exist apart from our works" (*L* 362).

Stevens offers a different view of detachment in canto XIII.
This is "a poem that deals with the intensity of the imagination
unmodified by contacts with reality," Stevens wrote to Renato
Poggioli (*L* 785). While the mere thought of such detachment left
the strings cold in canto VII, there is no sense of coldness in canto
XIII. Detachment is seen in large, Hoon-like terms, "Expansions,
diffusions." The imagination does not wither from its lack of con-
tact with reality but is "sleek with a hundred chins." Far from
being seen as marginal because of its isolation, the imagination in
canto XIII is described as the "heraldic center of the world" (*CP*
172).

Both the rejection of detachment that is expressed in canto VII
and the feeling of centrality and power associated with the imagi-
nation "unmodified by contacts with reality" that is expressed in
canto XIII contrast with Stevens' attitude toward detachment in
canto XXVI. Here, Stevens evokes a sense of the imagination's
longing or "nostalgia" for reality. Writing to Hi Simons, Stevens
comments that "the imagination with its typical nostalgia for real-
ity tried to go back to recover the world" (*L* 364). Yet the imagi-
nation seems unable to recover the world, which remains a remote
and inaccessible "Utopia": "The swarm of thoughts, the swarm of
dreams / Of inaccessible Utopia" (*CP* 179).

The idea of detachment and the idea of the unpredictability of
the imagination's response to reality are not the only subjects in
"The Man with the Blue Guitar" that Stevens examines from dif-
ferent perspectives. He also circles round, for example, the idea of

man. In canto II he considers the "hero's head," in canto III "man number one," in canto X the political leader, "Whom all believe that all believe," in canto XXI man as a replacement for the idea of god, "A substitute for all the gods: / This self, not that gold self aloft" (*CP* 176), and in canto XXX man the actor: "From this I shall evolve a man. / . . . / Like something on the stage, puffed out" (*CP* 181). Another concept to which Stevens repeatedly returns is the moment in which what is played upon the blue guitar seems to be reality, the moment in which "The tune is space" and "The blue guitar / Becomes the place of things as they are" (*CP* 168), or in which "the blue guitar / After long strumming on certain nights / Gives the touch of the senses, not of the hand, / But the very senses as they touch / The wind-gloss" (*CP* 174–75). If what is played on the blue guitar seems to be reality, then the player of the blue guitar at these moments might feel, as Stevens writes in canto XXVIII, that he is a "native" in the world.

> I am a native in this world
> And think in it as a native thinks,
>
> .   .   .   .
>
> And things are as I think they are
> And say they are on the blue guitar.
>   (*CP* 180)

This sense of integration, of being a native, contrasts sharply with the feeling of alienation expressed in canto XVI: "The earth is not earth but a stone, / Not the mother that held men as they fell" (*CP* 173).

The movement of thought in "The Man with the Blue Guitar," one in which subjects are taken up and returned to in an unsystematic way, gives the poem a sense of continually looping back even as it spirals outward. This movement of thought, similar to the movement of thought in "Like Decorations in a Nigger Cemetery," expresses simultaneously both a sense of unity and of fragmentation and dispersal. The multiplicity of points of view and subjects pushes the poem toward chaos while the repeated return to certain subjects gives coherence to the whole. Though the movement of thought in "The Man with the Blue Guitar" is similar to the movement of thought in "Like Decorations in a Nigger Cemetery," the *unit* of thought is very different in the two poems. The stanzas of "Like Decorations," all of which, with one exception, have either three or four lines, are so compressed that they seem to show us not the process of thought but the product of thought. As A. Walton Litz has noted, the poem has a strong epigrammatic quality.[11] The cantos of "The Man with the Blue Guitar," in contrast, are much lengthier and give Stevens room to show us the process of thinking.

The greater length of the cantos also allows Stevens to utilize some local techniques to express both the organizing and disruptive power of art. For instance, Stevens uses the music of the verse to mock or undermine an argument that is being presented. The music thus allows him to work through an argument and then toss the whole thing up in the air and move on to another subject or to another aspect of the same subject. Canto I of "The Man with the Blue Guitar" illustrates this technique.

> The man bent over his guitar,
> A shearsman of sorts. The day was green.
>
> They said, "You have a blue guitar,
> You do not play things as they are."
>
> The man replied, "Things as they are
> Are changed upon the blue guitar."
>
> And they said then, "But play, you must,
> A tune beyond us, yet ourselves,
>
> A tune upon the blue guitar
> Of things exactly as they are."
>
> (CP 165)

Three of the five couplets are rhymed with the same end word, and except for the initial couplet, the entire canto is written in an iambic tetrameter whose regularity tends to speed up the tempo of the canto, draws our attention to the purely rhythmic aspect of the verse, and gives the canto an increasingly singsong quality. The repetitive rhymes, the couplet form, and the increasingly regular tetrameter rhythm of the section are reminiscent of the nonsense doggerel of Humpty Dumpty's poem in *Through the Looking Glass*.

> *"I sent a message to the fish:*
> *I told them 'This is what I wish.'*
>
> *The little fishes of the sea,*
> *They sent an answer back to me.*
>
> *The little fishes' answer was*
> *'We cannot do it, Sir, because ———' "*

"I'm afraid I don't quite understand," said Alice.
"It gets easier further on," Humpty Dumpty replied.[12]

Of course, Stevens' tetrameter line in the opening canto of "The Man with the Blue Guitar" does not thump as loudly as Carroll's, but the canto's accelerating tempo and its repetitive rhymes gesture toward the nonsensical and give the canto a playful feeling that acts as a counterpoint to the abstract dialogue about the relation between reality and the imagination. While the dialogue is clicking away, defining ever more precisely the nature of this relationship, the music of the canto is gently mocking this rational enclosure, reminding us that the nature of the interaction between reality and the imagination is not one that can be caught, at least for long, in the net of thought.[13]

The use of music to undermine an argument is a technique that Stevens had employed earlier in "The Comedian as the Letter C." In a letter to Ronald Lane Latimer, Stevens comments: "I suppose that I ought to confess that by the letter C I meant the sound of the letter C; what was in my mind was to play on that sound throughout the poem. While the sound of the letter has more or less variety, and includes, for instance, K and S, all its shades may be said to have a comic aspect. Consequently, the letter C is a comedian. . . . Moreover, I did not mean that every time the letter C occurs in the poem it should take the stage. The reader would have to determine for himself just when that particular sound was being stressed, as, for example, in such a phrase as 'piebald fiscs unkeyed,' where you have the thing hissing and screeching" (*L* 294). The partial line Stevens quotes comes from section V of "Comedian," "A Nice Shady Home." Here we are told that "the quotidian saps philosophers / And men like Crispin" (*CP* 42). But we are also told that the quotidian that surrounds Crispin is a very pleasant one. It is composed of "fruits laid in their leaves, / The tomtit and the cassia and the rose" (*CP* 42). Hence, the narrator concludes,

> the quotidian
> Like this, saps like the sun, true fortuner.
> For all it takes it gives a humped return
> Exchequering from piebald fiscs unkeyed.
> (*CP* 43)

The sense of the lines, I think, is this: though the quotidian does take from us, "saps," it also gives back, "a humped return," paying out, "exchequering," from the unlocked, "unkeyed," royal treasury, "fisc," of multicolored, "piebald," nature, that is, from the bountiful variety of nature—the tomtit, the cassia, and the rose. The *c* sounds of the line, "hissing and screeching" as Stevens puts it, have a comic effect that undermines any sense that this discovery about the quotidian is "Crispin's last / Deduction" (*CP* 43). As in canto I of "The Man with the Blue Guitar," the sound of the verse functions as "constant self-parody," allowing Stevens simultaneously to present ideas and to be critically detached from them. This critical detachment opens up the verse to new ideas, which are in turn examined and humorously undermined during Crispin's "simple jaunt" from Bordeaux to Yucatan to Carolina.[14]

The actual sound of the verse is not the only way that music provides a sense of critical detachment in "The Man with the Blue Guitar." Stevens' description of the sound of the blue guitar, of other instruments, or of the way in which the guitar is being played, can also suggest a critical stance toward the subject under consideration. For example, in canto X Stevens confronts "a politician, a soldier . . . the false hero" (*L* 789):

> behold
> The approach of him whom none believes,
>
> Whom all believe that all believe,
> A pagan in a varnished car.
>
> Roll a drum upon the blue guitar.
> Lean from the steeple. Cry aloud,
>
> "Here am I, my adversary, that
> Confront you, hoo-ing the slick trombones.
>   (*CP* 170)

Stevens writes of this figure, "I address him but with hostility, hooing the slick trombones. I deride and challenge him" (*L* 789). This attitude is conveyed by the roll of the drum upon the blue guitar and by the Bronx cheer of the trombones. In canto III, where Stevens takes up the idea of "man number one," the manner in which the guitar is played suggests his distaste for the idea, "To bang it from a savage blue, / Jangling the metal of the strings" (*CP* 166). And the idea of the imagination's detachment from reality, explored in stanza VII, leaves the "strings . . . cold on the blue guitar" (*CP* 168).

Another technique Stevens uses in "The Man with the Blue Guitar" to suggest critical distance from the ideas he is exploring is a kind of verbal irony, difficult to label but probably closest to what Muecke calls "impersonal irony,"[15] in which a speaker of limited perception fails to see the implications of the language he uses. For example, canto XX opens with the couplet, "What is there in life except one's ideas, / Good air, good friend, what is there in life?" (*CP* 175). In this dramatic setting, the speaker addresses the air, his "good friend," and asks, "What is there in life except one's ideas?" The answer to the question is given in the question itself. The "good air," the material world, addressed by our uncomprehending speaker is what there is in life besides ideas. The speaker continues:

Is it ideas that I believe?
Good air, my only friend, believe,

Believe would be a brother full
Of love, believe would be a friend,

Friendlier than my only friend,
Good air. Poor pale, poor pale guitar. . . .
                              (CP 175–76)

The speaker wistfully thinks that belief in ideas would be friendlier than the air, all the while acknowledging, but not truly understanding, that the air itself is his "only friend." It is perhaps not surprising that this song of poverty in the midst of plenty should evoke the comment, "Poor pale, poor pale guitar" (CP 176).

The loose, repetitive structures of "The Man with the Blue Guitar" and "Like Decorations in a Nigger Cemetery" seem to contrast sharply with the structure of a later long poem, "Notes toward a Supreme Fiction." Stevens' lengthiest *ars poetica* appears to be organized in the same manner that its ultimate predecessor, Aristotle's *Art of Poetry,* is organized, through classification and division. Stevens first divides his subject, a supreme fiction, into three major categories, "It Must Be Abstract," "It Must Change," and "It Must Give Pleasure." Each of these categories is then formally subdivided into ten cantos and each canto further divided into seven tercet stanzas. The method of organization and the formal symmetry of the poem might suggest that the movement of thought in "Notes toward a Supreme Fiction" is hierarchical and logical, that Stevens moves in the poem from one precisely delineated category to the next. But "Notes," as B. J. Leggett observes, "does not itself hold strictly to its three-part division."[16] A theme or idea introduced in one section is returned to and reexamined in the other two sections. For example, Stevens first introduces the idea of the irrational or nonsense in section I, "It Must Be Abstract."

We say: At night an Arabian in my room,
With his damned hoobla-hoobla-hoobla-how,

Inscribes a primitive astronomy

Across the unscrawled fores the future casts
And throws his stars around the floor. By day
The wood-dove used to chant his hoobla-hoo

And still the grossest iridescence of ocean
Howls hoo and rises and howls hoo and falls.
Life's nonsense pierces us with strange relation.
                                    (CP 383)

Neither the Arabian, whom Stevens identifies in his letters as the
moon *(L* 433), nor the sounds of the wood dove, nor the ocean's
fullest display of its colors, "grossest iridescence," has any meaning.
Each is a separate example of "life's nonsense." Yet, Stevens sug-
gests, the mind can relate these incidents to each other; "Life's
nonsense pierces us with strange relation." Stevens returns to the
irrational, meaningless, or nonsensical quality of reality in section
II, "It Must Change."

The poem goes from the poet's gibberish to
The gibberish of the vulgate and back again.
. . . .
It is the gibberish of the vulgate that he seeks.
                                    (CP 396–97)

Here Stevens focuses not on the mind's ability to bring the mean-
ingless aspects of reality into a relation, but on the poet's desire to
seek out and to express the "gibberish of the vulgate." He takes up
the theme again in section III, "It Must Give Pleasure," canto I,
where he writes that "the difficultest rigor is forthwith, / . . . to
catch from that / Irrational moment its unreasoning" *(CP* 398).
The idea that poetry expresses the irrational moment in its unrea-
soning is returned to again in the final canto of "Notes," where
Stevens describes reality as "the soft-footed phantom, the irra-
tional / Distortion, however fragrant, however dear" *(CP* 406)
and suggests that poetry results from experiencing, from "feeling,"

this irrational distortion. "That's it: the more than rational distortion, / The fiction that results from feeling" (*CP* 406).

The return to and reexamination of a theme in all three sections of "Notes toward a Supreme Fiction" suggests that the movement of thought in the poem is indirect, repetitive, and exploratory, not one that proceeds logically and that is strictly bound within categories. Stevens himself, in a letter to Hi Simons, points to the poem's oblique, darting, nonlogical movement of thought: "Even in a text expounding *it must change,* it is permissible to illustrate *it must give pleasure* without any law whatever" (*L* 445).

This repetitive and indirect movement of thought can be seen not only *among* the sections of "Notes toward a Supreme Fiction" but also *within* them. For example, the central idea of section II, as the title tells us, is change. However, Stevens begins the section by considering the idea of repetition without change. "The bees came booming as if they had never gone, / As if hyacinths had never gone" (*CP* 389). His feeling about this lack of change is expressed unambiguously. "It means the distaste we feel for this withered scene / Is that it has not changed enough. It remains, / It is a repetition" (*CP* 390). Canto II takes the opposite perspective, repetition as constant change. To the bees in canto I who came booming as if they had never gone, Stevens contrasts the "Booming and booming of the new-come bee" (*CP* 391). The eternal return of spring is not a repetition as canto I defines it; it is a "beginning, not resuming." Canto III, which recounts the parable of the statue of General Du Puy, returns to the perspective of canto I, the absence of change. The statue represents a sense of historical reality, and "lawyers in their promenades" approach it "To study the past" (*CP* 391). Yet the reality that the statue represents is so remote from the present that the lawyers doubt whether the general ever could have lived, been "true flesh" at all. "There never had been, never could be, such / A man. The lawyers disbelieved" (*CP* 391). The doctors suggest that "the General / The very Place Du Puy, in fact, belonged / Among our more vestigial states of mind" (*CP* 391–92). Because the statue cannot change as reality changes, it is "rubbish in the end" (*CP* 391).

The first three cantos address the ideas of change and the absence of change. In canto IV Stevens considers a new topic, the origin of change. He speculates that change originates from a dependence of opposites on each other.

> Two things of opposite natures seem to depend
> On one another, as a man depends
> On a woman, day on night, the imagined
>
> On the real. This is the origin of change.
>   (*CP* 392)

Stevens describes this dependence of opposites on each other as an intimate, at times passionate, union. Winter and spring "embrace." Morning and afternoon are "clasped together." North and South make an "intrinsic couple," and the sun and rain are "like two lovers / That walk away as one in the greenest body" (*CP* 392). Canto V considers another "intrinsic couple," the planter and the island. Stevens' shift of perspective here is abrupt, even harsh. The idea expressed at the end of canto IV is the erotic union of all things in change: "The partaker partakes of that which changes him. / The child that touches takes character from the thing, / The body, it touches. The captain and his men / Are one and the sailor and the sea are one" (*CP* 392). This idea is followed by the announcement in canto V of the death of one of the lovers.

> On a blue island in a sky-wide water
> The wild orange trees continued to bloom and to bear,
> Long after the planter's death.
>
>   (*CP* 393)

Stevens expresses in this canto a theme that he had taken up in "Esthétique du Mal" and to which he will return in "Large Red Man Reading," death as a poignant separation from the earth seen as inamorata. "An unaffected man in a negative light / Could not have borne his labor nor have died / Sighing that he should leave the banjo's twang" (*CP* 393). In contrast to the meditations on the origin of change and on change and death, canto VI returns to the idea examined in cantos I and III, repetition without change.

> One voice repeating, one tireless chorister,
> The phrases of a single phrase, ké-ké,
> A single text, granite monotony,
>
> . . . .
>
>   the sparrow is a bird
>
> Of stone, that never changes.
>
>   (CP 394)

What appears to be unchanging, though, will itself be subject to change. "It is / A sound like any other. It will end" (CP 394).

The movement of thought in this section, one in which Stevens explores a subject from one perspective, moves to a second, loosely opposed perspective, loops back to explore an implication of the first perspective, introduces a third perspective on his subject, considers another aspect of this perspective, again loops back to the first perspective, and so forth, repeats the indirect and repetitive movement of thought in the poem as a whole. This movement of departure and return, of looping back while spiraling outward, itself replicates the movement of thought in "The Man with the Blue Guitar" and "Like Decorations in a Nigger Cemetery." Like them, "Notes toward a Supreme Fiction" revolves around while endlessly fragmenting the ideas that serve as its meditational center. The final words of the third section describe well this endless process of revolution and fragmentation. "You will have stopped revolving except in crystal" (CP 407).

Stevens' last long poem, "An Ordinary Evening in New Haven," turns from the overt formality of "Notes toward a Supreme Fiction" to the looser, more casual organization of "The Man with the Blue Guitar" and "Like Decorations in a Nigger Cemetery." There is no division in "Ordinary Evening" into categories such as "It Must Be Abstract" or "It Must Give Pleasure." Like those three poems, "An Ordinary Evening in New Haven" does not progress logically or set forth any argument. As Ronald

Sukenick writes, "[T]here is no argument to the poem, nor progression of any kind."[17] Again as in the other poems, the movement of thought in "Ordinary Evening" is indirect, oblique, associational. Concepts are introduced and then returned to and reexamined. In canto II, for example, Stevens considers how much the self contributes to reality. It is "So much ourselves" that we are unable to tell apart our ideas about reality from the reality that causes the ideas, "the bearer-being of the idea" (*CP* 466). This thought, how much reality is a composition of the self, is the point of departure for canto III. "The point of vision and desire are the same" (*CP* 466). We see reality as we desire to see it. The poet, "*un amoureux perpétual*" (*NA* 30) of reality, is the one to whom we "pray" to transform our hard, bleak world into a beautiful one. "It is to the hero of midnight that we pray / On a hill of stones to make beau mont thereof" (*CP* 466). The remainder of the canto investigates desire, the force that shapes our vision of the world. Stevens suggests that desire can bring a kind of peace or solace to the heart because desire, unlike love, does not seek to possess and hence cannot be frustrated at never attaining what it seeks.

> And next to love is the desire for love,
> The desire for its celestial ease in the heart,
>
> Which nothing can frustrate, that most secure,
> Unlike love in possession of that which was
> To be possessed and is. But this cannot
>
> Possess. It is desire, set deep in the eye.
>
> (*CP* 467)

In canto IV the focus shifts from "the hero of midnight" and the "beau mont" to the "man who has fought / Against illusion" and the "plainness of plain things." This plainness is felt to be a "savagery," uncongenial to the self and requiring an appeasement by the imagination that is equally "savage." Canto V, in contrast, shifts away from the plain sense of things and back to the perspective of cantos II and III: "Reality as a thing seen by the mind, /

Not that which is but that which is apprehended" (CP 468). The thought that reality is a thing seen by the mind leads here not to a sense of the mind's estrangement from reality. Rather, Stevens expresses the mind's acceptance of and pleasure in the way the imagination shapes the real.

> A great town hanging pendent in the shade,
> An enormous nation happy in a style,
> Everything as unreal as real can be.
>   (CP 468)

These themes, taken up in the early cantos, are returned to later in the poem. For example, cantos VIII and IX return to the perspective of canto IV, the plain sense of things. "We fling ourselves," Stevens writes in canto VIII, "constantly longing, on this form. / We descend to the street and inhale a health of air" (CP 470). And in canto IX he writes: "We keep coming back and coming back / To the real: to the hotel instead of the hymns / That fall upon it out of the wind" (CP 471). While the focus on plain reality links cantos VIII and IX with canto IV, cantos VIII and IX express a very different feeling than does canto IV about this plain reality. In canto IV the self seeks relief from the plainness of plain things, whereas in cantos VIII and IX the self expresses its desire for plain reality. "We fling ourselves . . . on this form" (VIII) and keep "coming back / To the real," to the "hotel" bereft of any of the imagination's songs, "hymns" (IX).

Stevens will also return in later cantos to the idea that perhaps reality is only that which is apprehended by the mind. The starting point of canto V, for example, "reality as a thing seen by the mind," is echoed in the opening of canto XXVIII.

> If it should be true that reality exists
> In the mind
>
>   .   .   .   .   .
>   it follows that

Real and unreal are two in one: New Haven
Before and after one arrives.

(CP 485)

And the thought that concludes canto II, that the self composes the reality it perceives, is taken in a different but related direction in canto XXIX. Though both cantos are linked by their focus on how much the self contributes to the reality that it perceives, canto II emphasizes the impossibility of separating our perception of reality from reality itself, while canto XXIX turns away from "confused illuminations and sonorities" and emphasizes instead the enormous power of the imagination, its domination of reality through language, "an alteration / Of words that was a change of nature" (*CP* 487).

The overall movement of thought in "An Ordinary Evening in New Haven" is similar to the movement of thought in "The Man with the Blue Guitar," "Notes toward a Supreme Fiction," and "Like Decorations in a Nigger Cemetery." A theme is introduced, looked at from a second angle, a second theme is taken up, the first theme is returned to and looked at from yet a third angle, the second theme is then returned to and reexamined, and so forth. As in the three other poems, this movement of thought expresses a sense of "artfully ordered confusion." The poem circles around or loops back to the ideas that are its meditational center, even as these ideas are endlessly differentiated in the poem's revolutions.

Chapter 5

Irony in the Late Poetry of Wallace Stevens

[T]his artistic ability of man *par excellence*—he has it in common with everything that is. He himself is after all a piece of reality, truth, nature.

—Nietzsche

Stevens writes in *The Necessary Angel* that for each individual certain subjects are "congenital."

> A man's sense of the world is born with him and persists, and penetrates the ameliorations of education and experience of life. His species is as fixed as his genus. For each man, then, certain subjects are congenital. (*NA* 120)

It is perhaps not surprising, then, to find Stevens returning in the late poetry, that is, *The Auroras of Autumn,* published five years before Stevens' death in 1955, and *The Rock,* first published in *The Collected Poems* (1954), to ideas that he had explored in the earlier work. A number of these ideas are taken up in one of Stevens' very late poems, "St. Armorer's Church from the Outside."

In "The Noble Rider and the Sound of Words," Stevens cites Pareto's epigram that "history is a cemetery of aristocracies" (*NA* 35). Stevens' work suggests that history is a cemetery of outdated beliefs, systems, or ideologies. One such ideology is symbolized by St. Armorer's Church. The religious belief that it represents was once vital. The church "was once an immense success. / It rose loftily and stood massively" (*CP* 529). In "To an Old Philosopher in Rome," Stevens considers the grandeur that might be possible were the church still an "immense success." For Santayana, on the

verge of dying, between "Rome . . . and that more merciful
Rome / Beyond" (*CP* 508), the material world is easily trans-
formed into the spiritual world. "[T]he figures in the street /
Become the figures of heaven" (*CP* 508). Yet the material world
is not denied but "enlarged" by the proximity of that "more mer-
ciful Rome," "every visible thing enlarged and yet / No more
than a bed, a chair and moving nuns" (*CP* 510). Though separate,
the two worlds complement each other and create "a kind of total
grandeur at the end" (*CP* 510). In "St. Armorer's" Stevens, echo-
ing a stance he had taken as early as "Sunday Morning," rejects the
religious belief that underlies the possibility of the kind of total
grandeur he contemplates in "To an Old Philosopher in Rome."
St. Armorer's Church has "lost its power to sustain us" (*NA* 7). It
is full of "holes," and "What is left has the foreign smell of plaster"
(*CP* 529), perhaps a direct allusion to the Rome of "To an Old
Philosopher in Rome." As an addition to the cemetery of out-
dated beliefs, St. Armorer's joins numerous other ideologies
whose demise is cataloged in the *Collected Poems:* the death of
Phoebus, "Let Phoebus slumber and die in autumn umber, /
Phoebus is dead," and the statue of General Du Puy, "rubbish in
the end," in "Notes toward a Supreme Fiction" (*CP* 381, 392);
"The death of Satan . . . / And, with him, many blue phenomena"
and "the logicians in their graves / . . . the worlds of logic in their
great tombs" in "Esthétique du Mal" (*CP* 319, 325); the "obsolete
fiction of the wide river in / An empty land; the gods that
Boucher killed; / And the metal heros that time granulates" in
"Asides on the Oboe" (*CP* 250); the "anti-master-man" who
"brushed away the thunder, then the clouds, / Then the colossal
illusion of heaven" in "Landscape with Boat" (*CP* 241); the "old
casino in a park" that replaced "nightingales, / Jehovah and the
great sea-worm" but which itself is now in ruin, "rain / Swept
through its boarded windows and the leaves / Filled its encrusted
fountains" of "Academic Discourse at Havana" (*CP* 142); and the
statue of "The Founder of the State" that is covered with mice in
"Dance of the Macabre Mice" (*CP* 123). In "St. Armorer's," as
often in Stevens' poetry, destruction is followed by creation.
Affirmation follows negation. As Stevens writes in "The Well

Dressed Man with a Beard," "After the final no there comes a yes / And on that yes the future world depends" (*CP* 247). If the destruction of St. Armorer's Church represents the "no," then the "yes" is represented by the chapel. It is "An ember yes among its cindery noes" (*CP* 529). The chapel is not a reformulation or rekindling of the ideology behind St. Armorer's. It is "No radiance of dead blaze" (*CP* 529). Rather, it is a new fictive construct created by the poet, "His own: a chapel of breath" (*CP* 529), and one that defines his own period and civilization. "The chapel rises, his own, his period, / A civilization formed from the outward blank" (*CP* 529). In defining the present period, the chapel fulfills "the need of each generation to be itself, / The need to be actual and as it is" (*CP* 530), a need Stevens had spoken of in "Of Modern Poetry," where poetry

> has to be living, to learn the speech of the place.
> It has to face the men of the time and to meet
> The women of the time. It has to think about war
> And it has to find what will suffice.
>
> (*CP* 240)

A new conception of reality can be thought of as the beginning of a new cycle of destruction and creation. But the chapel at St. Armorer's is not destined to become a future addition to the cemetery of ideologies. The chapel is "always beginning because it is part / Of that which is always beginning, over and over" (*CP* 530). That which begins over and over, as Stevens writes in "An Ordinary Evening in New Haven," is reality. Every day is new day; "The oldest-newest day is the newest alone" (*CP* 476). And he writes later in the poem that the sense of "original earliness" is a "daily sense" (*CP* 481). Like the element of which it is part, the chapel gives us "a new account of everything old" (*CP* 529). The architect of the chapel has learned the lesson of "Notes," section II, "It Must Change." The new account of reality remains new because it can change, "will soon change forms" (*CP* 529). Always beginning, the chapel is a continuing expression of the "dizzle-dazzle of being new" (*CP* 530). Unlike the constructs that cannot change and hence are destroyed, this construct, like the giant in "A Primitive Like an Orb," is "ever changing, living in change" (*CP* 443).

The theme of creation and destruction, expressed in "St. Armorer's" and in the earlier poetry, is explored further in "An Ordinary Evening in New Haven," canto XXIV. "In the genius of summer," after "they blew up / The statue of Jove among the boomy clouds,"

> There was a clearing, a readiness for first bells,
> An opening for outpouring, the hand was raised:
> There was a willingness not yet composed,
>
> A knowing that something certain had been proposed,
> Which, without the statue, would be new,
> An escape from repetition, a happening
>
> In space and the self, that touched them both at once
> And alike.
>
> (*CP* 482–83)

In blowing up the statue of Jove, an older conception of reality, like that represented by the statue of General Du Puy or St. Armorer's Church, has been destroyed. However, unlike other poems where destruction is followed immediately by the creation of another fiction, in canto XXIV of "Ordinary Evening" Stevens pauses to consider the moment *prior* to creation. There is an "opening for outpouring," not outpouring itself. There is a "willingness not yet composed," that is, a willingness to create prior to any actual composition. "The hand was raised," like a painter before the first brush stroke, a sculptor before touching the clay, a conductor before the first beat, a writer before pen touches paper. Though the canto focuses on the moment prior to creation, Stevens' description of the moment seems to suggest that the mind has a foreknowledge that a fiction will be created, "A knowing that something certain had been proposed," that the fiction will be "new" and will not be a repetition of the sense of reality just destroyed, "without the statue . . . / An escape from repetition," and that in this new fiction mind and outer will come together, "a happening / In space and the self, that touched them both at once / And alike." What is different about Stevens' meditation on the cycle of destruction and creation in this canto of "Ordinary Evening" is that he describes destruction and the prehistory of creation, not creation itself. It is as if Ozymandias, whom Stevens describes as always weaving a fictive covering, were to pause and reflect on what he is about to create before creating it.

Stevens' meditation on the prehistory of creation in canto XXIV of "Ordinary Evening" looks forward to his later meditation on the subject, "Long and Sluggish Lines."

> It makes so little difference, at so much more
> Than seventy, where one looks, one has been there before.
>
> Wood-smoke rises through trees, is caught in an upper flow
> Of air and whirled away. But it has been often so.
>
> The trees have a look as if they bore sad names
> And kept saying over and over one same, same thing.
>
> (CP 522)

These opening lines recall the sense of repetition that was described by the old seraph in "Notes," section II, canto I. He saw the jonquils the Italian girls wore in their hair, had seen them before in the bandeaux of the mothers, and would see them again. The bees came booming "as if they had never gone, / As if hyacinths had never gone" (CP 389). The distaste he feels for the scene "Is that it has not changed enough. It remains, / It is a repetition" (CP 390). The complaint that Stevens voices in "Notes" and "Long and Sluggish Lines" is one that was heard before in the long and sluggish lines of the *Harmonium* poem, "Indian River."

> The trade-wind jingles the rings in the nets around
>   the racks by the docks on Indian River.
> It is the same jingle of the water among the roots
>   under the banks of the palmettoes,
> It is the same jingle of the red-bird breasting the

orange-trees out of the cedars.
Yet there is no spring in Florida, neither in boskage perdu,
    nor on the nunnery beaches.

(CP 112)

And "Indian River" looks back to the complaint of monotony
voiced in "The Man Whose Pharynx Was Bad." "The time of
year has grown indifferent. / Mildew of summer and the deepen-
ing snow / Are both alike in the routine I know" (*CP* 96). Stevens
speculates in "Notes" (section II, canto IV) that opposition is the
origin of change, and in "Long and Sluggish Lines" "an opposite,
a contradiction" (*CP* 522) suggests the possibility of change. There
are earliest hintings that winter will give way to spring—"Baby-
ishness of forsythia . . . / The spook and makings of the nude mag-
nolia" (*CP* 522). The possibility of an awakening in nature leads
Stevens to speculate on the possibility of a parallel awakening of
the mind's creative power.

Wanderer, this is the pre-history of February.
The life of the poem in the mind has not yet begun.

You were not born yet when the trees were crystal
Nor are you now, in this wakefulness inside a sleep.

(CP 522)

The life of the poem in the mind has begun in canto XXIV of
"Ordinary Evening." It has not yet developed, but it has begun,
"something certain had been proposed" (*CP* 483). In "Long and
Sluggish Lines," in contrast, Stevens seems to describe a state prior
to beginning. "The life of the poem in the mind has not yet
begun." Though not yet begun, there is the potential for begin-
ning, represented by the mind's "wakefulness" even though it is
"inside a sleep."[1]

The cycle of destruction and creation, the idea that a fiction,
to be living, must change, the spiritual torpor that results from the
absence of change, the idea that poetry situates the self in the pres-
ent—all of these ideas in the late work are familiar to us from the

earlier work. Even the idea of the prehistory of creation can be
seen as a logical extension of Stevens' earlier explorations of the
idea of creation and destruction. But the late work does differ
from the earlier poetry. B. J. Leggett writes that Stevens' "earlier
tendency" was "to ennoble the individual imagination at the
expense of the external world."[2] This tendency changes in the late
work, which often turns away from the imagination and its con-
structs to the external. This shift in emphasis in the late work can
be illustrated by comparing the opening of "Notes" with the
opening of "The Auroras of Autumn." In "Notes" Stevens focuses
on the invention of a world. Though he acknowledges that reality
can have no final name, "But Phoebus was / A name for some-
thing that never could be named" (CP 381), the ephebe is given
the task of naming reality over and over. "The sun / Must bear no
name, gold flourisher" (CP 381). (This is perhaps the shortest
cycle of naming and unnaming in all of Stevens' poetry.) In each
naming, the poet gives us a new "invented world" (CP 380). In
each we see the real "in the idea of it" (CP 380). In contrast to
"Notes," "Auroras" asks us to approach the real apart from any
namings.

> This is where the serpent lives, the bodiless.
> His head is air. Beneath his tip at night
> Eyes open and fix on us in every sky.
>
> Or is this another wriggling out of the egg,
> Another image at the end of the cave,
> Another bodiless for the body's slough?
> (CP 411)

Stevens does not here focus on the destruction of one fiction, the
creation of another, and the new sense of reality that results from
the invention of a new fiction. He seeks not an "invented world"
but the flux of the real apart from any fictions, the serpent "Skin
flashing to wished-for disappearances / And the serpent body
flashing without the skin" (CP 411). Nor is he at all certain that he
has found the reality that he seeks. Borrowing an image from

Plato, Stevens writes that the body flashing without the skin could be "Another image at the end of the cave" (*CP* 411). Stevens had made the same point in the Ozymandias canto of "Notes." The world is always covered with the mind's fictive weavings. There is always another image at the end of the cave. What is different in "The Auroras of Autumn" is the mind's attitude toward this issue. Instead of accepting and enjoying the "invented world," the mind in "Auroras" expresses only a desire to get outside the cave, to find a reality that is not another image, another "fictive weaving."

This shift in emphasis from inner to outer raises questions in the later work about fictions and about creative activity that are very different from the questions raised about these two subjects in the earlier poetry. For instance, instead of asking whether the mind can view a construct as the real, Stevens will ask whether a construct, or whether creative activity itself, can direct the gaze of the mind outward, away from that which is created by the mind. He will ask if the outer can be encountered in the absence of any activity of the mind, whether creative or destructive. And he will explore the relation between the larger universe of flux and creative activity when the mind's stance toward its constructs is no longer one of belief. All of these questions point away from the two senses of irony that were described earlier. Attention to the outer runs counter to the subjectivism and isolation of, for example, "Tea at the Palaz of Hoon" or "A Rabbit as King of the Ghosts." The real often seems in the late work too precious, too much desired, for Stevens to withdraw from it. Indeed, so strong is his desire for the real that it persists even at the moment of death, as Stevens movingly attests in the very late poem "As You Leave the Room."

> Now, here, the snow I had forgotten becomes
>
> Part of a major reality, part of
> An appreciation of reality
>
> And thus an elevation, as if I left
> With something I could touch, touch every way.
>   (*OP* 117–18)

The late focus on the outer can also be seen as a turning away from that aspect of the irony of skeptical engagement in which the mind is seen as being able, through its constructs, to situate itself in the real. What sense of irony, then, does the late poetry express, and is this irony related in any way to romantic irony? Part of the answer to these questions is suggested in Stevens' exploration of the relation between fictions and the outer in his lyric of 1952, "The Poem That Took the Place of a Mountain."

> There it was, word for word,
> The poem that took the place of a mountain.
>
> He breathed its oxygen,
> Even when the book lay turned in the dust of his table.
>
> It reminded him how he had needed
> A place to go to in his own direction,
>
> How he had recomposed the pines,
> Shifted the rocks and picked his way among clouds,
>
> For the outlook that would be right,
> Where he would be complete in an unexplained completion:
>
> The exact rock where his inexactnesses
> Would discover, at last, the view toward which they had
>   edged,
>
> Where he could lie and, gazing down at the sea,
> Recognize his unique and solitary home.
>
>   (CP 512)

In the Ozymandias canto of "Notes," Stevens describes fictions as coverings. "A fictive covering / Weaves always glistening from the heart and mind" (CP 396). In creating fictions, the poet covers over blank reality. Stevens looks at fictions from the opposite perspective in "The Poem That Took the Place of a Mountain." Instead of seeing a fiction as that which covers the real, Stevens sees the fictive construct as the means by which the mind can gaze out at the flux of reality, the ocean. This stance

toward fictions is also different from the stance Stevens takes in
"The Snow Man." In that poem, it is through the reduction or
destruction of all fictive concepts that the listener "beholds" the
outer. In "The Poem That Took the Place of a Mountain," in
contrast, it is by constructing a fiction and not by destroying it that
the mind gazes outward. Paradoxically, creating a construct in
"Mountain" is an act of *un*covering.

Stevens writes in "The Noble Rider and the Sound of
Words" that the poet "creates the world to which we turn inces-
santly and without knowing it and . . . gives to life the supreme
fictions without which we are unable to conceive of it" (*NA* 31).
This idea, prevalent in the earlier work, is also expressed in the
later poetry. Stevens writes in "Someone Puts a Pineapple
Together," "This is everybody's world. / Here the total artifice
reveals itself / As the total reality" (*NA* 87). And it is the power of
the imagination to create the "supreme fictions," the fictive con-
structs that are the world in which we dwell, that he beautifully
reaffirms in one of his last poems, "Final Soliloquy of the Interior
Paramour."

> We say God and the imagination are one . . .
> How high that highest candle lights the dark.
>
> Out of this same light, out of the central mind,
> We make a dwelling in the evening air,
> In which being there together is enough.
>   (*CP* 524)

Stevens rejects in "The Poem That Took the Place of a Moun-
tain" the idea that the mind finds a dwelling place or home in the
constructs it creates. In "Mountain," not the construct but the sea
is described as "his unique and solitary home." In part, the mind
finds a home in its constructs because it believes in them. Though
aware that what it believes in is a fiction, the mind believes in the
construct anyway. Perhaps it is because Stevens in "Mountain" no
longer looks at home as that which is constructed by the mind but

as that which lies apart from the mind that belief does not seem to be an issue in the poem. The construct serves a function; through it the mind gazes at the sea, and the adequacy of the construct is determined by how well that function is fulfilled, not by its power to sustain the mind's belief.

In creating the mountain, Stevens increases the distance between himself and the ocean. He narrates in the poem a climb upward, first recomposing the pines and then "picking his way among the clouds." One aspect of the irony of detachment is the idea that in creative activity the self separates itself from the real. Though "Mountain" does show the self being lifted above the real through creative activity, the self does not experience a sense of separation from reality. To the contrary, by constructing a fiction that allows him to gaze at his "unique and solitary home," he discovers the "outlook that would be right" and hence feels "complete in an unexplained completion."

Stevens writes in "The Idea of Order at Key West" of the artist's desire to order reality through art, "The maker's rage to order words of the sea" (CP 130), and of art's power to satisfy this desire. The words of the singer "Mastered the night and portioned out the sea, / Fixing emblazoned zones and fiery poles" (CP 130). Neither of these aspects of creation is present in "Mountain." Nowhere does Stevens speak of the desire to order reality through art, nor is the ocean "portioned out" by the creation of this fiction. Indeed, the ocean is completely unaffected by his creative activity. In "Key West" the maker orders words of the sea, while in "Mountain" the maker only gazes on the ocean, yet these two poems share one similar view of art. Both emphasize the powerful aftereffect of creative activity. Just as the words of the singer master the night even after the singing has ended, so the poet in "Mountain" continues to breathe the "oxygen" of the poem he creates "even when the book lay turned in the dust of his table."

One idea expressed in "The Poem That Took the Place of a Mountain," that constructive rather than destructive activity can direct the gaze of the mind toward the outer, is carried to perhaps its logical extreme in "The Plain Sense of Things."

After the leaves have fallen, we return
To a plain sense of things. It is as if
We had come to an end of the imagination,
Inanimate in an inert savoir.

. . . .

Yet the absence of the imagination had
Itself to be imagined. The great pond,
The plain sense of it, without reflections, leaves,
Mud, water like dirty glass, expressing silence

Of a sort, silence of a rat come out to see,
The great pond and its waste of the lilies, all this
Had to be imagined.

                        (*CP* 502–3)

At first glance "The Poem That Took the Place of a Mountain" and "The Plain Sense of Things" appear to be opposed in the way in which they direct the gaze of the mind outward. In the former, Stevens constructs a fiction in order to look at the sea, while in the latter, he speaks of the elimination of all fictions, "after the leaves have fallen," and human projections that reflect our image, "without reflection." The opposition between the two poems, however, is not an opposition of construction and reduction but one of creative technique. Instead of evoking the plain sense of things by creating a construct, Stevens evokes the outer in "Plain Sense" by imagining not simply the absence of any construct, but the absence of the faculty that creates the constructs. Paradoxically, though, the imagining of the absence of the imagination is itself a powerful expression of the creative activity of the imagination, "the absence of the imagination had / Itself to be imagined" (*CP* 503). The poem seems to uncover the plain sense of things through a kind of creative anticreativity, the imagination imagining its own absence. Though they do so in different ways, both "The Poem That Took the Place of a Mountain" and "The Plain Sense of Things" explore how the creative activity of the imagination might expose what it had in earlier poems covered over.

It is by means of a construct, "There it was, word for word," that the mind gazes on the flux of reality, the ocean, in "The Poem That Took the Place of a Mountain." In "Things of August," canto II, words are also thought of as the means by which the mind can encounter the outer.

> We make, although inside an egg,
> Variations on the words spread sail.
>
> . . . .
>
> Spread sail, we say spread white, spread way.
> The shell is a shore. The egg of the sea
>
> And the egg of the sky are in shells, in walls, in skins
> And the egg of the earth lies deep within an egg.
>
> Spread outward. Crack the round dome. Break through.
> Have liberty not as the air within a grave
>
> Or down a well. Breathe freedom, oh, my native,
> In the space of horizons that neither love nor hate.
>
> (CP 490)

Stevens does not envision language in canto II of "Things of August" as the material out of which he will construct a vantage point from which to gaze on the outer, as he does in "The Poem That Took the Place of a Mountain." Rather, he views language as a destructive force that will allow him to break free to the world outside. Words, once set in motion, "words spread sail," continue to "Spread outward" until they crack through the shell of the egg, an image used, as in "The Auroras of Autumn," to symbolize the world constructed by the mind, and we "Breathe freedom . . . / In the space of horizons that neither love nor hate," that is, until we encounter a universe stripped of all human myths, whether these myths view the universe as benevolent, "love," or malevolent, "hate." Because it shows the mind being directed toward the outer through destructive activity, this canto of "Things of August" may recall "The Snow Man." In "The Snow Man," however, words are an obstruction to the mind's encounter with the outer. The first reduction in that poem is the removal of the language with which the mind has beautifully decorated the winter scene. In canto II of "Things of August," in contrast, words are the vehicle by which the mind reaches toward the outer.

While breaking through the shell of the egg is seen as an act that liberates the mind in "Things of August," the destruction of the mind's constructs is not always seen in such exhilarating terms. In "The Beginning," the loss of these constructs evokes an elegiac response.

> So summer comes in the end to these few stains
> And the rust and rot of the door through which she went.
>
> The house is empty. But here is where she sat
> To comb her dewy hair, a touchless light,
>
> Perplexed by its darker iridescences.
> This was the glass in which she used to look
>
> At the moment's being, without history,
> The self of summer perfectly perceived,
>
> And feel its country gayety and smile
> And be surprised and tremble, hand and lip.
>
> This is the chair from which she gathered up
> Her dress, the carefulest, commodious weave
>
> Inwoven by a weaver to twelve bells . . .
> The dress is lying, cast-off, on the floor.
>
> Now, the first tutoyers of tragedy
> Speak softly, to begin with, in the eaves.
>
> (CP 427–28)

The fictive dress of summer that is "Inwoven by a weaver to twelve bells" recalls an image that Stevens uses throughout his career—that of the poet as weaver. In "To the One of Fictive Music," addressing the beloved, reality, he writes that "of the music summoned by the birth / That separates us from the wind and sea, / . . . none / Gives motion to perfection more serene /

Than yours . . . / In the laborious weaving that you wear" (*CP* 87). The image is repeated in "Notes," where Ozymandias speaks of the fiction that "weaves" from the heart and mind. And it is recalled in "The World as Meditation" through Stevens' allusion to the *Odyssey*, in which Penelope weaves and unravels a tapestry while she waits for Ulysses. Stevens' own Penelope, thinking of her beloved Ulysses, weaves her image of him by "Repeating his name with its patient syllables" (*CP* 521). "The Beginning" also echoes motifs that are associated with weaving. The summer as a being "without history" recalls the idea that every fictive weaving offers a new discovery of reality, that each is a beginning, "without history." In "Notes," Nanzia Nunzio asks Ozymandias to "Clothe me entire in the final filament, / So that I tremble with such love so known" (*CP* 396). In "The Beginning," the self of summer, "perfectly perceived," will also "tremble," and does so, at least in part, for the same reason that Nanzia Nunzio trembles, from "such love so known" expressed through the poet's fictive weaving. Typically, an elegy begins with an expression of loss and ends with an expression of consolation or renewal. "The Beginning" follows this ancient pattern. The loss of the fictive dress of summer, "The dress is lying, cast-off, on the floor," gives way, as the title implies, to a sense of renewal. Discarding earlier imaginings is not an ending but a beginning, the start of a new poetic mode, tragedy—"Now, the first tutoyers of tragedy / Speak softly, to begin with, in the eaves" (*CP* 428).[3]

Stevens rewrites "The Beginning" in larger terms in "Puella Parvula." Like "The Beginning," "Puella Parvula" bids farewell to summer's imagined garment. "Every thread of summer is at last unwoven" (*CP* 456). The images in "Puella Parvula," like the images in "The Beginning," recall earlier poems. Marie Boroff has noted that "The elephant on the roof and its elephantine blaring, / The bloody lion in the yard at night or ready to spring" (*CP* 456) recall the elephant and the lion of "Notes," section I, canto V, while the flame in the final stanza of "Puella Parvula" recalls the aurora borealis of "Auroras." "He opens the door of his house / On flames" (*CP* 416–17).[4] "Puella Parvula" differs from "The Beginning," though, in the strength of its renewal. The quiet,

"Speak softly, to begin with," of "The Beginning" is replaced in "Puella Parvula" by the trumpeted power of the imagination. "Over all these the mighty imagination triumphs / Like a trumpet" (*CP* 456).

While unweaving is seen in "The Beginning" and "Puella Parvula" as a leave-taking that leads to a renewing, in "In a Bad Time," reduction leads only to the contemplation of creative activity.

> For him cold's glacial beauty is his fate.
> Without understanding, he belongs to it
>
> . . . .
>
> What has he that becomes his heart's strong core?
>
> He has his poverty and nothing more.
> His poverty becomes his heart's strong core—
> A forgetfulness of summer at the pole.
>
> (*CP* 426–27)

Stevens had contemplated a similar fate fifteen years earlier in "The American Sublime."

> And the sublime comes down
> To the spirit itself,
>
> The spirit and space,
> The empty spirit
> In vacant space.
>
> (*CP* 131)

He asks in the poem what sustains the spirit, given this emptiness. "What wine does one drink? / What bread does one eat?" (*CP* 131). These questions, unanswered in "The American Sublime," receive their response in "In a Bad Time." Emptiness itself sustains the spirit. "His poverty becomes his heart's strong core" (*CP* 427). Perhaps it is the strength drawn from poverty that leads to the contemplation, though not enactment, of renewed speech at the end of the poem, where Stevens instructs Melpomene, the muse of tragedy, to "Speak loftier lines" (*CP* 427).

Even this hint of renewal is absent from Stevens' very late poem, "Vacancy in the Park."

> March . . . Someone has walked across the snow,
> Someone looking for he knows not what.
>
> It is like a boat that has pulled away
> From a shore at night and disappeared.
>
> It is like a guitar left on a table
> By a woman, who has forgotten it.
>
> It is like the feeling of a man
> Come back to see a certain house.
>
> The four winds blow through the rustic arbor,
> Under its mattresses of vines.
>
> (*CP* 511)

Earlier, in "The Sun This March," Stevens looked at March as a brightening, a turning of the spirit, a beginning. "The exceeding brightness of this early sun / Makes me conceive how dark I have become, / And re-illumines things that used to turn / To gold in broadest blue, and be a part / Of a turning spirit in an earlier self" (*CP* 133–34). March will again be a time of stirrings in "Not Ideas about the Thing but the Thing Itself," where Stevens writes that "At the earliest ending of winter, / In March, a scrawny cry from outside / . . . was / A chorister whose c preceded the choir. / It was part of the colossal sun" (*CP* 534). "Vacancy in the Park" rejects this earlier and later sense of warmth and beginning in March. The poem conveys only a sense of absence. In the first couplet, the person is unidentified, is not present, and even the object of the search is unknown. This sense of absence is amplified in the following three similes. The boat has not only pulled away, it has disappeared. The guitar has been left behind, and even its memory has been obliterated. In the simile of the fourth couplet, the past, represented by the house the man has come to see, seems opaque, unknowable. The final image of the poem, the wind blowing through the rustic arbor, recalls the image of the wind "blowing in the same bare place" in "The Snow Man." The arbor provides no shelter from the wind, which blows through it from all four directions. Absence in "Vacancy in the Park," though, does not evoke a sublime response from the spirit, as it does in "The Snow Man." Unlike "In a Bad Time," the poem does not suggest that the spirit can draw strength from its poverty. Nor does the poem express the kind of stoic acceptance of the cold that Stevens describes in the last stanza of "Like Decorations in a Nigger Cemetery."

> Can all men, together, avenge
> One of the leaves that have fallen in autumn?
> But the wise man avenges by building his city in snow.
>   (*CP* 158)

The chill wind at the close of "Vacancy in the Park" elicits neither spiritual nor creative stirrings.

Both creative and destructive artistic activity can direct the mind in Stevens' later work toward the outer. The two activities can be seen, for example, in "The Poem That Took the Place of a Mountain" and in "Things of August," canto II. In the former poem, the mind, through the fiction it creates, gazes at the ocean, whereas in the latter poem the mind uses words to break through the shell to horizons that neither love nor hate. In "The Countryman" Stevens considers a third way in which the mind might encounter the outer, through the absence of any activity, whether creative or destructive. "Swatara . . . / A countryman walks beside you."

> He broods of neither cap nor cape,
> But only of your swarthy motion,
> But always of the swarthy water,
> Of which Swatara is the breathing,

The name. He does not speak beside you.
He is there because he wants to be
And because being there in the heavy hills
And along the moving of the water—

Being there is being in a place,
As of a character everywhere,
The place of a swarthy presence moving,
Slowly, to the look of a swarthy name.
                                        (CP 428–29)

In this poem, as in several of the late poems, Stevens uses the river
as a symbol of being. In "This Solitude of Cataracts" he writes of
"the flecked river, / Which kept flowing and never the same way
twice, flowing / Through many places, as if it stood still in one"
(CP 424). In "Metaphor as Degeneration" Stevens writes that
"The swarthy water / That flows round the earth and through the
skies, / Twisting among universal spaces, / Is not Swatara. It is
being" (CP 444). And in the penultimate poem of the *Collected
Poems*, "The River of Rivers in Connecticut," Stevens describes
"a river, an unnamed flowing, / . . . The river that flows nowhere,
like a sea" (CP 533). Though in "The Countryman" Swatara is
"the breathing, / The name" of this river of being, it is not by
naming (or by unnaming) that Stevens evokes its presence. The
persona of the poem is silent. "He does not speak beside you." He
meditates, "broods," on the motion of the water. Silence can be
thought of as an eschewing of artistic activity, whether construc-
tive or destructive. With silence, words neither "spread sail" until
they break through the shell to the outer nor do they, "word for
word," build a mountain that offers a view of the ocean. It is
through this silent meditation on being, and not through creative
activity, that Stevens becomes in the poem a "countryman" of the
great river.
     The silent meditation on being in "The Countryman" looks
forward to "St. John and the Back-Ache." St. John argues that
presence is felt in the effect made by "A sudden color on the sea"
and is not evoked by the "big-brushed green" (CP 437); that is, it

is not evoked by the painter's brush. It is felt in the sudden change from summer to autumn and not in the artistic expression of this change, "the unravelling of her yellow shift" (*CP* 437). This unraveling recalls the unraveling of the fictive dress of summer in both "The Beginning," "The dress is lying, cast-off, on the floor" (*CP* 428), and "Puella Parvula," "Every thread of summer is at last unwoven" (*CP* 456). The persona Stevens describes in "The Countryman" evokes being by meditating on it. In "St. John and the Back-Ache," however, Stevens considers a different relation between thinking and being. Here, "Presence" "fills the being *before* the mind can think" (*CP* 436; emphasis added).

A fourth way in which Stevens evokes the outer is expressed in "The River of Rivers in Connecticut." That poem, as Helen Vendler writes, is a "self-adjuration, by an old man[,] . . . to write more and yet more poems, calling the unnamed river by more and more names."[5] The flux of being in "River of Rivers" is indistinguishable from the particulars of the landscape. The "great river"

> is not to be seen beneath the appearances
> That tell of it. The steeple at Farmington
> Stands glistening and Haddam shines and sways.
> (*CP* 533)

Stevens' namings here are very different from his namings in "Notes toward a Supreme Fiction." To name in "Notes" is to bring forth an "invented world." In contrast, naming in "The River of Rivers" evokes being directly. Stevens' creative activity in "The River of Rivers" is also different from the kind of creativity expressed in "The Poem That Took the Place of a Mountain," where the construction of a fiction does not directly name being, but rather allows the self to gaze upon it. In calling the river of being by more and more names, Stevens continues in this poem the recitation he began in "Large Red Man Reading":

> he sat there reading, from out of the purple tabulae,
> The outlines of being and its expressings, the syllables of its
>   law:

Poesis, poesis, the literal characters, the vatic lines.

(CP 424)

In neither "St. John" nor in "The Countryman" do we see the self exercising its creative power. "St. John" focuses on the moment "before the mind can think," while the persona in "The Countryman" does not utter a single word. The absence of creative activity in the self, though, does not necessarily mean that the self is incapable of creating. Stevens often affirms the creative power of the self even as he writes about the difficulty of expressing that power. In "Auroras," for example, the "scholar of one candle" sees the aurora borealis and "feels afraid." The fear expressed in the canto is not caused by doubts about whether the self has creative power. It does, the "one candle." The fear is that the greater magnitude of nature's creativity will overwhelm the expression of that power in the self. Stevens, that is, fears that the self will lose what Bloom, commenting on "Auroras," calls the "great battle of the mind against the sky."[6] In "The Man Whose Pharynx Was Bad," the issue, again, is not whether the self has creative power but the stultifying effect of monotony on the exercise of that power. The same relationship between creativity and monotony is implied in "Notes," section II, "It Must Change." In what must be one of his darkest poems, "Looking across the Fields and Watching the Birds Fly," Stevens looks not at threats to the self's creative activity, but at whether the self does in fact have creative power of its own.

Mr. Homburg begins his exploration of this issue by observing that the human process of "thinking away the grass, the trees, the clouds" is only what nature does and by hypothesizing that nature is a kind of mental activity or meditational process.

> [T]here may be
> A pensive nature, a mechanical
> And slightly detestable *operandum,* free
>
> From man's ghost, larger and yet a little like,
> Without his literature and without his gods . . .

(CP 517–18)

Stevens writes in *The Necessary Angel* that Focillon's *The Life of Forms in Art* is "one of the really remarkable books of the day" (*NA* 46), and Stevens' description of nature as a cosmic imagination or meditation may be his adaptation of Focillon's idea of the "mobile life of external forms operating according to imaginative laws" that are completely independent of the human mind.[7] Though nature operates in "Looking across the Fields" independently of the mind, we are not separate from nature.

> No doubt we live beyond ourselves in air,
>
> In an element that does not do for us,
> So well, that which we do for ourselves, too big,
> A thing not planned for imagery or belief,
>
> Not one of the masculine myths we used to make.
> (*CP* 518)   ·

We "live beyond ourselves in air"; that is, we have a material existence in the world that is independent of, "beyond," our constructs about reality. The real "does not do for us, / So well, that which we do for ourselves." What we do for ourselves, as Nietzsche observes, is make reality habitable through the creation of constructs. "Pensive nature" in "Looking across the Fields" creates nothing that helps us accommodate ourselves to reality. Indifferent to our needs, it is a "slightly detestable *operandum*." The reality that we inhabit and that is beyond our formulations about it, "Not one of the masculine myths we used to make," is one of random and formless change, "A transparency through which the swallow weaves, / Without any form or any sense of form" (*CP* 518). Our knowledge and understanding of this changing reality is limited to our physical responses to it, "What we know in what we see, what we feel in what / We hear" (*CP* 518). The material quality of existence is beyond any supernatural, "mystic," disputation. It defines "what we are." Thinking, too, is seen as an integral part of the total natural process. "And what we think, a breathing like the wind, / A moving part of a motion, a discovery / Part of a discovery, a change part of a change, / A sharing of color and being part of it" (*CP* 518). The process of nature is the source of our thoughts, which reflect its motion.

> We think, then, as the sun shines or does not.
> We think as wind skitters on a pond in a field
>
> Or we put mantles on our words because
> The same wind, rising and rising, makes a sound
> Like the last muting of winter as it ends.
>
> (*CP* 518–19)

Mr. Homburg concludes his speculation by reversing his opening hypothesis. Reality is not "pensive" but is merely making an "affectation" of mind.

> The spirit comes from the body of the world,
> Or so Mr. Homburg thought: the body of a world
> Whose blunt laws make an affectation of mind,
>
> The mannerism of nature caught in a glass
> And there become a spirit's mannerism.
>
> (*CP* 519)

Our spirit comes from nature, "the body of the world," whose laws affect mind. This mannerism of nature is caught in a glass, that is, mirrored in the human mind, and becomes the mannerism of the human spirit.[8] But either of Mr. Homburg's propositions strip the self of its own creative power. Whether the human spirit is seen as reflecting nature as mind or as reflecting nature making an affectation of mind, it is subsumed within the natural process. As Milton Bates writes, "In Mr. Homburg's scheme of things, human thought is merely a function of nature's mechanical 'thinking' and the poet's verse an automatic and predictable response to natural stimuli."[9] There is no place in Mr. Homburg's meditation for individual creative activity. The "new scholar," reflecting on this "fantasia," "seeks / For a human that can be accounted for" (*CP* 519) and seeks in vain.

The issue explored in "Looking across the Fields and Watching the Birds Fly," that of the self's creative power, had been raised earlier in "The Man with the Blue Guitar," canto XIX. Writing to Renato Poggioli about the canto, Stevens comments, "I want, as a poet, to be that in nature, which constitutes nature's very self. I want to be nature in the form of a man, with all the resources of nature=I want to be the lion in the lute" (*L* 790). "Looking across the Fields" explores a similar proposition. Thinking and creating in that poem express "nature's very self." "We think, then, as the sun shines or does not. / . . . we put mantles on our words because / The same wind, rising and rising, makes a sound / Like the last muting of winter as it ends" (*CP* 518–19). But in canto XIX of "The Man with the Blue Guitar," Stevens envisions a kind of individual creative activity that is absent from "Looking across the Fields." "I want to face my parent and be his true part. I want to face nature the way two lions face one another—the lion in the lute facing the lion locked in stone. I want, as a man of the imagination, to write poetry with all the power of a monster equal in strength to that of the monster about whom I write. I want man's imagination to be completely adequate in the face of reality" (*L* 790). What the scholar in "Looking across the Fields" seeks but cannot find is the imagination that is "completely adequate in the face of reality."

The way in which the self is questioned in "Looking across the Fields" is very different from the way it is questioned in either the irony of detachment or the irony of engagement. For Hegel and Kierkegaard, the self, to be real, must recognize and accept a reality that exists apart from the self. When the ironist negates reality, he brings the self into question because he destroys the ground of the self's own actuality. This challenge to the self, implied in all of Stevens' poems in which the self escapes from the real, is voiced in canto XV of "Blue Guitar." "Things as they are have been destroyed. / Have I?" (*CP* 173). It is not the self's reality but the stability of its identity that is questioned in Schlegel's concept of irony. Schlegel describes the ironist as engaged in a never-ending process of "self-destruction" and "self-creation" (*LF* 147, no. 37). Self-destruction occurs when the mind skeptically examines existing concepts of the self. But even as the mind casts off these concepts, it creates and commits itself to new ones. Because this process is an ongoing one, the self can never *be* a self. It can never acquire a final and unchanging identity. It can only continue to *become* a self. While both of the senses of irony described above challenge the self, neither asks, as "Looking across the Fields" does, whether the self has any creative power of its own.

Two poems in Stevens' late work can be read as responses to the conception of the self in "Looking across the Fields." Both reject the idea that the self has no creative power and yet both, like "Looking," view self and world as aspects of a single, dynamic universe. The first, "The World as Meditation," can be seen as a direct answer to the search by the new scholar in "Looking across the Fields" for "a human that can be accounted for."

Is it Ulysses that approaches from the east,
The interminable adventurer? The trees are mended.
That winter is washed away. Someone is moving

On the horizon and lifting himself up above it.
A form of fire approaches the cretonnes of Penelope,
Whose mere savage presence awakens the world in which
    she dwells.

She has composed, so long, a self with which to welcome
    him,
Companion to his self for her, which she imagined,
Two in a deep-founded sheltering, friend and dear friend.

The trees had been mended, as an essential exercise
In an inhuman meditation, larger than her own.
No winds like dogs watched over her at night.

She wanted nothing he could not bring her by coming
    alone.
She wanted no fetchings. His arms would be her necklace
And her belt, the final fortune of their desire.

But was it Ulysses? Or was it only the warmth of the sun
On her pillow? The thought kept beating in her like her
    heart.

The two kept beating together. It was only day.

It was Ulysses and it was not. Yet they had met,
Friend and dear friend and a planet's encouragement.
The barbarous strength within her would never fail.

She would talk a little to herself as she combed her hair,
Repeating his name with its patient syllables,
Never forgetting him that kept coming constantly so near.

                                              (*CP* 520–21)

Penelope's reimagining of the world recalls "Notes" in several ways. First, the meeting between Ulysses and Penelope is seen as an intimate one. "His arms would be her necklace / And her belt, the final fortune of their desire." These words almost directly repeat Nanzia Nunzio's words to Ozymandias. "I am the spouse. She took her necklace off / And laid it in the sand. As I am, I am / The spouse. She opened her stone-studded belt" (*CP* 395). Second, as in the Ozymandias canto, the process of reimagining in "The World as Meditation" is seen as a never-ending one. Penelope talks to herself, "Repeating his name with its patient syllables, / Never forgetting him that kept coming constantly so near." Her repetition of his name, the present participle, "repeating," emphasizing the ongoing nature of this activity, is the same kind of endless fictive weaving that Ozymandias speaks of. "A fictive covering / Weaves always glistening from the heart and mind" (*CP* 396). Third, though Ulysses keeps coming constantly so near, he also seems to be present. "Yet they had met, / Friend and dear friend." Penelope's desire for Ulysses' presence seems to be satisfied even as it remains unfulfilled. That her desire is satisfied even as it is endlessly perpetuated by her namings of him recalls the idea, expressed in the Ozymandias canto of "Notes," that a fiction both satisfies desire and delays its satisfaction. In both "Notes" and "The World as Meditation," fictions are prothalamions that are their own epithalamions.

But the act of reimagining in "The World as Meditation" is also very different from Stevens' earlier reimaginings. Instead of creating a fiction that is accepted as the real, Penelope asks whether her composition is anything *other* than the real. "But was it Ulysses? Or was it only the warmth of the sun / On her pillow?" This is the question that "Looking across the Fields and Watching the Birds Fly" answered in the negative. There, the composition is only "the warmth of the sun." The spirit, coming from the body of the world, mechanically repeats nature's movement. "We think . . . as the sun shines" (*CP* 518). In "The World as Meditation" Stevens associates Penelope with nature. Her "barbarous strength" recalls the "green barbarism" (*CP* 31) of Yucatan in section II of "The Comedian as the Letter C." Though Penelope is associated with nature, Stevens carefully avoids making her meditation *only* the warmth of the sun. Her meditation is inseparable from nature and yet her reimagining of the world is her own individual composition. "It was Ulysses and it was not." That is, it was her own construct, Ulysses, and it was not her construct; it was the warmth of the sun. Her meditation and the "inhuman meditation" of nature are inseparable and yet are not identical. Individual creative activity remains an irreducible element within the total process of reality. Because she expresses this irreducible creative power of the self, Penelope might be thought of as the human figure whom the new scholar seeks in "Looking across the Fields and Watching the Birds Fly."

The view of creativity expressed in "The World as Meditation," that individual creative activity is inseparable from but not identical with the overall process of nature, was anticipated in the final canto of "An Ordinary Evening in New Haven."

> These are the edgings and inchings of final form,
> The swarming activities of the formulae
> Of statement, directly and indirectly getting at,
>
> Like an evening evoking the spectrum of violet,
> A philosopher practicing scales on his piano,
> A woman writing a note and tearing it up.
>
> It is not in the premise that reality
> Is a solid. It may be a shade that traverses
> A dust, a force that traverses a shade.
>
> (*CP* 488–89)

As in "The World as Meditation," Stevens does not focus in "Ordinary Evening," canto XXXI, on the result of creative activity, the "leaves" that "came and covered the high rock," as he puts it in "The Rock" (*CP* 526). He focuses rather on the activity of creation. Each of the images in the penultimate stanza of the canto conveys a sense of "Flickings," "general fidget," "edgings and inchings"—the swarming activity of the formulae of statement and not statement itself. Evening becomes not a single color, violet, but is differentiated into "the spectrum of violet." Practicing scales is an endless, repetitive activity. A woman is writing a note and tears it up, perhaps to start again. The sense of activity is emphasized by the verbs in the stanza. All are present participles— "evoking," "practicing," "writing," "tearing." Both natural activity, "an evening evoking," and human activity, "A philosopher practicing . . . / A woman writing," are seen as part of a total reality that itself is a force, in motion. Reality "may be a shade that traverses / A dust, a force that traverses a shade." Though Stevens suggests in canto XXXI of "Ordinary Evening," as he does in "The World as Meditation," that creative activity is part of a larger process of change, canto XXXI differs from "The World as Meditation" in the way in which this view is expressed. In canto XXXI there is no debate about whether individual creative activity reflects an inner or an outer reality. "But was it Ulysses? Or was it only the warmth of the sun / On her pillow?" The question does not even arise. Rather, human activity in canto XXXI is simply accepted as part of, but not identical with, the moving force of nature.

Stevens' view of poetry in canto XXXI of "Ordinary Evening" might be seen as a response to the self-criticism he had expressed earlier in the poem.

> This endlessly elaborating poem
> Displays the theory of poetry,
> As the life of poetry. A more severe,
>
> More harassing master would extemporize
> Subtler, more urgent proof that the theory

Of poetry is the theory of life,

As it is, in the intricate evasions of as.
(CP 486)

How is "as" an evasion? Simile posits a relation between two things while denying that the relation is one of identity. As Jacqueline Brogan writes in her study, *Stevens and Simile,* "In simile . . . one thing is said only to resemble another, never to *be* another; the two are always two and yet are joined *as* one by that resemblance."[10] Simile, then, simultaneously gestures toward identity, unity, and closure while forever deferring or evading them. But Stevens does not mean by "the intricate evasions of as" that unity, identity, and closure are evaded by the single figure of simile. "As" refers to the entire process of figuration or invention. Figuration is the ongoing edgings and inchings of final form that never reach final form. How, then, is figuration as postponement and delay "life as it is"? To delay closure indefinitely means that there is ongoing movement, and, as Stevens tells us in *Harmonium* in the simplest possible way, "Life Is Motion" (CP 83). Stevens' view of figuration as part of the ongoing process of reality, a view he expresses in canto XXXI of "Ordinary Evening," can be seen as his attempt to offer subtler, more urgent proof that the theory of poetry is indeed the "theory of life, / As it is, in the intricate evasions of as."

The focus on the outer in the late poetry can be seen as a turning away from that aspect of the irony of engagement in which the mind, through its constructs, situates itself in the real. Other aspects of Stevens' irony of engagement, though, are seen in the late work. Both "The Beginning" and "Puella Parvula," for example, bid farewell to earlier imaginings, and both anticipate further activity by the imagination. Neither treats us to an instance of this activity, yet the pattern of reduction and renewal is a familiar one.

Other late poems, however, do not express this pattern of reduction and reimagining. "Things of August," canto II, and "The Countryman," for example, are poems of reduction without renewal. One uses the power of words to break free of our conceptual limitations to the outer, while the other encounters the outer through silence. "In a Bad Time" and "Vacancy in the Park" are also poems of reduction. These poems, however, do not show the mind in the act of reduction. Rather, they begin in a reduced state: poverty, vacancy, cold. Schlegel describes the ironist as one who, by criticizing the mind's own limited creations, gains a feeling for the universe. "We must rise above our own love and be able to destroy in our thoughts what we adore; if we cannot do this, we lack . . . the feeling for the universe."[11] These late poems have an affiliation with this aspect of Schlegel's concept of irony because through reduction they turn the mind to the outer and allow it to gain a "feeling for the universe." This turn to the outer through reduction has been seen before in the mind's beholding of "the nothing that is" in "The Snow Man." Stevens' late poems, though, show how varied his response is to a universe without human projections. In "In a Bad Time," for example, the bare universe is seen as a source of strength. "His poverty becomes his heart's strong core" (*CP* 427). In canto II of "Things of August" the mind's encounter with horizons stripped of all myths is an exhilarating moment of freedom, while in "The Beginning," the absence of the mind's constructs, "The dress is lying, cast-off, on the floor," evokes an elegiac response.

For Schlegel the mind's creative and destructive activity is an analogue to the natural process of creation and renewal. As Anne Mellor writes, "Having ironically acknowledged the fictiveness of his own patternings of human experience, [the ironist] romantically engages in the creative process of life by eagerly constructing new forms, new myths. And these new fictions and self-concepts bear with them the seeds of their own destruction. They too die to give way to new patterns, in a never-ending process that becomes an analogue for life itself."[12] This aspect of Schlegel's concept of irony is not explored in the earlier poetry but is recalled in poems such as "The World as Meditation" and "An Ordinary Evening in New Haven," canto XXXI, where the mind's individual creative and destructive activity is explicitly seen as replicating these processes in the natural world. Though "Notes" expresses a sense of ongoing creation and destruction, the emphasis in that poem is on the "invented world" and not on linking the process of invention to the universe at large, as it is in "The World as Meditation" and canto XXXI of "Ordinary Evening." From this perspective, "The Poem That Took the Place of a Mountain" can be seen as a poem of transition, one that looks back to "Notes" and forward to "The World as Meditation." Like "Notes," it focuses on the result of creative activity, the fiction created by the mind. Unlike "Notes," however, it does not view a fiction as a construct in which the mind finds its home. The ocean, chaotic reality, is identified in this poem as the mind's "unique and solitary home." In "The Poem That Took the Place of a Mountain," as in "The World as Meditation," the gaze of the mind is directed outward. In "Mountain," though, the activity of creating a fiction is not seen as an analogue to the dynamic flux of nature, as it is in "The World as Meditation." Stevens builds the construct in "Mountain" simply to gaze at his "unique and solitary home." In "The World as Meditation," in contrast, Stevens shows us that through the process of creating a fiction, the mind discovers that it is at home in the ever-changing universe.

Afterword: Romantic Irony and Postmodernism

> It is not necessary to slay your father, time will slay him, that is a virtual certainty. Your true task lies elsewhere.
>
> Your true task, as a son, is to reproduce every one of the enormities touched upon in this manual, but in attenuated form. You must become your father, but a paler, weaker version of him.
>
> —Donald Barthelme

Romantic irony in both its Schlegelian and its Hegelian and Kierkegaardian senses swirls through the literature, philosophy, and criticism of the fin de siècle and modern periods. Huysmans, early Eliot, Babbitt, and Glicksberg, for instance, express (and in the case of Babbitt and Glicksberg excoriate) the latter sense of irony, while Frost, Yeats, and Nietzsche express an irony that is affiliated with Schlegel. Stevens' work expresses both of these senses of irony and the irresoluble conflict between them. Is romantic irony, though, also part of the postmodern landscape? One response to this question is suggested by a Donald Barthelme short story. The title of the story, "Kierkegaard Unfair to Schlegel," is itself revealing. Barthelme does not merely name Kierkegaard and Schlegel, he describes their relation, one of misinterpretation and conflict. The title suggests, then, that Barthelme's interest lies in the differences between these two great theorists of irony.

Kierkegaard's view of irony is taken up first.

Q: You are an ironist.
A: It's useful.

Q: How is it useful?
A: Well, let me tell you a story.[1]

The story A tells is of living in a rented house in Colorado. The house had "what seemed to be hundreds of closets and we immediately discovered that these closets were filled to overflowing with all kinds of play equipment" (163). A jokes about "the presence of all this impedimenta" (163). His joke, however, has an amazing effect. "The shuffleboard sticks, the barbells, balls of all kinds—my joke has, in effect, thrown them out of the world. An amazing magical power!" (164). He becomes "curious about how [his] irony actually works—how it functions" (164). He picks up a copy of Kierkegaard's *The Concept of Irony* and gives in mock academic fashion (even quoting from, with page numbers, Capel's translation of *The Concept of Irony*), a summary of Kierkegaard's views on the subjectivity of the ironist, his infinite absolute negativity, and the "animosity" between the ironist and existence. According to A, Kierkegaard believes that in *Lucinde* "Schlegel has constructed an actuality which is superior to the historical actuality and a substitute for it" (165). Hence, *Lucinde* becomes a "victory over the world" and not a "reconciliation" with it (165). A remarks that he finds "it hard to persuade [himself] that the relation of Schlegel's novel to actuality is what Kierkegaard says it is," and he comments that "Kierkegaard is here unfair to Schlegel" (165).

But Schlegel is not the only one to whom Kierkegaard may be unfair. Kierkegaard's description of irony, its power to displace phenomenal reality, is an accurate account of A's irony, which, as he says, throws things "out of the world" (164). A realizes that Kierkegaard would also disapprove of his irony, and in response to this disapproval, he tries to "annihilate" Kierkegaard. "But mostly I am trying to annihilate Kierkegaard in order to deal with his disapproval. Q: Of Schlegel? A: Of me" (166).

Barthelme offers in the story a second description of irony, one that does not suggest that "Quote the whole of existence has become alien to the ironic subject unquote page 276" (165).

A: But I love my irony.
Q: Does it give you pleasure?
A: A poor . . . A rather unsatisfactory. . . .
Q: The unavoidable tendency of everything particular to
    emphasize its own particularity.
A: Yes.

(167)

The words, "Q: Does it give you pleasure? A: A poor . . . A rather
unsatisfactory," were spoken earlier in the story. A has described
an imagined encounter with a girl on a train. Q interrupts.

Q: That's a very common fantasy.
A: All my fantasies are extremely ordinary.
Q: Does it give you pleasure?
A: A poor . . . A rather unsatisfactory . . .

(161)

The repetition links irony and fantasy, that is, the creative power
of the artist. This second description of irony does not express an
antagonism between the artist and existence. Far from throwing
things "out of the world," irony here points toward and empha-
sizes the actual, the "tendency of everything particular to empha-
size its own particularity" (167). A commented earlier that he
could not persuade himself that the relation between Schlegel's
novel and actuality is one of animosity, but he does not tell us
what he thinks the relation is. This later exchange between Q and
A indirectly defines A's view of the relation between *Lucinde* and
existence.

Barthelme's story not only echoes the Schlegelian and the
Hegelian and Kierkegaardian senses of romantic irony, but pre-
sents them in the same relation that they are presented in Stevens
and in modernism in general, in unresolved contradiction. One
response to being uncomfortable in the world, and A remarks that
the house in Colorado is "uncomfortable" (164), is to ironize the
world out of existence, to throw things "out of the world."

Barthelme does not deny either the existence of this type of irony or that, as he says, "It's useful" (163). He does, however, also present a radically different sense of irony, one in which the mind turns to the particulars of existence.

The presence of, and conflict between, these two senses of irony can be seen in other contemporary writers. Alan Wilde argues that the postmodern ironist is not "poised judicially above the world he surveys," but is "typically involved *in* . . . that world."[2] The ironist's attitude toward the random and contingent universe he or she inhabits is one of acceptance. Wilde argues further that while surfictionist writers such as Raymond Federman and Ronald Sukenick express this sense of irony, they also, though in covert fashion, withdraw from and displace the world. "In short, even as they revel in the world's chaos, these writers deny the world its specificity and provocations. . . . Fictions like *Take It or Leave It* and 'The Death of the Novel' . . . intend suspensiveness, indeed proclaim their acceptance of contingency and absurdity."[3] But "in the covert, substitutive orders they create, the Surfictionists recall . . . nothing so much as the aesthetic manifestos of the early decades of the century."[4] Though in a more "covert" way than Barthelme, Sukenick and Federman express both of the senses of irony that Barthelme describes in "Kierkegaard Unfair to Schlegel." One turns toward the world, the other away from it. And as in Barthelme, these two senses of irony remain in opposition.

The conflict between these two ironic stances can also be seen in contemporary poets such as John Ashbery. David Shapiro has shrewdly observed that "In Ashbery's work there is neither unmastered nor mastered irony. There is the constant process of *mastering irony*."[5] That is, Ashbery is neither completely withdrawn from the world, "unmastered irony," nor completely situated in the world, "mastered irony." ("When irony has first been mastered," Kierkegaard writes, "it undertakes a movement directly opposed to that wherein it proclaimed its life as unmastered. Irony now limits, renders finite, defines, and thereby yields truth, actuality, and content" [*CI* 338].) The two ironic stances remain in opposition, and Ashbery's poetry explores the space between them, "mastering irony." This exploration of the space between an irony of detachment and an irony of engagement points to one of Ashbery's affiliations with Stevens, whose work also explores the space between these two ironic poles.

We are too close to the literature of our time to be able to identify with any sense of assurance its central concerns. Barthelme's intricate juxtaposition of an irony that throws things out of the world with one that turns to the world, Sukenick's and Federman's expression of both an irony of engagement and an irony of detachment, and Ashbery's ongoing exploration of the space between an irony that lifts the self above the world and one that situates the self in the world—all suggest that, whatever its final significance, the conflict between the Schlegelian and the Kierkegaardian and Hegelian senses of romantic irony is at least part of the matrix of postmodern literature.

Notes

Stevens' work is abbreviated in my text as follows:

CP   *The Collected Poems of Wallace Stevens*. New York: Alfred A. Knopf, 1954.
L   *Letters of Wallace Stevens*. Ed. Holly Stevens. New York: Alfred A. Knopf, 1966.
NA   *The Necessary Angel: Essays on Reality and the Imagination*. New York: Alfred A. Knopf, 1951.
OP   *Opus Posthumous*. Ed. Milton A. Bates. Rev. Ed. New York: Alfred A. Knopf, 1989.
SP   *Souvenirs and Prophecies: The Young Wallace Stevens*. Ed. Holly Stevens. New York: Alfred A. Knopf, 1977.

Introduction

1. For a discussion of how Aiken and Untermeyer view irony in Stevens see Melita Schaum, *Wallace Stevens and the Critical Schools* (Tuscaloosa: University of Alabama Press, 1988), 33–56. In *After the New Criticism* (Chicago: University of Chicago Press, 1980), Frank Lentricchia describes the ironic self-consciousness that, in his view, leaves Stevens enclosed within the mind. (Cited hereafter in my text as *ANC*.) For J. Hillis Miller, Stevens' work expresses an infinitely unstable irony that points to the limits of human knowledge and that rejects the possibility of any fixed meaning. See "Stevens' Rock and Criticism as Cure," *Georgia Review* 30, nos. 1–2 (spring–summer 1976): 5–31, 330–48. Cited hereafter in my text as *SR*.

2. Lilian R. Furst, *Fictions of Romantic Irony* (Cambridge: Harvard University Press, 1984), 239.

3. D. C. Muecke, *The Compass of Irony* (London: Methuen, 1969), 182.

4. Søren Kierkegaard, *The Concept of Irony with Constant Reference to Socrates,* trans. Lee M. Capel (Bloomington: Indiana University Press, 1965), 292. Cited hereafter in my text as *CI*.

5. Irving Babbitt, *Rousseau and Romanticism* (Boston: Houghton Mifflin, 1919), chap. 7. Cited hereafter in my text as *RR*.

6. Charles I. Glicksberg, *The Ironic Vision in Modern Literature* (The Hague: Martinus Nijhoff, 1969), 97.

7. Candace D. Lang, *Irony/Humor: Critical Paradigms* (Baltimore: Johns Hopkins University Press, 1988), 50.

8. Furst, *Fictions of Romantic Irony,* esp. 236–37.

9. Gary J. Handwerk, *Irony and Ethics in Narrative: From Schlegel to Lacan* (New Haven: Yale University Press, 1985), 5.

10. Handwerk, *Irony and Ethics,* 15.

11. David Perkins has discussed romantic irony in Frost in "Robert Frost and Romantic Irony," *South Carolina Review* 22, no. 1 (fall 1989): 33–37. See Anne K. Mellor, *English Romantic Irony* (Cambridge: Harvard University Press, 1980), esp. 185–89, for a discussion of romantic irony in Yeats.

12. Mellor, *English Romantic Irony,* 187.

13. On Lasserre and his relation to Hulme and Babbitt see Michael H. Levenson, *A Genealogy of Modernism: A Study of English Literary Doctrine 1908–1922* (New York: Cambridge University Press, 1984), esp. 80–102. Levenson's entire study is apposite to my point here.

14. T. J. Jackson Lears, *No Place of Grace: Antimodernism and the Transformation of American Culture, 1880–1920* (New York: Pantheon Books, 1981), xi.

15. Samuel P. Hays, *The Response to Industrialism: 1885–1914* (Chicago: University of Chicago Press, 1957), 3.

16. Lears, *No Place of Grace,* xv.

17. James Longenbach, *Wallace Stevens: The Plain Sense of Things* (New York: Oxford University Press, 1991), 4.

18. Longenbach, *Wallace Stevens,* 5.

19. George S. Lensing, *Wallace Stevens: A Poet's Growth* (Baton Rouge: Louisiana State University Press, 1986), 62–63.

20. For a discussion of romantic irony in Byron and Keats, see Mellor, *English Romantic Irony,* 31–108. Stuart M. Sperry has discussed its expression in these two poets and in Shelley in "Toward a Definition of Romantic Irony in English Literature," in *Romantic and Modern: Revaluations of Literary Tradition,* ed. George Bornstein (Pittsburgh: University of Pittsburgh Press, 1977), 3–28. See Clyde de L. Ryals, *A World of Possibilities: Romantic Irony in Victorian Literature* (Columbus: Ohio State University Press, 1990), and Lloyd Bishop, *Romantic Irony in French Literature from Diderot to Beckett* (Nashville: Vanderbilt University Press, 1989), for discussions of romantic irony in the Victorian and French authors mentioned above.

21. B. J. Leggett, *Early Stevens: The Nietzschean Intertext* (Durham, N.C.: Duke University Press, 1992); Milton J. Bates, *Wallace Stevens: A Mythology of Self* (Berkeley and Los Angeles: University of California Press, 1985), 234–65;

J. S. Leonard and C. E. Wharton, *The Fluent Mundo: Wallace Stevens and the Structure of Reality* (Athens: University of Georgia Press, 1988), 103–39.

22. Albert Gelpi, *A Coherent Splendor: The American Poetic Renaissance, 1910–1950* (New York: Cambridge University Press, 1987), 6.

Chapter 1

1. Norman Knox, *The Word Irony and Its Context, 1500–1755* (Durham, N.C.: Duke University Press, 1961), 12–13.

2. Knox, *The Word Irony*, 6.

3. Knox, *The Word Irony*, 12.

4. Wayne C. Booth, *A Rhetoric of Irony* (Chicago: University of Chicago Press, 1974), 235.

5. *Nichts ist verschiedener als Satire, Polemik und Ironie.* Friedrich Schlegel, *Literary Notebooks 1797–1801,* ed. Hans Eichner (London: Athlone Press, 1957), 64, no. 506. My translation.

6. Friedrich Schlegel, *Friedrich Schlegel's Lucinde and the Fragments,* trans. Peter Firchow (Minneapolis: University of Minnesota Press, 1971), 148, no. 42. Hereafter cited in my text as *LF.* Citations include fragment numbers as appropriate.

7. Furst, *Fictions of Romantic Irony,* 29–30.

8. Translated by Hans Eichner in *Friedrich Schlegel* (New York: Twayne, 1970), 71.

9. Ernst Behler, *Irony and the Discourse of Modernity* (Seattle: University of Washington Press, 1990), 89.

10. M. H. Abrams, *Natural Supernaturalism: Tradition and Revolution in Romantic Literature* (New York: W. W. Norton, 1971). Cited hereafter in my text as *NS.*

11. Mellor, *English Romantic Irony,* 13.

12. G. W. F. Hegel, *Aesthetics: Lectures on Fine Art,* trans. T. M. Knox (Oxford: Clarendon Press, 1975), 1:64–69. Cited hereafter as *A.* Unless otherwise noted, all quotations will be from volume 1.

13. See. G. W. F. Hegel, *Lectures on the History of Philosophy,* trans. E. S. Haldane (London: Kegan Paul, Trench, Trubner and Co., 1892), 3:506–12; *The Philosophy of Right,* trans. T. M. Knox (Oxford: Clarendon Press, 1942), 101–3; *Lectures on the Philosophy of Religion,* trans. E. B. Speirs and J. Burdon Sanderson (1895; rpt. New York: Humanities Press, 1962), 3:183–85; *The Philosophy of Mind,* trans. from *The Encyclopedia of the Philosophical Sciences with Five Introductory Essays* by William Wallace (Oxford: Clarendon Press, 1894), 301–2.

14. Robert L. Perkins, "Hegel and Kierkegaard: Two Critics of Romantic Irony," *Review of National Literatures* 1, no. 2 (fall 1970): 232–54.

15. Søren Kierkegaard, *Either/Or,* trans. David F. Swenson and Lillian Marvin Swenson, revisions by Howard A. Johnson (1944; rpt. Garden City:

Anchor-Doubleday, 1959), 1:300. Cited hereafter in my text as *E/O*. Unless otherwise noted, all references will be to volume 1.

16. Muecke, *The Compass of Irony*, 246.

17. Eichner, *Friedrich Schlegel*, 77.

18. Quoted by Walter Jackson Bate in his discussion of romantic subjectivity in *From Classic to Romantic: Premises of Taste in Eighteenth-Century England* (1946; rpt. New York: Harper and Row, 1961), 165.

19. Søren Kierkegaard, *Concluding Unscientific Postscript*, trans. David F. Swenson and Walter Lowrie (Princeton: Princeton University Press, 1941), 226.

20. Translated by Eichner in *Friedrich Schlegel*, 71.

21. My discussion of Schlegel's concept of romantic form and of the expression of this concept in *Lucinde* is indebted to Eichner, *Friedrich Schlegel*, 44–90. My quotation is from p. 53.

22. Paul de Man, "The Rhetoric of Temporality," in *Interpretation: Theory and Practice*, ed. Charles S. Singleton (Baltimore: Johns Hopkins Press, 1969), 202.

23. Mark C. Taylor, *Kierkegaard's Pseudonymous Authorship: A Study of Time and the Self* (Princeton: Princeton University Press, 1975), 331.

24. Taylor, *Kierkegaard's Pseudonymous Authorship*, 278.

25. Taylor, *Kierkegaard's Pseudonymous Authorship*, 268.

26. Loyd D. Easton, "Hegelianism in Nineteenth-Century Ohio," *Journal of the History of Ideas* 23, no. 3 (July–September 1962): 356.

27. *The American Hegelians*, ed. William H. Goetzmann with the assistance of Dickson Pratt (New York: Knopf, 1973), 4–5.

28. Goetzmann and Pratt, *The American Hegelians*, 5.

29. My short summary of the history of the St. Louis Philosophical Society is indebted to Loyd Easton, "Hegelianism in Nineteenth-Century Ohio," 355–78.

30. Paul Russell Anderson and Max Harold Fisch, *Philosophy in America: From the Puritans to James with Representative Selections* (New York: D. Appleton-Century Company, 1939), 472–73.

31. Anderson and Fisch, *Philosophy in America*, 473, 476.

32. Easton, "Hegelianism in Nineteenth-Century Ohio," 355.

33. Walt Whitman, *Prose Works 1892*, ed. Floyd Stoval (New York: New York University Press, 1963), 1:281. *Prose Works 1892* is part of *The Collected Works of Walt Whitman*, ed. Gay Wilson Allen and Sculley Bradley.

34. Whitman, *Prose Works 1892*, 1:259.

35. Whitman, *Prose Works 1892*, 2:421. Whitman's use of the "Hegelian formulas," particularly in regard to his "doctrine of the union of self and nation," has been discussed by Kathryne V. Lindberg, "Whitman's 'Convertible Terms': America, Self, Ideology," in *Theorizing American Literature: Hegel, the Sign, and History*, ed. Bainard Cowan and Joseph G. Kronick (Baton Rouge: Louisiana State University Press, 1991), 233–68.

36. Walt Whitman, *Leaves of Grass*, ed. Harold W. Blodgett and Sculley Bradley (1965; rpt. New York: W. W. Norton, 1968), 274.

37. Henry A. Pochmann, *German Culture in America: Philosophical and Literary Influences 1600–1900* (Madison: University of Wisconsin Press, 1957), 310.

38. Pochmann, *German Culture in America*, 311, 312.

39. Stephen Crites, "Hegelianism," *The Encyclopedia of Philosophy*, ed. Paul Edwards (New York: Macmillan Publishing and The Free Press, 1967), esp. 3:457.

40. J. K. Huysmans, *Against the Grain (A Rebours)*, translator unidentified (1931; rpt. New York: Dover Press, 1969), 20, 21–22. Cited hereafter as *AR*.

41. *The Artist as Critic: Critical Writings of Oscar Wilde*, ed. Richard Ellmann (New York: Random House, 1969), 434.

42. Peter Ackroyd, *T. S. Eliot: A Life* (New York: Simon and Schuster, 1984), 35–36.

43. See Eliot's essay in *Irving Babbitt, Man and Teacher*, ed. Frederick Manchester and Otis Shepard (New York: G. P. Putnam's Sons, 1941), 101–4.

44. Lyndall Gordon, *Eliot's Early Years* (1977; rpt. New York: Farrar, Straus and Giroux, 1988), 39–40.

45. *The Letters of T. S. Eliot*, ed. Valerie Eliot (New York: Harcourt Brace Jovanovich, 1988), 1:23.

46. Gordon, *Eliot's Early Years*, 43.

47. T. S. Eliot, *The Complete Poems and Plays, 1909–1950* (New York: Harcourt, Brace and World, 1971), 3. All of my quotations from Eliot's poetry are taken from this edition.

48. Ackroyd, *T. S. Eliot*, 47.

49. Isaiah Smithson, "Time and Irony in T. S. Eliot's Early Poetry," *Massachusetts Studies in English* 8, no. 2 (1982): 39–52. While Smithson's conclusions about Eliot are similar to my own, we arrive at our conclusions from different paths.

50. T. S. Eliot, *Selected Essays* (New York: Harcourt, Brace and World, 1964), 15. Cited hereafter in my text as *SE*.

51. The spirit of Eliot's critique of subjectivity can be seen in cultural studies such as Christopher Lasch's *The Culture of Narcissism: American Life in an Age of Diminishing Expectations* (New York: Warner, 1979). His description of the narcissistic personality—his "doubts" about "the reality of his own existence," his "deeply antisocial" isolation, his self-absorption, "the world is a mirror" of the self (22, 23, 38)—echoes characteristics of the personality of the aesthete/ironist as it is portrayed in Hegel, Kierkegaard, Huysmans, and early Eliot. As in Eliot, Lasch's response to this subjectivism is to turn to the outer. Excoriating the mental-health community for pandering to the narcissistic personality, Lasch writes, "It hardly occurs to them . . . to encourage the subject to subordinate his needs and interests to those of others, to someone or some cause or tradition outside himself. 'Love' as self-sacrifice or self-abasement, 'meaning'

as submission to a higher loyalty—these sublimations strike the therapeutic sensibility as intolerably oppressive" (42). Subordination to a "cause or tradition outside himself"—the words are almost identical to Eliot's own words written over fifty years before when he asked for individuals to give "allegiance to something outside themselves."

52. Friedrich Nietzsche, *Human, All Too Human,* trans. Marion Faber with Stephen Lehmann (Lincoln: University of Nebraska Press, 1984), no. 16. Cited hereafter in my text as *H* with aphorism number.

53. Friedrich Nietzsche, *Philosophy and Truth: Selections from Nietzsche's Notebooks of the Early 1870's,* ed. and trans. Daniel Breazeale (Atlantic Highlands, N.J.: Humanities Press, 1979), 82–83. Cited hereafter in my text as *PT* with page and, if appropriate, aphorism number.

54. Friedrich Nietzsche, *The Will to Power,* trans. Walter Kaufmann and R. J. Hollingdale (New York: Random House, 1967), no. 473. Cited hereafter in my text as *WP* with aphorism number.

55. Arthur C. Danto, *Nietzsche as Philosopher* (New York: Macmillan, 1965), 116.

56. Paul de Man, *Allegories of Reading: Figural Language in Rousseau, Nietzsche, Rilke, and Proust* (New Haven: Yale University Press, 1979), 130.

57. For a discussion of Schlegel's concept of *Witz* and its relation to the eighteenth-century concept of wit, see Mellor, *English Romantic Irony,* esp. 8–10.

58. Joan Richardson, *Wallace Stevens: The Early Years, 1879–1923* (New York: William Morrow, 1986), 68.

59. Richardson, *Wallace Stevens,* 68.

60. June 8, 1993 letter to author from the Harvard University Archives.

61. Richardson, *Wallace Stevens,* 61.

62. Bates, *Wallace Stevens,* 249.

63. Reverend Arthur P. Hanley has written of Stevens' conversion to Roman Catholicism. ("A Letter from Father Hanley on Stevens' Conversion to Catholicism," *Wallace Stevens Journal* 18, no.1 (spring 1994): 3–5. "Archbishop at the time told me not to make his (Wallace's) conversion public, but the sister and the nurses on the floor were all aware of it and were praying for him" (5). Though it is impossible to prove the negative, that Stevens did not convert, the case for conversion is not a strong one. As McCann herself points out, "There is no one who has testified to his [Stevens'] actual baptism as a Roman Catholic except Father Hanley" (4). Helen Vendler has summarized the case against conversion in *"In Memoriam* Holly Stevens," *Wallace Stevens Journal* 16, no. 2 (fall 1992): 213–14.

64. Alan Wilde, *Horizons of Assent: Modernism, Postmodernism, and the Ironic Imagination* (Baltimore: Johns Hopkins University Press, 1981), 10.

65. Wilde, *Horizons of Assent,* 36.

66. Paul A. Bové, *Destructive Poetics: Heidegger and Modern American Poetry* (New York: Columbia University Press, 1980), 113.

67. Bové, *Destructive Poetics*, 97.

Chapter 2

1. William Carlos Williams, "Yours, O Youth," in *Selected Essays of William Carlos Williams* (1954; rpt. New York: New Directions, 1969), 33–34.

2. Stéphane Mallarmé, "Music and Literature," in *Mallarmé: Selected Prose Poems, Essays, and Letters*, trans. Bradford Cook (Baltimore: Johns Hopkins University Press, 1956), 48.

3. Stéphane Mallarmé, "Crisis in Poetry," in *Mallarmé*, 42.

4. Ezra Pound, "Vorticism," *Fortnightly Review*, September 1914; rpt. *Gaudier-Brzeska: A Memoir* (New York: New Directions, 1974), 86–87, 89.

5. "Another Weeping Woman" was first published in *Poetry* 19, no. 1 (October 1921). That Williams' poetry fundamentally clings to experience while Stevens' verse evades "local quiddities" is argued by Hugh Kenner in *A Homemade World: The American Modernist* (New York: William Morrow, 1975), 50–90.

6. Ezra Pound, "A Few Don'ts," *Poetry* 1, no. 6 (March 1913); rpt. in "A Retrospect," in *Literary Essays of Ezra Pound* (New York: New Directions, 1968), 4–7.

7. Translated by Eichner in *Friedrich Schlegel*, 71.

8. William James, *Pragmatism*, ed. Fredson Bowers and Ignas K. Skrupskelis (Cambridge: Harvard University Press, 1975), 17–18.

9. William James, *Pragmatism*, 31.

10. William James, *Pragmatism*, 32.

11. The influence of James on this and other poems in *Harmonium* has been described by Margaret Peterson in *Wallace Stevens and the Idealist Tradition* (Ann Arbor, Mich.: UMI Research Press, 1983).

12. Eleanor Cook, *Poetry, Word-Play, and Word-War in Wallace Stevens* (Princeton: Princeton University Press, 1988), 177.

13. Stevens' use of metaphor to evade the overwhelming presence of nature has been discussed by Jacqueline Vaught Brogan in *Stevens and Simile: A Theory of Language* (Princeton: Princeton University Press, 1986), 72–116.

14. Carl Woodring, *Nature into Art: Cultural Transformations in Nineteenth-Century Britain* (Cambridge: Harvard University Press, 1989), 82.

15. Sperry, "Toward a Definition of Romantic Irony," in *Romantic and Modern: Revaluations of Literary Tradition*, 3–28.

16. Barbara Fisher, *Wallace Stevens: The Intensest Rendezvous* (Charlottesville: University Press of Virginia, 1990), xxiv.

17. For a discussion of this essay in the context of Stevens' growing

engagement with the Second World War, see Alan Filreis, *Wallace Stevens and the Actual World* (Princeton: Princeton University Press, 1991), esp. 21–28.

18. The deconstructive literature on Stevens is too extensive to list here. For useful overviews of deconstructive approaches to Stevens, see Alex Argyros, "The Residual Difference: Wallace Stevens and American Deconstruction," *New Orleans Review* 13, no.1 (spring 1986): 20–31, and Schaum, *Stevens and the Critical Schools,* 100–128.

19. Longenbach, *Wallace Stevens,* 131.

20. This side of the "many-sided self one encounters in reading *Harmonium*" is discussed by James C. Ransom, "Fable in *Harmonium*'s 'Adult Make Believe,'" *Wallace Stevens Journal* 16, no. 1 (spring 1992): 37–52.

21. Ransom, "Fable" 41.

22. Oscar Wilde, "Impressions du Matin," in *Aesthetes and Decadents of the 1890's: An Anthology of British Poetry and Prose,* ed. Karl Beckson (New York: Random House, 1966), 242.

23. "Mr. Whistler's 'Ten O'Clock,'" in James Abbott McNeill Whistler, *The Gentle Art of Making Enemies,* 2d ed. (1892; rpt. New York: Dover Publications, 1967), 151.

24. Bates, *Wallace Stevens,* 104.

25. Paul de Man has discussed this aspect of romantic irony in "The Rhetoric of Temporality," in *Interpretation: Theory and Practice,* esp. 202.

26. B. J. Leggett, *Wallace Stevens and Poetic Theory: Conceiving the Supreme Fiction* (Chapel Hill: University of North Carolina Press, 1987), 24–25.

27. Mellor, *English Romantic Irony,* 11.

28. Mellor, *English Romantic Irony,* 4.

29. My synopsis of Plotinus' thought is indebted to Abrams, *NS,* esp. 146–54.

30. Helen Vendler, "The Qualified Assertions of Wallace Stevens," in *The Act of the Mind: Essays on the Poetry of Wallace Stevens,* ed. Roy Harvey Pearce and J. Hillis Miller (Baltimore: Johns Hopkins Press, 1965), 163–78.

31. The relationship between "To Autumn" and a number of Stevens' poems, including "On the Road Home," has been explored by Helen Vendler in *Part of Nature, Part of Us: Modern American Poets* (Cambridge: Harvard University Press, 1980), 20–40.

Chapter 3

1. The error was apparently caused by O'Connor's misreading of a tribute to Eliot in *The Harvard Advocate* 125 (December 1938). O'Connor's error is discussed by Thomas Vance in "Wallace Stevens and T. S. Eliot," *Dartmouth College Library Bulletin,* n.s. 4, (December 1961): 37–44. Holly Stevens writes in *L* 677, n. 3 that Stevens' description of his relation to Eliot was confirmed by Eliot in a letter to her.

2. Stevens' antithetical relation to Eliot has yet to be fully mapped. Even Harold Bloom restricts himself in *Wallace Stevens: The Poems of Our Climate* (Ithaca: Cornell University Press, 1977) to a summary of Stevens' epistolary polemic against Eliot, to fairly brief remarks about the anti-Eliotic aspects of "The Creations of Sound," "Extracts from Addresses to the Academy of Fine Ideas," and "Esthétique du Mal," and to sentence-length contrasts, scattered throughout his study, between the poets.

3. Bloom, *Wallace Stevens*, 65.

4. The elaborate defense mechanisms by which Stevens protects the pleasurably isolated self from interpersonal entanglings have been described by Mark Halliday in *Stevens and the Interpersonal* (Princeton: Princeton University Press, 1991).

5. Quentin Anderson argues in *The Imperial Self: An Essay in American Literary and Cultural History* (New York: Knopf, 1971) that the "failure of the fathers" has given us the American tradition of "incorporation." Emerson, Whitman, and Henry James all attempt "to incorporate the whole, to take the whole into consciousness" (ix). Hoon's absorption of the world into himself suggests that Stevens can be seen in terms of this tradition. "The Snow Man" reminds us, though, that his relation to it is not an uncritical one.

6. Bloom, *Wallace Stevens*, 137, 138.

7. See Stevens' letter to Renato Poggioli (*L* 783), where he identifies Zervos' conversation with Picasso as the source of his quotation.

8. Zervos' conversation with Picasso was originally published in *Cahiers d'Art* 5, no. 10 (1935). It is reprinted in *Picasso on Art: A Selection of Views*, ed. Dore Ashton (New York: Viking, 1972), 7–13. My quotation is from p. 8. The importance of this issue of *Cahiers d'Art* to Stevens' aesthetic in "The Man with the Blue Guitar" has been discussed by Glen MacLeod in *Wallace Stevens and Modern Art: From the Armory Show to Abstract Expressionism* (New Haven: Yale University Press, 1993), 57–78.

9. Helen Vendler, who also sees desire without an object as the central issue of "Chaos in Motion and Not in Motion," argues that the poem expresses "one of the fundamental miseries of the old" (15). "[T]here is no diminution in desire: there is only a loss of belief in a possible object adequate to desire" (15). See "Apollo's Harsher Songs: 'Desire without an Object of Desire,'" *AWP Newsletter*, May 1979; rpt. *Wallace Stevens: Words Chosen out of Desire* (Knoxville: University of Tennessee Press, 1984), 10–28.

10. Harold Bloom writes in *A Map of Misreading* (New York: Oxford University Press, 1975) that "a poem is written to escape dying. Literally, poems are refusals of mortality" (19). While Bloom's thesis is supported by Stevens' irony of detachment, his irony of skeptical engagement suggests that not all poems make this refusal.

Chapter 4

1. Friedrich Schlegel, *Dialogue on Poetry and Literary Aphorisms,* trans. Ernst Behler and Roman Struc (University Park: Pennsylvania State University Press, 1968), 86. Cited hereafter in my text as *DP.*

2. Mellor, *English Romantic Irony,* 19.

3. Eichner, *Friedrich Schlegel,* 88.

4. Mellor, *English Romantic Irony,* 19.

5. See Beverly Coyle, *A Thought to Be Rehearsed: Aphorism in Wallace Stevens's Poetry* (Ann Arbor, Mich.: UMI Research Press, 1983), and Leggett, *Early Stevens,* 149–77.

6. In his study of Stevens and Nietzsche, *Early Stevens,* Leggett makes a similar point. "Neither style nor convention (stanza or line lengths, rhythm, etc.) nor 'theme' pulls these passages [of "Thirteen Ways"] together into anything approaching sustained and coherent thought or feeling. . . . The possibility that the form of the poem itself implies the *absence* of an overarching unity in which each look at the blackbird finds its place would have been a difficulty for several decades of Stevens' criticism" (171). Though the poem lacks an "overarching unity," it is not without coherence. "In order to give this sense of the multiplicity of seeing, the poem must isolate each perspective while indicating that they are all directed toward the same general subject" (170).

7. Coyle, *A Thought to Be Rehearsed,* 57. The relation between the simple pleasures of eating and drinking and what Stevens called "the normal" has been explored by MacLeod in *Stevens and Modern Art,* esp. 46–53. For an opposing perspective on Stevens as a highly discriminating consumer, see Frank Lentricchia, *Ariel and the Police: Michel Foucault, William James, Wallace Stevens* (Madison: University of Wisconsin Press, 1988), 196–244. Lentricchia argues that Stevens' delight in expensive food and in rare collectibles expresses the special kind of desire generated by "first-world consumer capitalism" (204). This desire is also seen in the late poetry, which Lentricchia describes as "a form of gourmandizing" (204). The late work is an "epic of bourgeois interiority, wherein the life of the spirit is hard to distinguish from the special sort of desire stimulated in the time and place of first-world consumer capitalism: when the life of the spirit is subjected to endless need for the new which alone can break us out of the grooves of boredom" (204).

8. Coyle, *A Thought to Be Rehearsed,* 58.

9. Coyle, *A Thought to Be Rehearsed,* 56.

10. Helen Vendler, *On Extended Wings: Wallace Stevens' Longer Poems* (Cambridge: Harvard University Press, 1969), 65.

11. A. Walton Litz, *Introspective Voyager: The Poetic Development of Wallace Stevens* (New York: Oxford University Press, 1972), 111–12.

12. Lewis Carroll, *Through the Looking Glass*, in *Alice in Wonderland: Authoritative Texts of Alice's Adventures in Wonderland, Through the Looking Glass, The Hunting of the Snark*, ed. Donald J. Gray (New York: W. W. Norton, 1971), 166–67.

13. Stevens need not have had Lewis Carroll specifically in mind. James Rother has discussed the influence of American nonsense writers on Stevens' style in "American Nonsense and the Style of Wallace Stevens," *Bucknell Review* 23, no. 2 (1977): 164–86.

14. For a lengthier discussion of how the sounds of "Comedian" offer a commentary on Crispin see Martha Strom, "The Comedian as the Sounds of the Letter C," *Wallace Stevens Journal* 11, no. 1 (spring 1987): 21–31.

15. Muecke, *The Compass of Irony*, 64–86.

16. Leggett, *Stevens and Poetic Theory*, 90.

17. Ronald Sukenick, *Wallace Stevens: Musing the Obscure* (New York: New York University Press, 1967), 167.

Chapter 5

1. The theme of inception in Stevens' very late poetry has been explored by Helen Vendler in *On Extended Wings*, 309–14.

2. Leggett, *Wallace Stevens and Poetic Theory*, 198.

3. This pattern in the late poetry has been studied by Charles Berger, who writes that many of "the final poems aim not to complete the career so much as to prolong it. . . . Sometimes this involves turning against the completed forms of art belonging to one's own past. . . . Disparaging what has already been fashioned clears ground for new work." See *Forms of Farewell: The Late Poetry of Wallace Stevens* (Madison: University of Wisconsin Press, 1985). My quotation is from p. 146.

4. Marie Borroff, "Wallace Stevens: The World and the Poet," in *Wallace Stevens: A Collection of Critical Essays*, ed. Marie Borroff (Englewood Cliffs, N.J.: Prentice-Hall, 1963), 21–22.

5. Vendler, *Wallace Stevens: Words Chosen Out of Desire*, 77.

6. Bloom, *Wallace Stevens*, 271.

7. Leggett has explored the influence of Focillon on Stevens in *Stevens and Poetic Theory*, 142–201. The phrase quoted is from p. 178.

8. My summary of the poem's argument is generally indebted to Ronald Sukenick's reading of the poem in *Wallace Stevens*, 189–91.

9. Bates, *Wallace Stevens*, 272.

10. Brogan, *Stevens and Simile*, 125–26.

11. Translated by Eichner in *Friedrich Schlegel*, 71.

12. Mellor, *English Romantic Irony*, 5.

Afterword

1. Donald Barthelme, "Kierkegaard Unfair to Schlegel," in *Sixty Stories* (New York: Dutton, 1982), 163. Page numbers cited hereafter in my text.

2. Wilde, *Horizons of Assent,* 166.

3. Wilde, *Horizons of Assent,* 137, 143–44.

4. Wilde, *Horizons of Assent,* 144. See especially pp. 136–47, where Wilde lays out in detail these conflicting aspects of Federman's and Sukenick's work.

5. David Shapiro, *John Ashbery: An Introduction to the Poetry* (New York: Columbia University Press, 1979), 13.

Index of Stevens' Work

General Index

Abrams, M. H., 12, 89
Ackroyd, Peter, 45
Aesthetics (Hegel), 13, 15–16
Aiken, Conrad, 1
Alcestis Press, 141
Alcott, Bronson, 32
Allegories of Reading (de Man), 53
"Ancient Tragical Motif as Reflected
   in the Modern, The"
   (Kierkegaard), 27
Arabesken, Die (Goethe), 125
Aristotle, 149
Arnold, Matthew, 5, 46
Art of Poetry, The (Aristotle), 149
Ashbery, John, 6, 192–93
Aspasia, 18
Athenaeum Fragments (F. Schlegel), 1,
   11, 126
A Rebours (Huysmans), 5, 41; expres-
   sion of romantic irony in, 35–40, 60

Babbitt, Irving, 2, 3, 40, 56, 189;
   expression of romantic irony in,
   33–34
Barthelme, Donald, 6, 189–92
Bates, Milton, 5, 56, 84, 179
Baudelaire, Charles, 5, 40, 84
Beckett, Samuel, 3, 57
Behler, Ernst, 12
Blanschard, Brand, 33
Bloom, Harold, 95, 101, 177

Booth, Wayne, 10
Borges, Jorge Luis, 3, 57
Boroff, Marie, 171
Bové, Paul, 57
Brogan, Jacqueline, 185
Brokmeyer, Henry, 32
Browning, Robert, 5, 46
Bubu de Montparnasse (Philippe), 40
Byron, George Gordon, 5

Cahiers d'Art, 109
Calvino, Italo, 3
Capel, Lee M., 190
Carlyle, Thomas, 5, 46
"Carlyle from American Points of
   View" (Whitman), 33
Cézanne, Paul, 65
Church, Henry, 56, 87
Concept of Irony, The (Kierkegaard), 4,
   13, 15, 19, 21–23, 25–26, 29, 34,
   109, 190
Concluding Unscientific Postscript
   (Kierkegaard), 24
Conway, Moncure, 33
Cook, Eleanor, 68
Corot, Jean, 140–41
Coyle, Beverly, 134
Crates, 18

Dante, 56, 112
Davidson, John, 2